RUNAWAY JOE

RUNAWAY JOE

A Murder, A Hidden Identity,
A Six-Decade Manhunt

Pavel Barter

First published in the UK in 2026 by Eriu
An imprint of Bonnier Books UK
5th Floor, HYLO, 105 Bunhill Row,
London, EC1Y 8LZ

This book is a work of Non-Fiction. Some names may have been changed to
respect the privacy of those mentioned.

A CIP catalogue record for this book is available from the British Library.

Trade Paperback ISBN: 978-1-80444-257-9

Also available as an ebook and an audiobook

1 3 5 7 9 10 8 6 4 2

Typeset by IDSUK (Data Connection) Ltd
Printed and bound in Great Britain by CPI (UK) Ltd, Croydon CR0 4YY

The authorised representative in the EEA is
Bonnier Books UK (Ireland) Limited.
Registered office address:
Block B, The Crescent Building
Northwood, Santry
Dublin 9, D09 C6X8
Ireland
compliance@bonnierbooks.ie
www.bonnierbooks.co.uk

To Elaine

Thank you for joining me on the adventure

'If you were to talk to a hundred people who knew Joe Maloney every single one of them would describe him differently. I don't know anybody who really knows Joe. I don't know if that person exists. He was more than a chameleon. He was a man of many faces.'

– Joseph Picciotti, Fairport Village Police Chief

Contents

Prologue

The Package   1

1. June and Joe   7

2. A Toxic Recipe   27

3. Ten Days of June   43

4. Dragnet   55

5. Never-Never Man   71

6. Master of the Manor   91

7. The Children   115

8. Shooting from the Hip   127

9. Forgive Us Our Debts   145

10. Meet Me on Killiney Heath   161

11. A Question of Identity   173

12. Jailbreak 193

13. The Dirty Pool 209

14. Twisted Odyssey 225

15. Behind the Wall 241

16. Enter the Bounty Hunter 249

17. Where I Live, I Don't Exist 257

18. Footprints in the Snow 283

Epilogue

June 297

Acknowledgements 301

Prologue
The Package

May 1967

JUNE MALONEY PULLED HER OLIVE-GREEN CHEVROLET CORVAIR TO A HALT OUTSIDE THE HOUSE ON THE CORNER OF THE QUIET SUBURBAN STREET. It was 4pm. June – 26 years old, slightly built, freckles, vibrant red hair – looked out the window to see the familiar tree-lined streets and yards separated by white picket fences. There had been barbeques with neighbours during the summer; gossip across snow ploughs in winter; happy memories from the early days of her marriage. But those were in the past. Her situation with Joe had been impossible and untenable for years. The ragged stitch marks in the white convertible roof above her head, where his knife had torn through two months previously, served as a reminder of this.

June turned off the engine. Joey, her little boy, got out of the passenger seat and ran up the steps, past the maple tree in the yard which held the swing his father built for him and to the front door. Joey was four years old but not for much longer. The following day he was turning five, and although he was too young to understand why his mom and dad had separated, he definitely didn't object to their plan to hold two birthday parties in his honour.

June followed him from the car to her former home, a two-storey building with a white trim and gable roof. As much as she didn't want to be here, she was determined to make this work for her kids. June was a head nurse at Rochester's Genesee Hospital and she knew how to care for others. Now she was learning how to look after herself. It had been over two months since she left this house and the man within it. Wanda, her friend, a kind and newly married 19-year-old who lived opposite June's new apartment on Lyell Avenue, was minding Joey's sister, 18-month-old Patti-Ann, while June took Joey to his father. June had been unhappy for a long time, but she was turning a corner. Maybe Joe could see that too? The debts, threats, intimidation and lies. The madness. It had been a nightmare. She'd made a fresh start. Maybe he could be civil and accept she'd met another man.

The birthday party was underway when June stepped into the living room.

At least a dozen people were here, including June's 23-year-old brother Dale Fisk and his wife-to-be Gladys MacDiarmid. The couple were recently engaged, and June's estranged husband had offered to host the party partly in celebration of the engagement. Joey opened his presents and June gravitated towards a group of her nursing colleagues in attendance with their children. They included Carol Reckahn and her son. Joe was in the centre of proceedings, soaking up attention as usual. He was six feet two inches tall and a redhead like June, but while she was reserved and quiet, he was a whirlwind of activity: orchestrating proceedings, regaling the guests with tall tales while simultaneously acting as bartender.

Now he was towering over June and Carol where they sat.

'What do you want to drink?'

'I'm driving,' said Carol. 'I'll just have a beer.'

He looked at June. 'Want your regular?'

She nodded.

Joe disappeared into the kitchen and emerged minutes later with Carol's beer and June's screwdriver, a cocktail of orange juice and vodka, which he served in a water glass decorated with a blue-brown pattern. Dale and Gladys had the same. The adults sat and talked while the children played with Joey's toys. The guests knew about the conflict and June and Joe's separation, but the subject was not raised, and, to everyone's relief, June's most of all, Joe was being civil. He went outside to start a charcoal fire, fried up steaks and served food. He fixed June a second drink in the kitchen: this time a Manhattan, made with whiskey, sweet vermouth and bitters.

After dinner, June and Joe stepped out of the room. Dale overheard them arguing about her car – information he later recounted in police testimony. June fell quiet and went upstairs. A few minutes later Joe followed her, prompting June to return to the living room.

'I don't feel so good,' she whispered to her brother.

She looked tired and drowsy, like she'd had too much to drink.

'The Manhattan was awfully strong,' she told him. 'I couldn't even finish it.'

At 6pm, two hours after June arrived at 190 Eastmoreland Drive in the southern district of Rochester in upstate New York, she left the party with her son Joey. A few minutes into the drive back to her apartment, she pulled the car to the side of the road near Strong Memorial Hospital and started to cry.

'What's wrong, Mommy?' asked Joey.

June didn't respond. She just sat there and sobbed. After crying for several minutes, she wiped her face, started the engine and continued on her way.

February 2025

Joey, 62, opened the manila envelope and out spilled the guts of the past: personal artefacts of his biological father, Joe Maloney, before he went on the run in 1967. Joey inspected Joe's birth certificate, his passport, a vaccination certificate. A wallet containing business cards and addresses. Photographs of Joe as a baby, a young man, an adult. Pictures of Joey and Patti-Ann when they were children and a portrait of June in her nurse's uniform. Joey traced his finger over the indentations of Joe's name on a Gulf Travel credit card.

Decades had passed since Joey last saw his birth father, but as he looked at the registration for Joe's prized 1965 red Ford Mustang, memories returned. This package, like so many revelations about Joe Maloney, reached Joey through unexpected channels. Jim Memmott, a columnist for Rochester newspaper *Democrat & Chronicle*, had run into his lawyer Robert 'Chip' Presutti and got to talking. Chip's late father was Thomas Presutti, a celebrated criminal defence lawyer in Rochester who'd acted as Joe Maloney's attorney.

When Thomas died, Chip inherited his father's files, including this archive, which Joe left behind when he went on the run. Since Chip was never Maloney's lawyer and his father was dead, client-attorney privilege no longer applied.

'Chip doesn't want the stuff,' Memmott wrote to Gary Craig, another *Democrat & Chronicle* reporter who covered Maloney's case decades beforehand and revisited the story after

RTÉ, Ireland's national broadcaster, released a podcast series on the case in 2024.

'Do you? Or are there members of Maloney's family who would want it? A strange turn in the never-ending saga of *Runaway Joe*.'

Joey thumbed through more items from the envelope as I watched from across a table at his home in Florida. My interest in the case began after I read a memoir by Gillian Hussey, a judge in Ireland who had dealt with Joe's case. That interest evolved into my RTÉ *Documentary on One* podcast which was a sensation – two million downloads and broadcasting awards in Ireland and Europe – but when it was over Joe still felt to me like an enigma, a cipher, and I was continuing the investigation in the hope of unravelling more answers for a book.

This package of ancient ephemera only enhanced the mystery. There were no explanations here about Joe Maloney's motives, only inconsistencies and fabrications that made him seem more opaque. There was a foreign UK address listed on Joe's passport, issued in June 1959 when Joe was 23: 2625 Liverpool Street, Newmarket, England. A search on Google revealed no street of that name in Newmarket. There was a US Army ID card, describing Joe as a Second Lieutenant, and a US Army social security card with an address of Fort Jackson in South Carolina. Joe had never been in the army.

These forgeries were expertly crafted, indecipherable to the casual observer as fakes.

There were also items here belonging to June: details about her retirement annuity and her nurse registration certificates. Within Joe's package was an invoice from Strong Memorial Hospital posted on 13 June 1967, a week after June's death and Joe's arrest on a charge of murdering her with a poisoned cocktail. The bill described the hospital costs for June's care from the time of her admittance until her death. The total came to $1,601.95, which was covered by her Blue Cross nursing insurance. '$0.00 patient payment paid', stated the letter, '$0.00 balance due'. The price of a life had been settled and the matter was over, according to the receipt. But it was not.

Not by a long shot.

1.

June and Joe

WARD HORACE FISK WAS A MAN OF FEW MEANS BUT MUCH ROUTINE. Every morning he left his home – a weathered dark-brown shingled building, paint flaking off the siding, situated next to a nursing home on Route 98 – and walked the quarter mile to Earl Harding's farm, where he worked as a labourer picking apples and cherries in the orchards. Come lunchtime he'd walk back home, where his wife was waiting for him with lunch prepared. Then he'd be off again to the farm until evening. You could set your clock by him, the neighbours used to say.

Ward was born 1891 in Carlton, Orleans County, on the shores of Lake Ontario in upstate New York to a first-generation immigrant father from England. In 1928, he married Laura Marie King, known to her friends as Marie, from Albany in New York. Census records over subsequent years show Ward moving around the local area, where he sought work on farms, scraping a living during the dark days of the Great Depression and the

Second World War. By 1950, Ward and Marie had moved into a dilapidated farmhouse in Gaines, a rural area north of Albion village.

Albion was a fertile land. The first settlers who arrived here grew corn and tomatoes. Farmers on the road south to Batavia grew potatoes and onions. The village, named after an ancient poetic description of Great Britain, sprung up in the early 1820s, when it was chosen as a major stop on the Erie Canal, the longest artificial waterway in North America, stretching 363 miles between Albany and Buffalo. Immigrant workers flocked to the region to build the canal, and Italian engineers carved up local quarries in Medina using sandstone to construct huge three-storey buildings at the heart of Albion. Businesses and industries blossomed in the environs. By the early 1900s Albion's population had grown to 5,000, and for the most part its melting pot of denizens coexisted peacefully. They intermingled and intermarried. The only thing that separated them was wealth. Poorer families tended to be found on the margins of the village and many of them were like Ward, working as tenanted farm labourers.

Ward and Marie Fisk had two children: June Rosalee was born 1940 and Dale followed four years later. Marie supplemented the family income with a job at the nursing home next door, but the family never managed to escape poverty, and there were spells in which they couldn't afford a car. The Fisks were private people who tended not to engage with the local community. Some neighbours suspected their marriage was unhappy. June, though, was a gentle soul. People who knew her at school described her as quiet: thin with a light complexion, freckles and naturally curly dark-red hair.

'The way she walked, her toes always pointed out,' said Linda Chamberlain, one of June's classmates. 'She'd be swinging along and her right foot would swing to the right and her left foot to the left. Isn't it funny how you think of these things?'

Kay Walter, another classmate at Albion High School, described June as neat and making the most of what she had. 'I remember her wearing clothes that were . . . I don't think that the family had a lot of money.' What June lacked in money, she made up for with a generous demeanour. She may have been poor but she was content to play the cards she'd been dealt.

Rochester, 30 miles east of Albion on the southern shores of Lake Ontario, went through a metamorphosis after its birth in the late 1700s. The city's watery topography – the Genesee River, waterfalls and access to the Erie Canal – made it an ideal location for milling and gave it the nickname 'Flour City'. With the arrival of the Industrial Revolution it became something else entirely. George Eastman established his Kodak business here, bringing photography to the masses and revolutionising consumer technology. In 1906, a printing business called the Haloid Photographic Company set up shop in the city. It was later renamed Xerox. Immigrants – Italians, Irish, Dutch, Greeks and Poles – flooded here to find work in the manufacturing and technology industries, and by 1930 the population had expanded to over 300,000.

Among those newcomers was a couple from the midlands of Ireland. Joseph Maloney was born 1903 in Roscrea, County Tipperary. His wife Winifred was born 1909 and came from Raheen, a small townland in County Laois, only a few miles away from Joseph. The Rochester City Directory of 1934 showed the couple living at 43 Richard Street. The following year they moved to a larger home on 669 Linden Street in Swillburg, a working-class neighbourhood in the southeast part of the city, perhaps to make room for their first son, Joseph Michael Maloney who they called Joe, born on 4 September 1935.

Joseph Senior worked as an attendant at Rochester State Hospital, a psychiatric institution described in those days as an asylum. By 1940, he'd been promoted to night watchman. After briefly being drafted during World War Two, Joseph returned to his hospital job, and although the work was unlikely to have been as backbreaking as Ward Fisk's farm labour, Joseph's salary, pension and promotion inducements were oceans apart.

The Maloneys certainly led a comfortable existence. They lived on the bottom floor of a two-storey detached house and rented out the top floor. There was a wraparound porch with white railings on both floors and a patchy lawn out front. The neighbourhood was peaceful, residential and a block away from Clinton Avenue, where all the stores were. Neighbours remembered the Maloneys as a loving couple who walked arm in arm through the neighbourhood to attend mass at the Blessed Sacrament Church. Winifred had one more child, James, in 1937. She would have preferred more children, but ill health stood in her way.

Neal Dunkleberg first met Joe around 1944, when they were eight or nine years old. Neal lived on Meigs Street, three or four blocks away from Linden, and although they attended different schools (Neal to a public school, Joe to a Catholic one) they spent weekends and summers together. Joseph Senior worked at the State Hospital nights and slept during the day, so the kids had to be quiet when they were hanging out.

'I slept over at Joe's house a couple of times,' recalled Neal. 'He slept over at my house a couple of times. His mother was a very pleasant woman. She always treated me nicely. Fed me occasionally. Of course, my mother fed Joe occasionally.'

Joe, Neal and fellow neighbourhood ne'er-do-well Warren Daansen rarely spent much time at home, though. When they weren't at school, they were outside looking for adventure and making forts in the 150-acre Highland Park.

'We dug a cave about 20 to 25 feet in the side of the hill,' said Neal. 'The soil we dug out was washing downhill into this gentleman's back yard. Eventually the police showed up and we stopped digging. Youthful nonsense.'

Young Joe showed a propensity for mischief and trouble. He stole leftover beer from pubs for kicks and terrorised his brother James. On one occasion, Joe fired an arrow up into the air with a bow and it came within inches of skewering James upon its return to earth. James always had a more reserved personality. 'Jim wasn't as goofy as Joe,' remembered Neal. 'He wouldn't hop and skip, holler and yell as much as Joe did.'

Another story involved Joe setting off his father's service pistol and narrowly missing a friend with the bullet. Joe was spoiled from a young age, reckoned some family members, and allowed to get away with mayhem. But sometimes his dad put his foot down. Joseph Senior and Winifred took Joe back to their home turf, the Tipperary-Laois midlands area of Ireland, on a few occasions when he was a child. During one visit Joe was misbehaving.

'Joe Maloney Senior had a relative in law enforcement in Ireland,' said Robert Connors, whose mother was Joe Maloney's first cousin. Joseph convinced his policeman relative to 'lock Joe up overnight in a jail cell to teach him a lesson'.

Connors paused. 'Apparently it didn't work.'

Joe's childhood contemporaries in Rochester gave him the nickname Crazy Joe, but they didn't dare call him this to his face. Neal described him as capturing people's imaginations: 'Somebody who's fearless but also dangerous. He liked to go places, liked to do things. He annoyed some people pretty well and would get in fights now and again with the other kids in the neighbourhood.'

Neal knew how to push his buttons.

'I called him "Goofy" occasionally. I used to make fun of the Irish just to upset Joe. He could put on an Irish accent and I'd put on a German accent and we'd yell at each other occasionally.'

As a teenager Joe grew tall: over six feet in height. Despite his intelligence, good looks and flamboyance, he made few friends. Joe lived in a dream world. He fantasised about having an older brother and joining the Irish Republican Army, and he had an obsession with militaria. His imagination spiralled in every direction and manifested itself as lies.

'Joe was superb at lying,' Neal told me for the podcast series *Runaway Joe*. 'Joe would lie about everything, every day, even when we were kids. He seemed to have been born with a knack for coming out with a story. And come out with stories he did.' Sometimes the lies were so convincing, so alluring, that Neal and Warren played along with them. Joe to them was like an actor playing a role. But for the kids who knew him fleetingly, Joe just seemed weird, and so they avoided him.

'He didn't get tight with very many people,' said Neal. Instead, he formed 'intense, transient friendships. People were fascinated by him, but as soon as they found out he was full of crap and you couldn't believe a word he said, they tended to pull away.' Even his best friends found themselves second guessing their interactions with Joe. But Neal knew him well: 'I didn't take anything Joe said for granted unless I had other data: proof, if you will.'

* * *

Thirty miles west, life was very different for teenagers growing up in the smaller confines of Albion village. It was a tight local community where everybody knew everybody, and teenagers were largely trusted and left to their own devices. June Fisk attended the local elementary school, which had one entrance door for boys and another for girls, before graduating to Albion High School, which held around a hundred students. June was studious, and her classmates liked her, but her quietness, shyness and geographical distance (living in Gaines, five miles north of the village) dislocated her from the popular cliques.

June found a close friend in Carol Severns, a girl in her school year whose family owned Ray's Diner, a popular restaurant in Albion, and whose mother taught at Albion High. Carol, like June, was reserved, and they had much in common.

'I think we both were [quiet],' Carol recalled. 'June was always a very positive person. We spent quite a bit of time together. She'd come to my house on Friday nights to sleep over. I'd go to her house to sleep over. We spent many nights staying at each other's houses.' The Fisk's poverty may have been a contributing factor to June not fitting in with other kids at school, but it meant nothing to Carol. 'Monetary value for things like that didn't impress me. Maybe it did other people, but it didn't impress me. And it certainly didn't seem to affect her happiness. She almost always had a smile on her face.'

Sleepovers at Carol's place opened up the rich social world of Albion for June. Carol's parents' restaurant was only four blocks from their house, and sometimes they went there to eat. 'That was no novelty for me,' said Carol. 'I was brought up as a restaurant kid, so I spent a lot of time there.' But for June it was both a novelty and a joy. Right opposite Ray's Restaurant, on Albion's North Main Street, was the Rialto Theatre, which showed movies every night and matinees on Sunday. Teenagers paid fifteen cents to see James Dean in *East of Eden* or Kirk Douglas in *20,000 Leagues Under the Sea* with buckets of popcorn and candy. 'There was a balcony, but we usually stayed downstairs,' Carol recalled. The Orleans drive-in cinema opened on the west side of Albion in 1955 with Glenn Ford in *The Violent Men* and John Payne in *Raiders of the Seven Seas*.

Carol and June went to the roller-skating rink on the east edge of the village, on Route 31 (an east–west road going through Albion). In the winter, locals flooded the rink so they could ice skate on it. 'They usually had somebody there who maintained and shovelled the ice,' said Carol. 'There was a hut which had a potbelly stove in it and a wooden floor, and the person who was taking care of things usually had a fire going in there. You came in with your skates on, sat down on a wooden bench, warmed up and then went back outside again. Skating was free. It was a village rink, so they didn't charge anything.'

During the summer, the friends rode bicycles to swimming areas like the creek at the eastern edge of Route 31, not far from the skating rink and a mile and a half from Carol's home. A stream had been dammed up here and picnic benches were installed alongside slides and swings. 'The village didn't maintain a lifeguard,' said Carol. 'The dam was maybe three feet high. So if you were more than three feet in height you were safe. We'd swim there for however long we wanted to and then ride our bikes back home again.'

June lived far from these amenities, but she shared them with Carol when they spent time together in the village. 'I think she was too far out and she lived on a main north–south road, so it probably wouldn't have been safe for her to walk [into Albion].'

Carol's father owned a Packard automobile dealership, so her mother always had a car to collect or drop off June, and there were occasions when June's family had wheels of their own. Carol has a distinct memory of sitting in the backseat of June's car. 'Her mother was driving and they'd just installed a traffic light at the top of a hill. This car was standard shift.

She stopped for the traffic light and then had trouble getting it started again. She didn't clutch out fast enough and started rolling back down the hill!'

The mid-1950s, when June and Carol came of age was a golden era for American music and a heyday for rock 'n' roll. In May 1956, when June was 15 turning 16, chart singles included Elvis Presley's 'Heartbreak Hotel', Carl Perkins's 'Blue Suede Shoes', Little Richard's 'Long Tall Sally', and Frankie Lymon and the Teenagers' 'Why Do Fools Fall in Love'. A few weeks later, in early June, Elvis released 'Hound Dog', liberating a generation of teenagers and shocking their elders with his hypnotic hips. The girls spent a lot of time hovering over turntables and devouring the latest 45 vinyl record. Albion had a record store and they hung out here to listen to latest releases. June's school had plenty of music events too – free dances in the gymnasium with sounds furnished by a ten-piece orchestra and 'record hops' hosted by local charity organisations.

June was no extrovert, but she was active in school, participating as a cheerleader and singing in Glee Club as part of a chorus led by the austere Mrs Mary Trumble. Religion gave her another social outlet. Albion's diverse ethnic mix was felt through its places of worship: Roman Catholic churches for the Italians and the Irish, a Presbyterian church for the Scots, an Episcopal church for the English, and Methodist and Baptist churches for the American settlers who had travelled to the region from across the continent. June and Carol were Presbyterian and shared the same Sunday school teacher throughout high school. The teacher taught Latin and was a guidance counsellor at Albion High, where her husband was principal.

'She was there for us if we had a problem in high school,' said Carol. 'We could always go and talk to her. She was there for us every single Sunday, year after year.' The two friends were not overly religious, but they loved the sense of community the church brought to their local area.

In April 1956, Albion High School held a matchmaking event, which promised teenagers the opportunity to have 'their dreams fulfilled'. The rules of this 'Sadie Hawkins Race' were not complicated. Girls had to chase boys, and if a girl caught a boy 'he had to escort her to the box lunch on Friday night,' according to a description in Rochester's *Democrat & Chronicle* newspaper. 'Any boy who didn't want to be chased and caught could buy an immunity ticket, which would discourage any would-be boy snatchers.' Boys who were caught did not have to worry about spending money on their accidental dates, added the article, 'because the lunch was free'.

June did not attend. She had already fallen for someone. She was dating John Jones, a tall, quiet fellow a year older than June, whose father was minister at the Presbyterian Church.

In the summer of 1956, the governing body of Presbyterian churches in the Rochester area conducted a 'caravan tour' of the southern states, allowing local teenagers to visit Presbyterian colleges with a mind to attending one after graduation. Carol and June were among the juniors invited to participate and, to June's delight, John Jones was going too.

'We got on a bus and started south and hit a number of church colleges,' recounted Carol. 'We stayed in dorms there and had tours of the campus. We got as far south as Tennessee and North Carolina, but it was pretty exciting to go that far. Here we were, freshmen and sophomores in high school, and we were going off on this trip. It was something that a lot of kids didn't get a chance to do.'

Certainly not a girl like June, whose family struggled to make ends meet.

The trip lasted almost two weeks, and June turned 16 while she was on the road. The *Democrat & Chronicle* printed a photograph of five of Albion's 'caravaners' upon their return in July. Carol and June are at either ends of the picture, smiling happily at each other. John is gazing at June with a soft, adoring expression. 'I don't think anybody who went on that tour ever went to a Presbyterian college,' said Carol. 'But that's OK.'

When she returned to Albion High after that summer, June Fisk blossomed. The school had societies like the Future Teachers and Future Farmers that allowed students to explore potential career opportunities. June was an enthusiastic member of the Future Nurse's Society; she made visits to local clinics and hospitals, where she observed medical professionals and undertook auxiliary tasks. She and John Jones drifted apart – he left high school a year before her – but her future was mapping out.

For her last two years of high school, from the autumn of 1957 through to 1959, June travelled the couple of miles to school every day with Kay Walter, a girl who was in the same year as her at school. 'I lived across the road diagonally from June, probably 100 yards across the street,' said Kay. 'I wasn't a close friend. We didn't run back and forth to each other's houses. But my father, who had a business in the town and had a pickup truck, would take us to school. So every day she came out of her house and hopped in the truck and away we went. She was very nice.'

Carol Severns remembers June as a person who had everything to live for, someone with whom she shared magical times in her adolescence and early adult life.

'June,' said Carol. 'She was always such a positive, happy person.'

* * *

Joe was never going to last long at Aquinas Institute. Much to the annoyance of his parents, he was expelled from the prestigious Catholic school and sent to Monroe High School to finish out his education with his pals Neal Dunkleberg and Warren Daansen. Outside of class, Joe and Warren continued to get up to mischief, on one occasion reactivating a disused Civil War cannon in the dead of night and waking up the whole of Rochester. Kathy Daansen, Warren's wife, recalled visiting Warren's mother's house and seeing two cannonballs in the basement, which the boys kept as mementos. Joe, Warren and another local miscreant, John Chiswick, roamed the city's second-hand shops looking for munitions and gun parts, which they'd reconstruct into Frankenstein armaments.

As much as he longed to unleash hell on a battlefield, Joe was too unstable, too impulsive for a career in the armed forces. Upon graduating in 1953, Neal was posted to the Air Force in England, where he worked as a nuclear weapons specialist in Lakenheath and Mildenhall during the Cold War. Warren served as a pilot during the tail end of the Korean conflict. But Joe? He failed all military entry tests and settled for a six-month stint in the National Guard, an unflattering demotion that he told no one about. This was the extent of his military career, although in his mind, the eternal fabulist, it never got in the way of his stories of wars on foreign shores and conquests of native maidens that he'd relate to anyone within earshot. In truth, Joe was stuck in Rochester while his younger brother Jim, the less adventurous sibling, was drafted as an aviation mechanic in the US Navy.

Joe drifted from job to job. He worked at a leather shop on South Clinton and at Xerox, where Jim (after completing his Navy service) rose through the ranks to become head of the Maintenance Section. When Joe was fired from these and other part-time occupations, Joe's father took pity and got him a job at Rochester State Hospital. Monroe County Insane Asylum, as it was known in the 1800s, before it changed its name, was situated on a 200-acre parcel of land and encompassed over 80 buildings, most of which were constructed during the 1930s, when the Great Depression triggered a mental health crisis in America, causing severe overcrowding at facilities across the US. As a security guard, Joseph Maloney Senior had keys to every nook of the premises, and Joe took full advantage: roaming the corridors, the social areas and even the basement in the dead of night. He learned the layout of the place.

But he was never able to hold down a job, even a job with his dad – his predilection for chaos always ruined everything. In 1955, Joe received his first criminal record, when police arrested him walking down South Clinton Avenue with a Thompson submachine gun, a popular weapon amongst Allied forces in World War Two (and mobsters of the Prohibition era, who nicknamed it the 'Chicago Typewriter'). He and Jim were taking the Tommy gun home, Joe told the cops, 'to figure out how it worked'. Joe pled guilty to possession of an unregistered weapon, received a three-year probation sentence and was paroled to his parents.

Neal was at that time in England for a stint of four years, and he heard about Joe's actions on the grapevine. He contacted Joe only once during his time in England, and that was when Neal's sister complained. 'Joe had said something to my sister Gail, and she wrote me a letter saying he said some nasty things to her. So I wrote him a note back saying, "Behave yourself, boy".'

Despite his propensity for cruelty, Joe was irrepressibly charming, and he used this trait to his advantage with women. Girlfriends came and went, but his relationship with Joan Agnes Howland, a 19-year-old with reddish-brown hair who'd been in the year below him at high school, was serious. Joan was in love, and she agreed to marry Joe despite early warning signs of his temper. Joan's father objected. She was the youngest of his children, too young for marriage, he thought. He'd heard the rumours about her fiancé. In particular a story about Joe picking up a female hitchhiker. Rumour had it Joe was showing off a gun to the hitchhiker and the gun accidentally discharged in the car, grazing Joe's foot and scaring the hell out of his passenger.

When Joan Howland and Joe were married in February 1955, Joe's parents attended, but Joan's father boycotted the event, sitting in his bedroom, sulking and smoking. Joe and Joan's marriage was turbulent from the beginning, and they separated after a year following an incident in which Joan supposedly fell over a coffee table and broke her nose. While she was in hospital Joan met an ex-con called William Firth. She took off with Firth to Florida, unaware until her arrival that she was pregnant with Joe's child. Karen was born on 5 April 1957. The divorce went through the following month, but within a few days of receiving the paperwork Joan was forced to return home to Rochester when her mother died. During that brief home stay she told Joe about Karen, and they rekindled their relationship.

Joan fell pregnant a second time, although this time she didn't tell Joe the child was his. They separated a second and final time, and Joan left Rochester to live with Firth.

Joe was delighted when his friends Neal and Warren returned from military service. Warren studied at the University of Rochester and found work at General Motors, helping the car company develop windshield wipers. Neal sold drugs – legal drugs – for a Californian pharmaceutical outfit called Ryker Laboratories and spent his working day calling into physicians, surgeons, hospitals and drug stores. When Neal had an argument with his parents he moved in with Joe at his family home on Linden Street for a few weeks, and then he and Joe rented their own place: a ground-floor apartment on Westminster Road in Rochester.

'It was an interesting stay,' recounted Neal. 'I did the cooking. Sometimes we would stop in for a hamburger some place. We would wander around town, have a drink here, a drink there. We'd hit some spots downtown and get asked to leave this bar and go over to that one. I woke up one morning to a sound in our little apartment we were living in and found he had a lady guest with him. She ended up in bed with me, actually. Those were pleasant days.'

By 1959, Joe had found his calling: demolition. Although his total experience in explosives was blowing up a bridge on a farm in Livingston County, an hour south of Rochester, he talked his way onto a job on the Inner Loop, the city's version of the Washington DC beltway. The expressway circled the city and had been under construction since the early 1950s. Joe, a man of sudden enthusiasms, revelled in the destructive power of dynamite, but his fellow construction workers questioned his sanity, and they reignited his childhood nickname, Crazy Joe. Was it wise to give explosives to this lunatic? Joe certainly did himself no reputational favours with his choice of transport: a decommissioned ambulance that he bought in auction, cleaned up and called the 'Meat Wagon'.

* * *

When June Fisk graduated from Albion High in the summer of 1959, the world opened up to her – as much of the world that could be afforded to the daughter of a tenant farm labourer. Some of her contemporaries went to work at T.J. Lipton, a local factory that manufactured and packaged instant soup. Others gravitated to the Hunt-Wesson food canning plant. June knew exactly what she wanted to do with her life – and it wasn't working in a factory. June's experience in the Future Nurse's Society, her kind nature, excellent high school results and positive references from Albion High's principal, Charles D'Amico, won her a $750 nurses' training scholarship provided by the Orleans County Veterans organisation. A photograph of a smiling June celebrating her scholarship was featured in local newspapers, including the front page of the *Orleans Republican American*. June began her training at the Genesee Hospital School of Nursing, which offered a three-year programme that would qualify her as a New York State-registered professional nurse. June was excited by the opportunity to leave home in Albion and move into the student dormitories close to the city's downtown area.

Joan LaBue of Irondequoit NY was one of her fellow students at the nursing school. 'June was my size: small, five foot two,' recalled LaBue. 'She wasn't real bubbly, but she was friendly. She didn't have a lot of friends around her. She was very quiet. She was sweet and everything, just not as outgoing as the other girls. A little harder to know.'

LaBue got the sense that June's parents had an unhappy marriage, and she was correct. Ward and Marie's marriage had fallen apart, and Marie had left home. 'I think June did not come from a very good home life. She didn't talk much about her parents. The little she said about her mother, [I got the impression] they did not get along.'

But June came out of her shell at college and became part of a tight-knit group of friends, including Carol Reckahn. 'There was a group of about six of us that hung out together, and June was one of them,' said Reckahn. 'June was a very, very nice girl. She was very quiet. I would say attractive. She had beautiful red hair.'

Between their classes and work experience on hospital wards, the students didn't have much time off. Most of the girls, apart from one classmate from Ohio, who used to stay in the dorm over the weekend, returned to their family homes from Friday night to Sunday night. Reckahn's family lived in Medina, a few miles west of Albion. 'So June and I had something in common. I took her home a couple times during our time at nursing school. On weekends when I'd go home, I'd drop off June then pick her up again on Sunday.'

The School of Nursing was a multi-storey building. Above the first floor were the nurse dormitories, where men were not permitted. On the first floor was a residence hall featuring a large living room space, a fireplace and a piano, where residents and interns read and relaxed. One afternoon, Carol Reckahn was in the hall studying from a chemistry book when she noticed a young red-headed man in a laboratory coat with a stethoscope around his neck sitting opposite her.

'What are you looking up,' he asked.

'Meperidine,' replied Reckahn.

'Oh, I never heard of that.'

Reckahn was surprised. Every medical student knew about meperidine, a popular pain reliever. But the man seemed nice. He was tall, charming, good-looking. Years later Reckahn recalled: 'There was a connection there. He asked me if I wanted to go out. I said, "Why not?" I went upstairs, got changed and we went to a bar, had a couple drinks. He had a nice little sports car.'

Reckahn went on a few more dates with Joe Maloney. 'I can't remember the names of the places now, but I never went out to dinner with him or anything. We would just hop in his car and go for a drive.'

She liked Joe, but there was something strange about him. Joe took Carol Reckahn to his family home on Linden Street, and after introducing her to his mother he showed her his bedroom, where he'd plastered certificates and diplomas all over the walls.

There was a pilot's license, dated 1956, issued for a single engine private pilot; commendations for his status as a Second Lieutenant in the US Army; medical qualifications and all manner of salutations. None of it added up. How could a man who was barely 24 have done all these things? Then she wondered: 'Jesus, is he even a medical student?'

Carol felt a chill.

'They were all fictitious. He was a liar, you know, a downright liar.'

Joe's friends Warren Daansen and Neal Dunkleberg had both studied at the University of Rochester, and so Joe, who never liked being left out of anything, decided to do the same. He grilled Neal about the layout of the university and Neal, against his better judgement, gave his friend a tour of the campus and its library. In 1959, Joe got a new passport, on which he listed his occupation as a student. Then he set up an interview with the university's admissions officer, presented forged papers and told a story that he was a medical student from Dublin, Ireland, who had moved to Rochester to care for his ailing mother. The admissions officer, upon reading the paperwork and hearing Joe's Irish brogue (honed and polished from listening to his parents and trips to the motherland), bought the story and told Joe he was free to attend classes.

Neal rolled his eyes when he saw his roommate feverishly devouring the *Gray's Anatomy* reference book. Those medical night classes were costly, but Joe never paid a dime.

'He talked his way in,' said Neal. 'They admitted him, pending a check of his background. He was extremely intelligent. His intelligence made him readily able to grasp facts.'

That intelligence was not enough to get him through medical school. During anatomy classes, Joe persuaded his laboratory partner to do the dissecting while he read notes and pretended to be useful. In biochemistry he was totally lost after a couple of weeks.

'He was out of his depth,' said Neal.

Six months – two semesters – into Joe's tenure at the University of Rochester, papers arrived from Dublin revealing Joe's hoax, and he was kicked out of college. But by then the damage had been done, and June Fisk's fate was set in motion.

Carol was not with Joe for very long. His lies and strangeness were simply too much, and she refused to date him anymore. 'I said, "Hey, listen. I can fix you up with someone?"' June was the first one that came to mind, and she introduced her to him at a party. She didn't warn June about his eccentricities. Of course, she barely knew Joe and had no idea what he was capable of, she told me decades after these events.

'It left a lasting impression on me over all these years, because it could have been me. If I hadn't cut off the relationship and introduced him to June, it might have been me. I was the one that introduced Joe to June and I have regretted it every day since.'

2.

A Toxic Recipe

JUNE FISK WAS SMITTEN DURING HER FIRST FLUSH OF ROMANCE WITH JOE. He was adventurous and chivalrous – a bolt of lightning for this quiet country girl. Joan LaBue, June's classmate at Genesee nursing school, remembered him as tall, slim and attractive: a fast talker and a salesman who could make you believe anything. Marsha Curry had been in the year behind June at Albion High and was training to be a nurse. Marsha recalled Joe coming to the student dormitory to collect June for dates and found him outgoing and personable: 'Very friendly to everybody. People liked him, and if you were around the area, you would talk to him while he was waiting for June to come down to the residence hall. A very likeable guy.'

But the wild impulses that initially attracted June to Joe started to frighten her. She questioned his stability and confided in his friend and roommate Neal Dunkleberg, who 'tried to talk her out of marrying him. I said, "He's not the kind of guy you want to hang around with." I discussed his psychological peculiarities with June.' As far as Neal was concerned, this was not a betrayal of his friend but informed advice from years of experience witnessing the trail of destruction that Joe left behind him, particularly with women.

June didn't listen. Every time she had doubts, Joe charmed her all over again, and after completing her second year of training, mere months after they first met, she dropped out of nurse's school to follow Joe to California, where he had an offer to work for an Irish demolition contractor in San Carlos. 'She ran away,' said Joan LaBue. 'She more or less ran away and took off. She left nursing school and took off with him to California.'

The trip was a disaster. Joe's braggadocio about conquering California was bogus, and once again he was unable to hold down a job. A rental agreement from October 1961 showed the couple living in an apartment in the San Francisco area and described his job status as 'unemployed'. Two months later, Joe married June in Daly City, California. Joe was broke and jobless, and June was pregnant. By March of the following year, the same month Joe's mother Winifred died, the couple had been forced to return to Rochester. Their first child, Joseph Scott Maloney – Joey – was born on 28 May 1962.

June was now entirely financially reliant on Joe. In the summer of 1962, June's friends celebrated their graduation from nursing school, but June was noticeably absent from their group photographs. The world was leaving her behind. But June hid resourcefulness and determination behind her reserved façade. She persuaded the school to take her back and let her finish her final year. In a decision that cannot have been easy, she gave her baby boy Joey to a friend, an older woman called Catherine Blair, to care for while she returned to Genesee to complete her studies.

'June was a student nurse living in the dormitory at Genesee,' Catherine later told police in a sworn statement. 'The couple had no place to keep the child since Joe Maloney did not provide a home.' She cared for Joey for six months. 'Mister Maloney only came to my house once in [those] six months and when he came he only talked about himself. He gave no money at all for the support of the child, except once he gave me a 15 dollar cheque which proved to be no good.'

By the summer of 1963, the couple's finances were in better shape. June took Joey back into her fulltime care, graduated from school to become a qualified nurse and began working at Genesee hospital. Joe found steady employment in construction and set up his own demolition business, Joe Maloney Blasting Inc., which, to his delight, came with a certificate of fitness to 'set off and discharge high explosives in the city of Rochester'. The couple even managed to get a mortgage for a property on the corner of upmarket Eastmoreland Drive. Years later, the inhabitants of Eastmoreland became transient, but in the mid-1960s it was a local, generational neighbourhood where everyone knew each other. Joe befriended George Reiss, a detective and a captain in the Rochester police department who lived a couple of blocks away. George and Joe saw each other a lot, and Joe enjoyed socialising with a law enforcement officer. They were often in each other's houses, and Joe picked up George in his car and took him for a ride when he was scoping out new construction jobs.

'My brother and I both cut Joe's lawn,' Ed Reiss, George's son, recalled. 'During the summertime myself and George Junior would be at his house every couple of weeks. Joe would be at our house for neighbourhood parties too. I remember he was very tall, had red hair and he was a nice guy.'

Jack Borgese, another neighbour, remembered Joe speeding past on his huge black motorcycle and fussing over a new red

Ford Mustang and playing with his son Joey on the front porch. 'He'd give you the shirt off his back,' said Borgese. 'One time, I was out shovelling snow and he came by with his snow blower.' Joe insisted his neighbour use the snow blower to clear his driveway before Joe worked on his own. 'He was like that.'

The Maloneys frequently entertained guests. Marsha Curry was working alongside June on the sixth floor of Genesee hospital and remembered rowdy parties at their residence: 'It was the first time I ever got drunk!' Linda True Chamberlain, who went to school with June at Albion High, had a daughter the same age as Joey and brought her to the Maloney home for play dates. Linda's husband was of Scottish heritage, and he and Joe swapped notes about their Celtic motherlands. Joe recounted tales of his visits to Ireland over drinks and card games.

But Joe always struck Linda as strange. 'He was an odd person,' she said. 'He talked about death a lot.'

Not everyone in the neighbourhood fell for his charms. Joe was in long-running disputes (the origins of which are unknown) with a couple of neighbours. One of them, Charles Austin, was a retired cop. The other, Roger Marsocci, lived across the street from the Maloneys' home. Marsocci didn't mince his words in his appraisal of his neighbour. Joe, he said, was 'a very, very bad man'.

June's proficiency as a nurse did not go unrewarded. She was promoted to take charge of a ward at Genesee and then became head nurse for an entire floor on the west wing of the hospital, a position salaried at $8,000 per annum.

'June was smart,' said her friend and fellow nurse Joan LaBue. 'She was a good nurse. She worked straight evenings as a manager from 3pm to midnight, full-time, up there on the sixth floor. I had a baby. I just worked two or three days a week.

My husband was trying to establish a law practice during the day, and then I would go to work 6pm to midnight.'

June's shifts started rotating between nights and days, and her friend Catherine Blair cared for Joey during the day. June's downtime was spent baking and cooking for her husband and taking her son to church every other Sunday when she was off work. Behind the façade, however, her marriage was crumbling. Joe, according to Neal, was 'never a great believer in monogamy', and he usually had a girlfriend or two on the side.

'He had been a little abusive to June,' said LaBue. 'He could push her around a bit. I don't think she had enough confidence in herself to stand up to him or get rid of him and figure out, "I'll find somebody else".'

In the summer of 1964, June moved in with Catherine for six or seven weeks because Joe was 'entertaining a woman' in their home. June moved out of the house on Eastmoreland several times, in fact, but whenever she left he refused to counter the idea that she didn't want to be with him. Joe was relentless. He hounded her to return, waiting outside the hospital emergency room with flowers and apologies and stories of regret.

'He stalked her,' explained LaBue. 'I would see her at the hospital and she'd say, "Would you stay and have coffee with me because I know he's going to be waiting outside to talk to me" and she didn't want to talk to him.'

But June always relented and moved back in with her tormentor.

'He was diabolical,' said LaBue. 'I met him a couple of times, but I got to know him through people that knew him well that grew up with him. He was always a bit sadistic. He said he was always in trouble. He was not a nice kid. There was one fellow I dated for a little while who grew up in his neighbourhood with them. He said Joe used to take cats by the tail, swing them around and throw them into a tree. That's cruelty, right there.'

In 1965, the Maloneys' second child, Patricia Ann (Patti-Ann) was born, and Joe's unstable finances stretched the family thinner. Joe seemed incapable of holding down a job in construction, and his brief forays into sales never lasted long – employers usually found out that his qualifications were forgeries and his reliability was close to zero. He spent his sporadic pay cheques on needless purchases, and when he wasn't blowing his own wages he was burning through June's. One year it was a brand-new 1965 Ford Mustang; the next it was a new Ford pickup. Creditor letters mounted up at the Eastmoreland Drive residence. Marsha Curry worked the night shift at Genesee hospital and talked with June whenever they had a coffee break.

'The thing I remember is every night just about, June would have a tale of woe about Joe and things he was doing to her and the family,' said Marsha. 'A lot of financial problems. He would steal money from her and he would spend money on things he didn't have. Finances were a big thing. He was very irresponsible, and it made her life miserable.'

Joe was too consumed by his fantasies to care. One day Catherine Blair and her nephew were getting a lift in Joe's car when he showed them a US Army officer uniform on the backseat.

'That's mine,' he announced proudly. 'I was a Second Lieutenant.'

Catherine knew it was hokum and that his military experience consisted of a few months in the National Guard. On another occasion, Joe offered her drugs – he appeared to be hitting on her. 'Mister Maloney showed me a little silver box with something in it and told me if I tried it, it would give me a "way out feeling",' she later told police.

Cathy sometimes turned up at the house on Eastmoreland Drive to mind the kids while June was working and she found them both in bed at noon. 'Mister Maloney would tell me he didn't allow the boy downstairs and made them stay in bed. He would refer to them as "her kids".'

Neal believed Joe was fond of his children, and Joey in particular, but he was 'never close' to them: 'I don't think Joe could get close to other people'. By the mid-1960s, Neal was studying psychology at the University of Rochester. He thought Joe was 'a walking case study', and he wrote a paper about his friend for his Abnormal Psychology class.

'My professor was really interested. Joe never told the truth that I knew of. Or he rarely told the truth. He was an expert liar. I think a lack of conscience is a pretty good description. Joe ran his own life in his own way. I think a sociopath is a good description. A psychopath in some ways, but it didn't come out readily. You had to know him a while and find out some of the things he engaged in before you recognised him as a bit of a weirdo.'

Neal told Joe about his academic study of Joe's 'psychiatric peculiarities'. Joe wasn't annoyed. Far from it. 'He was very interested in it. He thought it was wonderful. Yes, he always loved the attention.'

For June, this was no laughing matter. Joe's financial control, his manipulative behaviour and his psychological abuse were textbook signs of domestic abuse. In the summer of 1966, Joe bought a cottage in Springwater, 40 miles south of Rochester, and the family moved there, but Joe walked out one day and didn't return. A penniless June had to get her brother Dale to help her move out.

'Joe used to play tricks on her,' recalled Marsha Curry. 'He would tell her things and tried to make her believe things that weren't true. He would lie to her about things and she never quite knew if she could believe what he was telling her. He just wasn't a very nice person. I remember always thinking, although I probably didn't say it to her, "Why doesn't she leave him? Why doesn't she get rid of him?"'

June told Neal she wanted to escape, for good this time, but she was afraid of what Joe would do. 'June confided in me that Joe had roughed her up a couple of times,' he said. 'He wasn't above jumping around hollering and yelling and looking very dangerous, and perhaps grabbing hold of you and shaking you.'

Neal wasn't afraid of Joe. He was far smaller than the burly Irishman, but he had stood up to him when he was intimidating Neal's sister, and now he did the same for June.

'Lay off her, Joe,' Neal told him. 'I'm warning you.'

'You're getting too pushy,' Joe yelled back. 'I'm living my own life.'

In October 1966, Joe's father, Joseph Senior, died. He bequeathed Joe $10,000 and all the personal property in the living room and dining room of the house on Linden Street. The rest of the estate including the house was to be distributed among the grandchildren. James, Joe's brother, was appointed executor of the will. Joe was by now hopelessly unemployed, and nobody wanted to hire him on account of his poor reputation. His wallet, which his lawyer's family posted to Joey decades later, was laden with credit notices: $30 owed to Gray's Carpet Cleaning; $34 to Tidy Didy; $1,517.61 to Atlantic Tug for the purchase of a bulldozer.

Joe, now 31 years old, was ignoring his debts and his family's needs and had become fixated upon his father's estate and questions around collateral from his ancestral homestead. In January 1967 he travelled to Ireland to meet with a solicitor, Patrick O'Connor in Roscrea, County Tipperary, to enquire about the estate. Joe left June and the children behind in Rochester with no money despite his $10,000 inheritance.

Catherine Blair was with June when she called the bank, 'which is what he told her to do. Mister Maloney had told her he had deposited $700. They told her she had less than $50.'

June was done, finished. This was the final straw. And this time she had an escape route. She'd begun seeing a man, Lee DiClemente: a handsome skier and all-round outdoorsman from neighbouring Canandaigua. DiClemente, with his Italian extraction and mop of black hair, had a roguish charm that earned him the nickname 'Marlboro Man'. His party trick was extinguishing cigarettes on the palm of his hand. His macho tendencies were offset by a sensitive side, which in later years would see him establishing an animal shelter in New Mexico. Unfortunately for June, he was also married. But she had run out of options. Broke and in need of help with the children, she moved in with her friend Catherine Blair after Joe returned from Ireland. When Joe learned about DiClemente, said Joan LaBue, 'that's when he really started getting nasty'.

Neal Dunkleberg agreed. 'Things really went bananas.'

One day, Joe phoned Neal asking him for help. Joe explained he'd fallen down the steps of the basement at Eastmoreland Drive and accidentally stabbed himself with a screwdriver. Neal arrived to find blood everywhere and Joe clutching his abdomen. Strong Memorial Hospital was the logical place to take him – it was only five minutes away from Eastmoreland – but Joe insisted they go to Genesee, where June was on duty.

Doctors were puzzled. Joe's puncture wound was surgical in precision. There was no tearing. The screwdriver had sheared a loop of Joe's small intestine but missed his bladder and major blood vessels. Neal was convinced Joe had inflicted the injury upon himself using the anatomical knowledge he picked up from medical school in a bid for his wife's sympathy.

* * *

While recovering from abdominal surgery in room 436 of the west wing of Genesee Hospital, Joe, demented with jealousy, hired a private investigation firm to monitor June and DiClemente's movements:

Client: Joseph Maloney
Female Subject: June R. Maloney
Male Subject: Lee DiClemente

Saturday, 4 March, 1967
8:00pm Both Operatives had the house at 190 Eastmoreland Drive staked out and the Female Subject was in the house, her residence.
9:15pm Male Subject entered the house at 190 Eastmoreland Drive; he was driving a white station wagon, license #5A-6969; as he entered the house the lights were on until 11:20pm
11:21pm It was checked by both Operatives and was found that the house was in total darkness by 11:25pm Both Operatives staked out the house for the entire night.

Sunday, 5 March, 1967
7:22am The Male Subject left the house. Male Subject drove South on Eastmoreland Drive, turned left onto Westmoreland Drive.

Wednesday, 15 March, 1967
3:30pm Both Operatives drove to Genesee hospital. Female subject came out of the hospital dressed in nurse's uniform and drove to her new residence 114 Christian Avenue [Catherine Blair's House].

7:30pm Female Subject came out of the house and drove her green Corvair, Licence #M9643, to the shopping centre, returning in 15 minutes, only to be met by the Male Subject, Mr DiClemente, and they both drove off together, she sitting right by his side. Upon entering the car: a kiss and embrace.

Such insights did nothing to quell Joe's feelings of rejection; they only fuelled his rage. After being released from Genesee hospital he lurked in the car park outside the hospital waiting for June to emerge from work. When she got into her car he sprang, a kitchen blade wielded high above his head. June slammed the lock on the door as Joe drove the knife through the white convertible canopy above her head. Screaming, she started the engine and put the accelerator to the floor. When she arrived home she called the police. Around the same time, March 1967, Joe tracked down DiClemente and tried to beat him up.

'Joe tried to kill me!' DiClemente told police.

William 'Bill' Mahoney, an officer with the Rochester police department, arrested Maloney and charged him with third-degree assault. But June and DiClemente withdrew their complaints and the police decided not to proceed with charges. It's not clear why they let him off the hook, but June appeared to be trying to keep the peace and was no doubt frightened of what he might do if she had him arrested. Joe, on the other hand, was unabashed by the involvement of the police and continued paying private detectives to surveil the couple.

June moved with her children out of Catherine Blair's house and into a small two-bedroom apartment in a new development called LeChase Manor, off Lyell Road to the west of the city. Joe continued his intimidatory tactics, breaking into June's apartment when she was out and leaving obvious signs of his presence.

He spread a rumour among her friends that he planned to booby trap her house with dynamite.

Joan LaBue's husband Gene was by now an attorney and agreed to help June. One day he came home and told his wife: 'You'll never guess who came to see me at my office.'

LaBue explained: 'Joe Maloney walked right in and gave Gene this sad story about how June was lying about Joe doing the things he did. Blah, blah, blah. Gene said if he hadn't known I had been telling the truth and that June was telling the truth he could have been taken in. Joe was that smooth of a talker. Gene asked him to leave the office when he realised who he was. Joe left without any trouble.'

Intimidation, violence and coercion. They'd all failed. Faced with the prospect of a restraining order, Joe tried another tactic: he begged for reconciliation. June wasn't interested. Joe was still not providing money for the support of their children. DiClemente suggested she also approach his attorney, Robert Agnello, who moonlighted as an assistant district attorney for Monroe County.

'My law office, Rosenbawn and Agnello, represented Mrs Maloney in regard to her marital difficulties,' Agnello wrote in a letter. 'The parties were physically separated and living apart. During the past few weeks, Mrs Maloney had indicated to our office that [Joe] had threatened her life because of the separation action that she had instituted.' Indeed, Joe fought the separation proceedings and avoided the marshals who tried to serve him papers. When one marshal tracked him down at a gas station, Joe convinced him he was his brother James. 'He had a basic ability to deceive,' said Agnello.

Eventually Joe appeared to give up. In an informal separation agreement, June was given custody of the children and Joe was allowed to visit them whenever he wanted.

The situation was not ideal, but maybe June could finally have some peace.

Wanda Mordenga was newly married and lived with her husband in an apartment directly across the hall from June at LeChase Manor. Wanda was 19, younger than 26-year-old June, but the women hit it off. 'We started talking and became friends,' said Wanda. 'It was like an older sister type thing. June was a slender woman with pretty red hair. A really attractive woman. And she was very nice. She was just a really nice lady, a great person. She was very kind. She was bubbly. She had a smile on her face most of the time.'

Wanda didn't have children of her own but was fond of Joey and Patti-Ann, and she left her apartment door open to allow the kids to run back and forth.

'June adored her kids. They were well behaved. I don't remember her yelling at them or telling them to sit down. She just went with the flow. She loved them so much. They were really good kids. Joey was very inquisitive. He was a smart kid.'

Joey had inherited his father's passion for vehicles and could identify the brand of pretty much any car, tractor or digger. Patti was 18 months old; Wanda remembered her as 'a little charmer. A tiny little thing. A sweetheart.' LeChase was a series of two-storey red-brick apartment buildings: a smaller, more modest abode than the Maloneys' suburban home eight miles away on Eastmoreland Drive. But June felt liberated here, and Wanda could see her friend emerging from her shell. June would return from Genesee hospital and relax while Wanda took the kids for a walk or would build makeshift forts for them outside using scraps from a nearby construction site. June invited Wanda to Tupperware parties, where the younger woman met some of June's fellow nurses.

'I think once she got away from Joe, she felt better,' said Wanda. 'She was happier.'

June was still dating DiClemente and, although he treated her well, Wanda didn't envisage the relationship lasting. 'It was just somebody she was with.' June never talked about her separation, but Wanda could see Joe was bombing June with a mixture of infatuation and threats. On one occasion, he sent her flowers. On another, Wanda heard him yelling at her in her apartment. 'June must have called the police, but they went to the apartment building next door instead of checking where the call came from. They just left. I guess everything settled down and Joe left.'

Wanda met Joe when he came to see the kids. 'I remember him being a big man: ruddy complexion. I would have to say he scared me a little bit. I don't think he's anybody to be pushed. Sometimes, the way he talked, he connived, it seemed like. His eyes were quite striking. Strange. He gave me a scary, eerie feeling.'

From a young age, Neal Dunkleberg had been fascinated with chemistry and the practical applications and intellectual challenges that accompanied science. It was his interest in explosives, in fact, that inspired Joe to work in the demolition trade. Neal kept a chemistry set in the basement of his parents' home at Meigs Street in Rochester: a makeshift laboratory that consisted of a table and shelves that held chemicals, tubes and a Bunsen burner. It was all he needed for experiments and party tricks.

'I had a little show that I put on where I had a beaker and I'd pour things into it and it would change colours, bubble, make a little smoke.'

In early May 1967, Joe turned up at Neal's door. Relations between the childhood friends were strained. Neal was not exactly June's number one confidante during the breakup with her husband, but he'd supported her and was never afraid to confront Joe over his behaviour. But Joe didn't appear to have come for a fight. Instead he wanted advice. A dog that belonged to his neighbourhood nemesis, the ex-cop Charles Austin, was infuriating him, he told Neal. The dog kept raiding his garbage, tipping over the trash cans and leaving a mess.

'Have you got some kind of poison that doesn't leave any trace? I'd shoot the damned thing but it belongs to a detective,' said Joe.

Neal thought about this for a moment. 'It's impossible – everything leaves a trace. How would you get the dog to drink it anyway?'

Joe shrugged. 'There's got to be something that leaves no trace?'

Then the conversation became theoretical and Neal and Joe discussed specific chemicals. Neal had cyanides and arsenics in his collection, but Joe showed particular interest in methyl alcohol, otherwise known as wood alcohol, a clear liquid used as a solvent and as anti-freeze in vehicles. It was colourless and highly toxic.

Neal didn't give him any. The encounter raised his suspicions, so he gave Joe 'something that smelled nasty to keep the dog away. I didn't give him any poison.'

When Joe left Neal wondered what he really wanted to do with the chemical.

'You see,' he later recounted. 'I knew him so well.'

Neal double-locked the side door that led to his laboratory and told his family members not to let anybody in without his explicit permission – in particular Joe Maloney.

3.

Ten Days of June

ON FRIDAY, 26 MAY 1967, THICK BLACK SMOKE OVER ROCHESTER RINSED THE SKY OF COLOUR. Fire fighters assembled on Troup Street in the west of the city, where flames tore through a row of garages and threatened a neighbouring barn and houses. A second fire simultaneously broke out at a four-car garage on Clinton to the south of the city: an incident that investigators blamed on adolescent arsonists.

As fires raged and sirens blared, Wanda Mordenga accompanied June Maloney on a trip to the local mall to find a cake for Joey's birthday. They left their neighbouring apartments in June's Corvair and June explained the plan en route. Joey's fifth birthday was not until Sunday, but Joe wanted to hold a party for him on Eastmoreland Drive. June, hoping to keep the peace, agreed to have it on Saturday and then she would hold her own party for Joey on Sunday with family and friends. They found a cake for

Joey and returned to the apartment building, the sky above them a darkened canopy.

The following day, Wanda took Patti-Ann's crib into her apartment so she could mind the infant while June took Joey to Joe's house. Not long afterwards, the phone rang.

'Hi Wanda, it's June. Why don't you and Tony come over with Patti-Ann to the party?'

Tony was Wanda's husband.

'No you go ahead and have a good time,' Wanda said. 'I'll put Patti to bed tonight if you like. We'll work everything out.'

'OK, that's fine.'

Wanda went about her day but then June arrived back earlier than expected, just after 6pm. Wanda thought June was behaving strangely. She wasn't walking properly and looked terrible. Joey ran into June's apartment with the toys from his birthday party. Wanda fetched Patti and brought her into the apartment. June staggered to a chair.

'June,' said Wanda. 'How many drinks did you have?'

'Wanda, I only had two.'

'Two drinks? You're acting kind of funny.'

'I know. I don't know what's wrong.'

Soon afterwards Joe turned up; June's mother and brother followed. Dale later told police: 'I was concerned about her condition and said I'd drive over and see how she was doing. I arrived at her house around 6:15pm. Joe Maloney seemed concerned. He'd been drinking but he appeared sober. I stayed at her apartment for about half an hour. She was normal and felt a little better. Wanda, the babysitter, was in June's apartment.'

Joe talked to June in hushed tones. She wanted to go to bed but he didn't want her to. He wanted to stay with her.

'No, you leave,' she said, bluntly.

Joe left with Dale to return to the house on Eastmoreland, where the party continued until around 1am. Wanda got up to go back to her apartment.

'I'll check on you during the night, June,' she told her friend.

'No, don't worry, I'm okay,' replied June.

June had a terrible night. She tossed and turned. Her stomach and abdomen hurt something crazy and she was nauseous, constantly getting out of bed to vomit. Sunday was her son's birthday, so she put on a brave face as her parents came to the apartment alongside Dale and his fiancée Gladys. Wanda and Tony came from across the hall and gave Joey an electronic game called *Operation*. The boy delicately used tweezers to extract the patient's funny bone and spare ribs, wrenched ankle and broken heart, trying not to set off the game's buzzer. His mother kept a brave face, but her deterioration was evident.

Later on that day, after the party, Wanda was in her apartment when she heard somebody talking in the hall. She looked out the door to see a man in the hallway with Joe.

Joe introduced him as a doctor. 'I've called him for June.'

Wanda wanted to visit June. Joe was hesitant, but the doctor said it was fine. June was in bed. She looked terrible; worse than the previous night.

'I'm not feeling good. Wanda, I have this awful headache.'

June told her she didn't want to be left alone with Joe. She wanted Wanda to stay: 'Don't leave me,' June pleaded. 'Don't leave yet.'

She told Wanda the doctor thought she had food poisoning, but June believed it was something else. She got out of bed to get aspirin from the bathroom. Wanda would later recall: 'We were in the bedroom talking and she didn't want me to leave her alone with Joe. She wanted me to stay with her. She was quite definite.

So I did. All of a sudden June stopped talking and she had, I would have to say, a fear look in her eyes. I looked over and Joe was standing in the doorway.'

Joe glared at Wanda with contempt. 'He didn't want me there. He did not want me there. But June didn't want me to leave her alone with him. I know that.'

But the situation felt intolerable, and Wanda eventually left. That night June's mother, Marie, came to the apartment to care for her while Joe had dinner with the children. Marie tried to convince June to go to the hospital but she refused, insisting she was alright.

The following morning – Monday, 29 May – Wanda witnessed Joe take June to Strong Memorial Hospital in his car. Ward and Marie, June's parents, stuck around for a while in the apartment to mind the children, then asked if Wanda could take over.

Joe initially told hospital staff he didn't know what was wrong with his wife. Doctors ran a battery of tests but couldn't find a cause for her condition, and she deteriorated further. They took a blood sample, which they sent to the Public Safety Laboratory with a request that it be analysed. Seeing this, Joe's story changed. He had an explanation. June was depressed due to work troubles and martial strain, and she had attempted suicide.

By the time Dale arrived that evening, June was unconscious. 'I talked with Joe,' June's brother later told police. 'He told me the details of what had happened. She was seriously ill. Thought she had taken poison. And Joe said, "Oh my God, why did she do this to herself? Why did she do this?"'

Joe told the same story to a doctor called Hugh Clarke. June had attempted suicide. How did Joe know? He'd seen a bottle of rubbing alcohol – a liquid solution used as a disinfectant and antiseptic, also known as surgical spirit – next to her bed. Dr Clarke took it upon himself to go to the apartment with Joe, but he couldn't find the bottle. The following morning, Tuesday, Dale arrived at Strong Memorial with Gladys to learn that June had fallen into a coma. Joe was beside her bed and seemed to know more about what happened.

'I've been down to the research library in the hospital and looked up alcoholic poisoning and read up on it,' declared Joe. 'I've been talking to the doctors and this is what they've come up with as a solution to what June has taken.'

Joe took Dale and Gladys to the library, where he pulled a book off a shelf and opened it at the toxicology section. 'Look: methyl alcohol,' he said. Ingesting the tiniest amount of this liquid also known as wood alcohol was highly dangerous, explained the book. It could cause vision problems and permanent damage to a person's central nervous system. It oxidized into formaldehyde, the main agent in embalming fluid, and effectively embalmed a person alive from the inside out. Dale was horrified. This is what was happening to his sister?

'Say nothing to the police,' Joe warned Dale and Gladys. The way he spun it, the authorities would turn family and friends against each other. June had made a terrible decision to end her life and now everyone needed to be united in their support for her.

'He said it was better not to talk to an attorney or the police,' Dale said. 'It would be better to keep quiet. If nothing was said about this publicly, it would be less apt to come out.'

Joe took aside members of hospital staff. 'My wife is a head nurse at Genesee hospital,' he told them. 'Please don't tell anybody about her attempted suicide. This could destroy her career.'

The staff and doctors bought his story, and the hospital didn't make a report to the police, despite this being a legal requirement in the event of a suspected poisoning. The hospital instead requested the results of the blood test be sent directly to them.

Wanda Mordenga, however, was not convinced. Later that week, Joe drove Wanda to visit June at hospital in his Ford Mustang, telling her: 'June tried to commit suicide, Wanda.' He placed the blame on June's boyfriend. 'It's Lee DiClemente's damned fault.'

Wanda was silent as they drove the six miles to Strong Memorial Hospital. 'He wasn't nervous,' Wanda recalled. 'I wouldn't call him nervous at all. He told me that they all thought June tried to commit suicide and Lee was the cause of it and this and that. I knew that wasn't the case. I didn't say anything. I don't recall saying anything back to him because I knew that wasn't true.' Joe was fishing to see what Wanda knew, but she stayed quiet. 'I was a 19-year-old kid. I didn't know what to do. So I didn't do anything.' When they arrived at the hospital, Wanda was shocked. June lay there: motionless as though she was only sleeping. She was pale and clammy.

'What will happen if I pulled this plug?' Joe asked a nurse who was in the room.

The nurse looked at him, surprised. 'She would die.'

Joe brought Wanda home from the hospital. Once again he raised the subject of June's attempted suicide and kept digging to see if Wanda thought anything different. Wanda said nothing but inside she was screaming.

'I knew it wasn't true. She would not commit suicide. You don't commit suicide if you're planning your life. Joey would have started school in September. You think she really wanted to put that on Joey? No. Not at all. She was making plans.'

* * *

Lee DiClemente was no angel. Like Joe Maloney, he had a talent for inventing stories and using his charisma to seduce the people in his orbit. In many ways, this Italian-American tough guy was the perfect nemesis for Joe. DiClemente was kicked out of high school, his parents were forever bailing him out of trouble and he never went to college. But he was a self-made man: a competitive skier who eventually established a ski resort in Naples, New York, at the southern end of Canandaigua Lake. DiClemente was also a hopeless womaniser who, at the time of his relationship with June, was living with his wife (a redhead like June) in an apartment in Seabreeze, a neighbourhood north of Rochester between Lake Ontario and Irondequoit Bay. DiClemente's wife was oblivious to his affair with June, and it was probably in his best interests to stay quiet, but his moral compass was made of stronger stuff. At 6:15pm on Tuesday, 30 May, the day after June was taken to hospital, DiClemente phoned his lawyer, Robert Agnello, at his home. DiClemente recounted how the Saturday beforehand, after Joey's birthday party at Joe's house, he had spoken to June over the phone.

'I don't feel good, I think he's trying to kill me,' June told him. 'Lee, I love you and I don't want to die. I feel wobbly and have trouble seeing. I think he put something in the drinks.'

DiClemente called her back at 1pm the following day and she told him Joe was in her apartment. 'She still felt about the same,' DiClemente told his attorney.

'Has he said anything to make you think he put anything in the drinks?' DiClemente asked June.

'No, but he's acting awfully funny,' replied June.

DiClemente asked if she wanted him to come over and pick her up.

'No, better not, he'll kill you.'

'I talked to her again that evening about 7pm,' Lee continued to Agnello. 'She felt worse. She said she had company, I assumed it was Joe. She couldn't keep anything down.'

DiClemente hung up. Agnello stared at the phone. He was representing June in her separation from Joe and knew what she'd been going through. He knew Joe was capable of pretty much anything. He picked up the receiver and called Strong Memorial Hospital to check that June was a patient there. She was, they told him, and her condition was critical. He then phoned Dr Waterhouse, who was apparently treating her, identified himself and asked more about June's condition. The medic was uncooperative.

The attorney called DiClemente back and instructed him to come to his office the following morning. That next day, Wednesday, he called John Little, the Monroe County district attorney, asking for advice. Little was not available, so he reported the matter to John Mastrella, an assistant DA, who in turn asked the lawyer to take it to Lieutenant Anthony Fantigrossi, a detective in Rochester police's Physical Crimes Unit. Agnello and DiClemente then travelled to the detective bureau, where the police initiated an investigation with their cooperation.

The first task of the investigators was to diagnose the blood sample taken from June in Strong Memorial. The medic at the Public Safety Laboratory 'could not understand why the hospital had sent the sample to him and was confused as to why the police were not contacted,' Agnello later wrote in a letter to the DA, John Little.

Lieutenant Fantigrossi travelled to the lab, picked up the blood sample and took it to Robert Greendyke of the Monroe County Medical Examiner's office. Greendyke was also surprised to learn that the hospital had made no attempt to report the incident to authorities, and he relayed his findings to police headquarters. The blood sample, taken on Monday, 29 May, the day June entered the hospital, revealed 0.04 g/dL methyl alcohol content.

'If enough methyl alcohol is ingested, the first thing to happen is blindness,' Greendyke explained to the cops. 'Then, as the brain eventually deteriorates and becomes like a sponge, the person dies.'

While Agnello and DiClemente were at the police station, Agnello's legal partner received a call from an attorney called William Power, who worked with Thomas Presutti, the lawyer who represented Joe in his marriage dispute. Power tried to convince Agnello's legal partner that there was nothing to see here: June Maloney tried to commit suicide and they were keeping it quiet at the hospital out of concern for her and her family's privacy. This only increased Lieutenant Fantigrossi's suspicions. He sent two detectives to Strong Memorial to check on June, and they found her in a coma with her doctors behaving uncooperatively.

Fantigrossi was increasingly sure Joe was involved. His department had handled Joe's knife attack on June a few months beforehand, and his suspicions grew after speaking to Charles Austin and George Reiss, the retired cop and lieutenant who were Joe's neighbours. The officers described Joe as a salesman: a person with 'a tremendous gift of the gab'.

'You might say he was a sub-contractor of sorts,' Reiss told Fantigrossi. 'He would look around and get jobs like roofing or operating heavy construction machinery by just asking different people and selling them on his supposed qualifications. Sometimes he would do some regular sales work but not for long.'

Over the next few days, the detectives questioned witnesses and people who knew June and Joe. Wanda, who was taking care of June's children with help from June's friend Catherine Blair, was in her apartment when the phone rang. It was Fantigrossi on one line and another cop – detective supervisor Bill Mahoney, the same officer who arrested Joe following his assault of her and DiClemente – on the other.

'How long have you known them? What was their relationship like? What has Joe told you?'

Wanda felt overwhelmed from their barrage of questions. She started answering then thought, 'I don't even know who I'm talking to' and hung up.

Soon afterwards Catherine Blair called.

'Wanda, the police are involved. They've called me too. They suspect Joe.'

'Oh, God,' said Wanda. 'What will happen to the kids?'

Fantigrossi and Mahoney arrived at Wanda's apartment to ask more questions.

'I know Joe but I'm not fond of him,' she told them. 'I'm afraid of him in a way.'

The detectives continued to question witnesses and collect evidence, and they sensed June's family were obstructing them. William Power, Maloney's attorney, contacted Fantigrossi's office to tell the lieutenant he represented Joe and that his client should not be spoken to unless his lawyers were present. Furthermore, he said he represented June's brother and mother, Dale and Marie Fisk, and Dale's fiancée, Gladys MacDiarmid. Power and Presutti, Rochester police later discovered, did *not* represent Dale or Gladys. Gladys 'would have gladly answered questions if she was contacted,' Agnello wrote in a letter to DA John Little. '[Gladys] was at the [birthday] party when Mrs Maloney was administered [the cocktails], but Lt Fantigrossi did not contact her because of Mr Power's statement that he represented her and she should not be questioned.'

Agnello and the detectives were in no doubt as to the source of this disinformation: Joe had convinced his attorneys to speak on behalf of June's family members. 'This guy could talk you right out of your shorts,' a furious Detective Mahoney told his colleagues.

Agnello would later describe Power's conduct as 'obstructing the investigation' and he was critical of Power's decision to 'conduct a search of Mr Maloney's house before the police had an opportunity to obtain a search warrant'.

On Friday, 2 June 1967, a search warrant was finally obtained and the police searched Joe's home with Joe and Power hovering in the background. Nothing was found.

* * *

When Neal Dunkleberg heard about June's illness his immediate thought was: what the hell has Joe done now? He travelled to Strong Memorial Hospital, where Joe was with June's mother in the waiting room. Joe scowled upon seeing his supposed best friend and practically strong-armed him out of the hospital. Neal returned later on when Joe was gone and sat with June for a while. She was motionless and breathing through a respirator. As soon as he got home he called the police. An investigation was already underway, they told him.

'Well,' Neal told them, 'I know something that you might not.'

But it was too late. June never regained consciousness. She died in Strong Memorial hospital on 5 June 1967, 10 days after her poisoning. Following her passing, the medical examiner, Robert Greendyke, undertook an autopsy, which confirmed findings from the earlier blood sample: June had been administered a lethal dose of methyl alcohol.

Catherine Blair came to Wanda's apartment to tell her the news of June's death.

'I just lost it,' recalled Wanda. 'June was a remarkable young woman. So full of life. This woman would not commit suicide. I bet all my life on it.'

Later that day she received a call from Albert Skinner, the Monroe County sheriff. 'Wanda, I want you to know that everything will be fine,' he said. 'I want you to come downtown to the sheriff's office.' Wanda's brother-in-law took her downtown.

'Oh my God, what could I have done to help her?' she exclaimed in the station.

'Nothing, Wanda. You couldn't have done anything to help her. It was too late.'

The police had an ulterior motive for taking Wanda to the station. On the afternoon of June's death, Joe Maloney was seen going into June's apartment directly opposite where Wanda lived. Three detectives – Lieutenant Anthony Fantigrossi and detectives Bill Mahoney and Norman Krapp – pulled up outside LeChase Manor. They walked down the corridor and knocked on June's door. There was no answer and the door seemed locked, but they heard a sound from inside. While his colleagues covered other exit routes around the building, Mahoney found an unlocked window to the apartment and climbed through with his gun drawn. Joe, the way Wanda heard it, was found hiding in a broom closet.

Four and a half hours after the death of June Maloney, Joe was arrested and brought to the local station, where he was booked, photographed, his fingerprints were taken and the 31-year-old was formally charged with murder.

4.

Dragnet

POISONING HOMICIDES ARE NOTORIOUSLY DIFFICULT TO PROVE, AND THE CASE OF JUNE MALONEY APPEARED TO BE THE FIRST OF ITS KIND IN MONROE COUNTY FOR OVER 30 YEARS. The investigators took an affidavit from Lee DiClemente and pieced together what they believed was a solid case to present to the grand jury. DA John Little would prosecute alongside his assistant DAs Robert Agnello and Eugene Bergin.

Agnello wrote in a letter to Little: 'I believed the evidence against Mr Maloney is sufficient to support a charge of murder in the First Degree, notwithstanding the total lack of cooperation from Strong Memorial Hospital and the interference in the investigation by Mr Power, Lt Fantigrossi's office did a remarkable job in putting the case together.' Agnello, privy to so much that occurred between Joe and June, laid out the chain of events in careful detail. 'The purpose of this lengthy explanation is to establish chronologically the course of events involved in the investigation with emphasis on the lack of cooperation from the staff of the Strong Memorial Hospital.' The attorney described Joe Maloney to the media as 'a very unusual guy who could charm the pants off a snake. A very dangerous guy.'

Joe was being held in Monroe County Jail, where he maintained Thomas Presutti and William Power as his legal representatives. He was in need of money and asked his attorneys to contact Patrick O'Connor, the barrister in Roscrea, Tipperary, whom he had met during his trip to Ireland earlier that year, to enquire about Joe's 'share of his father's estate and his property in Ireland'. Presutti wrote in a letter: 'We appreciate your aid in closing this estate as soon as possible.' There were no indications in his father's will that any such property existed.

The wheels of the judicial system creaked into motion. First there would be a preliminary indictment hearing in which prosecutors and witnesses presented evidence and testimony to a grand jury. The jury, acting on a majority rather than a unanimous verdict, could either dismiss the case or issue the indictment, pushing the case forward to a criminal trial. Then there was the matter of his children, five-year-old Joey and 18-month-old Patti-Ann. With June dead and Joe in custody, the kids were in limbo. During the making of the podcast series *Runaway Joe*, Wanda Mordenga told me about the moment when Joey found out what happened to his mom. Wanda had returned to her apartment from a visit to her mother's when the boy ran up the sidewalk, around the dirt and construction material where new apartments were being built.

'Wanda, my grandma said my dad killed my mom.'

What a thing to say to a child, thought Wanda.

Catherine Blair stepped in to look after the kids; she was staying in June's apartment. Her husband died in 1963. The 52-year-old woman had no children of her own, and she'd become attached to Joey and Patti-Ann, but social services had a foster family in mind for the children. The family lived in Canandaigua, New York, half an hour south of Rochester. The kids were taken to visit the family and returned that night to LeChase. The following day, the social worker came to bring them to their new home. Joey, old enough to realise what was happening, refused to go and locked himself in the bathroom.

'Wanda, please don't let them take me. Please don't let them take me,' the child pled from behind the door.

'And I had to let them take him,' Wanda recalled. 'I couldn't keep him. I felt so bad. I'll never forget that as long as I live. It broke my heart. That poor kid. And Patti-Ann was too little. She didn't know. But Joey knew what went on and everything, you know. My heart broke for him.'

Wanda pressed up on the other side of the bathroom door. 'Joey, you've gotta come out. You're going to go with this nice lady and she's going to help you. And you'll be OK.'

Joey finally emerged and the social worker helped him pack his belongings, which were not much: a suitcase containing a few clothes and the teddy bear he'd had since he was a baby. Wanda watched in the doorway as Joey and Patti were placed in the back seat of the social worker's car and were driven away. Wanda cried for days. She begged people in authority to let her adopt the two children – 'I think June would have wanted that' – but was told it would be best if she didn't. At 19 she was too young, and the kids needed a fresh start. 'I could understand that,' acknowledged Wanda, 'but it broke my heart.'

June's funeral service was held at a funeral home in Rochester. Wanda was too upset to attend, but alumni from Albion High School and some of the staff members at Genesee hospital came to show their respects. Kay Walter remembers going with others from Albion's class of 1959 and talking to June's brother Dale there.

Carol Severns, June's best friend during her high school years, had left the Rochester and Albion region by this time and did not hear about June's death until months later, but June's friends Carol Reckahn and Joan LaBue were in attendance.

Nobody discussed Joe, although his presence hung heavy over the funeral. Before they went to Mount Hope Cemetery, where June was buried, attendees could not help but notice the lurid floral arrangement on top of her casket. It read: 'From Your Loving Husband'.

On 16 June 1967, Joseph Michael Maloney was arraigned on a first-degree murder indictment at the Monroe County courthouse before Judge Harry Rosenthal. DA John Little presented the evidence to the grand jury with his assistants. Joe pled not guilty and was represented by his attorneys Presutti and Power, the latter describing his client in the courtroom as 'intelligent and reckless, taking risks other people wouldn't in his job as a dynamite contractor.' Among those testifying were doctors from Strong Memorial Hospital and June's brother, Dale Fisk. 'He had us and a lot of our friends convinced that [suicide] is what happened,' recounted Dale. 'Then the police came around and kind of shed light on it.'

Wanda was called to speak in court, although she was, by her own reckoning, an emotional mess. 'I was a basket case. I couldn't eat, I couldn't sleep. I was definitely devastated. [Before the indictment] they had to put me to bed. The doctor had to give me a prescription. Nineteen years old. To have something like that happen is very traumatic.'

Under cross-examination, Presutti and Power objected to Wanda's description of June's physical condition when she returned from Joe's party on Eastmoreland Drive.

'That's hearsay,' yelled Presutti.

Wanda lost her composure and started crying. More questions about June's condition were flung her way, and there were more interruptions during her responses. Eventually Wanda snapped back: 'Well, I know it's a fact. The fact was June was fine when she left the house and she wasn't fine when she came back.'

A lady in the public gallery yelled: 'Stop harassing her and give her a drink of water.' Wanda recalled: 'She felt bad for me. I felt bad for myself.'

Catherine Blair, June's friend and babysitter, brought a sobering presence to the courtroom. She painted a dark picture of Joe's coercive control and domestic violence.

'Last year [in 1966] Joe Maloney beat his wife around the face,' she told the jury in her sworn statement. 'He admitted to me after he denied it. I saw her and her face was sore and black and blue.'

Cathy also outlined an incident that took place a week before Joey's birthday.

'I was a passenger in Joseph Maloney's car and I was aware June and Joe had separated. While I was a passenger in the car, Joe Maloney asked me if June would come back. I said I didn't know. At one point in our conversation, Joe said he would do away with June and that they would not be able to pin it on him. He also stated to me, "If she doesn't come back I will make it so nobody else will want her".'

Lee DiClemente provided more details about Joe's alleged abuse, referring in his statement to an incident two weeks prior to June's death in which 'her husband was beating her up'. Lee called the police in Gates [the suburb of Rochester where June moved to] but 'they never even showed up'. Without Lee DiClemente putting his neck and his marriage on the line, none of this would have risen to the surface, Agnello told the courtroom.

Between the Monday when June was admitted and the following Monday when she died, 'no attempt of any kind was made by anyone at Strong [Memorial Hospital] to contact or report this incident to the police,' Agnello told John Little in a letter. 'If it had not been for the phone call I received from Mr DiClemente the day after Mrs Maloney went into the hospital neither the DA's office nor the police department would've had any knowledge of this incident. Consequently, Mrs Maloney's death may have gone unquestioned.'

June's friends were made aware of the importance of DiClemente's role: he was June's voice in court. 'Luckily because of that guy,' said Joan LaBue, 'that's how Joe got caught.'

The most damning testimony came from Gail Mann, the sister of Neal Dunkleberg. On 23 May, two days after Joe allegedly outlined his plans to 'do away with June' to Catherine Blair in her car, Joe visited the Dunklebergs' house 'between the hours of 5pm and 6:30pm'. Neal and the rest of the family were on vacation, and Neal's sister was home alone. Neal had given Gail strict orders not to let Joe near his laboratory, but Joe 'sweet-talked' the woman into letting him into the house.

'I need some chemicals in order to sterilize some instruments,' Joe told Gail. 'The stuff is in the cellar.'

A photograph of Neal's ramshackle laboratory in the Meigs Street basement was presented to the grand jury. In her testimony to Detective Bill Mahoney, which Mahoney deposed for the court, Gail stated the following: 'I gave the [methyl] alcohol to [June's] husband to sterilize some things . . . I poured some into a small mayonnaise jar and gave it to Joe.' Before Joe left, he told Gail not to tell anybody she gave him the poison – including her brother Neal. Joe phoned Gail on three subsequent occasions telling her not to reveal he'd taken the chemical. In one call he said he'd dropped the jar and it broke. 'But when I asked if he wanted more, he told me no, he had gotten it for himself somewhere else.'

When the topic of motive was raised in the courtroom, Agnello expressed his option that Joe never had any real love for June: 'He was fighting her because it was a matter of vanity and pride that she would reject him.'

Dale Fisk elaborated on this theory when he told police about a conversation he'd had with Joe two weeks prior to the party. Joe told Dale he was concerned about June's affair with DiClemente and believed she was pregnant with his child. June's autopsy did not reveal she was pregnant – but could Joe's bruised ego have pushed him over the edge?

The grand jury seemed to believe so. In their minds, the case was clear-cut. Joe Maloney, who'd made persistent threats to his wife's life, obtained a jar of methyl alcohol. Within days his wife was in a coma and then died, the autopsy ascertained, from methyl alcohol poisoning. The jury indicted Joe on a charge of first-degree murder, which opened the door for a criminal prosecution. Joe was to be held in Monroe County Jail pending further proceedings.

Neal Dunkleberg – who had seen Joe grow from an ebullient, adventurous, charismatic yet compulsive liar in his teenage years, to a deceptive and dangerous adult – knew that his and Joe's friendship was over following his sister's testimony.

'Well, you hate to see an old friend end up in jail, but Joe was such a disturbed person,' said Neal. 'So weird. So intelligent. Very manipulative. He was out of reality.'

*   *   *

The prosecutors prepared their case and lined up witnesses, including Carol Reckahn, June's friend who introduced Joe to June in 1961 and attended the birthday party at Joe's house. Then Joe's lawyers approached the court on his behalf. Joe wanted to be committed to the Rochester State Hospital psychiatric institution for assessment before trial. Presutti, his attorney, wrote to the judge: 'After discussing it with Mr Maloney, I request that he be sent to the hospital for a mental examination so that I may be assured of my own mind, after discussing this with him, that I can proceed with the defense in this matter.'

Prosecutor Eugene Bergin had no objection. He hadn't noticed Joe displaying any mental health problems during the indictment but these examinations were routinely sought before trial. On 8 September 1967, the court granted Joe's request, ordering he be committed to the hospital for a period of observation not to exceed 60 days. The hospital should report back to the court their findings on his fitness to stand trial.

Joe was admitted to the Rochester State Hospital four days later. The hospital campus and its three interconnected patient wards were built around an open central quad. There was the Howard Complex, built in a Spanish revival style, and the Walters Building, constructed in a Georgian Revival style. Elsewhere on the campus were buildings for staff accommodation, vehicles, a power station and a laundry facility. By the mid-1960s the hospital had 3,500 beds, making it the eighth largest psychiatric hospital operated by New York State, with an annual budget of $6 million. Patients included children, alcoholics, the elderly and chronically ill, and alleged criminals like Joe undergoing assessment.

Joe was seen by two psychiatrists: Dr Benjamin Pollock, assistant director of the hospital, and Dr Harold Feldman. Their task was to 'question the defendant to determine the question of his sanity and report to the court'. Joe was compliant, for the most part.

Rochester State Hospital, like most psychiatric institutions of its time, was a grim place, but the Rochester county chapter of the Red Cross made an effort to liven it up. Gray Ladies and Gray Men, Red Cross volunteers in operation since the First World War, provided frequent entertainment and recreation on site. They helped patients celebrate their birthdays, took part in reading programmes, managed the book cart, entertained troubled children and at Christmas distributed gifts and sang hymns by candlelight. Occasionally, the volunteers taught patients to square dance and held parties at which they played the piano or music on vinyl.

On the evening of 25 September 1967, less than two weeks after Joe was admitted, the Red Cross held one such dance on the fifth floor of the hospital. After the patients had made their way back to their rooms, staff realised that one of them was missing. Lance Lohm, a 16-year-old patient, described witnessing Joe standing in the ward hallway beside the exit door at around 7:50pm. Lohm turned away, and when he looked back, Joe was gone. During the dance, Lohm repositioned himself beside the window, where he witnessed Joe crossing the hospital quad lawn.

The Rochester police department hurriedly assembled. Across the road, on the other side of Elmwood Avenue from the hospital, was an unfinished building where Joe once worked as a labourer. They searched this building first, but there was no sign of Joe. A tip came through that a man in green pyjamas was spotted on East Henrietta, eight miles south of the State Hospital, but it must have been a red herring, because Joe was wearing a black sport coat, dark trousers, brown socks and loafers at the time of his disappearance.

Police staked out airports, fearing Joe's pilot's license (which he had on the wall of his bedroom at his parents' home on Linden Street) could be genuine and he might abscond via air. The homes of James Maloney, Joe's brother, and Joey and Patti-Ann's foster family in Canandaigua were also placed under surveillance. Police even checked the site of June's grave in Mount Hope Cemetery in case he was hiding out there. Investigators contacted Joe's network of friends, including Patricia Rich, a 'girlfriend of Maloney', according to Rochester district attorney case files. Larry McDonald, described in Rochester DA case files as a 'buddy of defendant', informed the police about an identifiable scar on Joe's abdomen (the injury that Neal Dunkleberg believed was self-inflicted). Wanda, June's friend and neighbour, was gobsmacked when state police called her at her mother-in-law's home to tell her the news. They'd visited her apartment at LeChase Manor and wanted to make sure she was safe.

'I was like, "Oh, man. He can't get away",' Wanda said. 'Nobody should get away with that. I don't remember being scared. Maybe angry.'

A police officer was sent to Rochester State Hospital to investigate Joe's disappearance and learned that Joe had planned to escape from the minute he got there. Joe told Lance Lohm, the boy who saw him leave the ward, that he had access to $3,000 and would give Lohm some of the money if he helped him.

'When Maloney first got to the hospital,' wrote a cop in his report, 'he planned an escape by taking one of the billiard balls from the billiard table, putting it into a sock and having his two friends distract the attention of the attendants while he hit them on the head with the weapon.'

Ultimately, Joe used his engineering skills to formulate an escape, crafting a key from parts of an electric razor and using this to pick a door lock on the fifth floor of the hospital. From there he made his way to the basement and out onto the lawn and to freedom. Joe, the police learned too late, knew the layout of the building. Unbeknownst to them, Joe's father had worked at Rochester State Hospital for decades as a night watchman.

Joe had worked there with his dad, roaming the corridors and exploring the staff areas, and this paid off in planning his escape. It was the reason why Joe requested to be committed to the hospital for assessment: it had all been part of his plan. George Reiss, the Rochester lieutenant and Joe's neighbour, was appalled when he heard about the escape. Alice Fisher, Reiss's daughter, distinctly recalled her father 'telling the police in Rochester when Joe was arrested and he was put into a mental hospital they better keep tabs on him because he would probably escape'.

He'd warned his fellow officers not to underestimate Joe Maloney.

Carol Reckahn was on edge. Night after night following Joe's escape an unmarked police vehicle was parked on the street a few doors along from her house in the event Joe might try to contact her, his former girlfriend, or James Maloney, Joe's brother, who lived on the same street. Joe never made an appearance at Reckahn's home. In any event, Reckahn and her husband moved soon thereafter from Rochester to Niagara Falls on the border with Canada. Even at a 90-mile distance from Rochester, Joe still haunted them. One evening, Carol's husband came home from work and asked Carol if she had any pictures of Joe.

'I don't know, why?'

'I remember you showing me a picture of him and he had red hair and freckles, right?'

'Yeah.'

'I think I just saw him in a diner when I stopped to get coffee in downtown Buffalo.'

Buffalo was only 20 miles from their home.

'Are you sure? Should we report it to somebody?'

'Well, the guy sitting next to me had black hair but he had his sleeves rolled up and he had red hair on his arms, very light red hair.

That didn't fit the picture and he kind of talked with an accent. There was just something about him.'

Reckahn and her husband reported the matter to the police and Lieutenant George Reiss, Joe's former neighbour, and another detective travelled to Buffalo to question them. They apprehended a suspect but it wasn't Maloney, although they weren't sure this was the same man who Reckahn's husband identified.

In the weeks following his escape, Joe phoned his attorney William Power a few times. The first call came through to Power's home at 4am on Wednesday, 27 September, two days after his escape. Joe said he was 'good' and had 'business matters' he had to take care of. There were two more calls on the following Saturday and Monday, in which Joe asked for the location of his children, Joey and Patti-Ann. Power told investigators he would not have revealed their location even if he knew it. Joe spent half an hour on each call and discussed the possibility of giving himself up.

'He had some idea that his escape might make authorities let him get bail,' Power said.

On Wednesday, 4 October, Joe phoned Power again. This time he agreed to give himself up but was uncertain where he should do it. 'We didn't want him shot if he was going to give himself up,' said Power, 'so we had to decide on Buffalo or Syracuse because he obviously was in the Southern Tier [a region of New York State]. He wanted Buffalo.'

Rochester police had tracked Joe's movements. The fugitive had hid in a vacant house in Rochester for two days after his escape. Then he left the city and fled to Hornell, a town 70 miles south. Now, just as Reckahn's husband suggested, he appeared to be hiding out in Buffalo. On Saturday, 7 October, Joe called his attorney and arranged to surrender at the Hotel Lafayette in downtown Buffalo. But he never turned up. William Power said he and a colleague waited for Joe for an hour at the hotel.

Eventually, Power's colleague 'went outside and saw two police cars, one on each end of the block'. Power recounted: 'We went back into the hotel and stewed. We told the police to let us pick him up. The police had been told to leave us alone – that we would get him and turn him in, in Buffalo.'

In Power's mind, the police scared Joe away. Joe never called again.

A week later the FBI joined the hunt for Joe Maloney. The bureau issued a federal warrant – a charge of unlawful flight to avoid prosecution – because they believed, in light of new information gathered by the Monroe County DA's office, he'd fled from the state of New York. They sent wanted posters, featuring his photograph and fingerprints, around the country and to foreign agencies such as the international policing organisation Interpol.

More details emerged of Joe's plans. During his brief time at Monroe County Jail, Joe confided in a fellow inmate, a drapery hanger by the name of John Tischer. Joe and Tischer played the two-handed card game Gin Rummy in their cell, Tischer told prosecutors.

'We played almost daily and he carried on conversations about what he would do when he left the jail. On several conversations, Joe Maloney stated he would get out on bail.' Once he got out, Tischer continued, Joe planned to cross the border into Canada and hop a boat to Australia. Then he would fly to Italy. 'This way, he claimed he would not need a passport. This way he could start his business over again and have his children join him. I have not heard nor seen him since I left the Monroe County Jail in July 1967.'

If this was Joe's true intention, it did not come to pass. Despite the FBI's involvement, two months after his escape from Rochester State Hospital, Joe Maloney still hadn't left the state.

*   *   *

On Sunday, 5 November 1967, at 7:30pm, Canandaigua police received a phone call. Two women who worked at Shamrock Gas Station on Route 332 north of the city claimed to have seen Joe at their service station. There was a light on in an abandoned trailer behind the station and they believed Joe was inside. When a deputy officer arrived to investigate, the man bolted into the night. By 9pm the area was swarming with 60 law enforcement officers, who searched the area on foot and in patrol cars. The search party, according to a report in Rochester's *Democrat & Chronicle*, was made up of units from the Canandaigua city police, the Ontario County Sheriff's Office, the Monroe County Sheriff's Office and the State Police. Shortly before midnight the State Police in Oneida brought bloodhounds to assist in the hunt. But there was no sign of Joe.

The FBI sent an agent to gather facts on the reported sighting. The agent couldn't find any fingerprints in the caravan, only a single unidentifiable shoe. When the agent questioned people in the area and showed them Joe's mug shot, witnesses confirmed it had been him. A reporter from the *Democrat & Chronicle* who looked similar to the suspect – 'a red-headed, blue eyed man like Maloney, about an inch shorter than the 6 foot 2-inch fugitive, weighing about ten pounds less' – was paraded before those same witnesses in a police line-up.

'They perceptively noted minor differences in appearance,' stated the reporter, 'including Maloney's scar under one eye and his permanent crease in his forehead.'

Canandaigua was where Joey and Patti-Ann were staying with their foster parents while under police guard. Had Joe tracked them down or was his presence there a coincidence? Either way, Joe's collateral in Rochester was evaporating. Authorities took control of the mortgage of his Eastmoreland Drive home and obtained a court order allowing its sale. A small office property, also in Joe's name, was put on the market. Joe had nothing, it appeared, other than the clothes on his back, although when William Power rounded up his client's personal goods he discovered information to indicate that Joe had a 'substantial estate' in his mother's name in the midlands of Ireland. (There was no mention of this estate in the package that his son Joey received in 2025.)

Joe seemed to be chaotically flailing from one local bolthole to the next: surely it was only a matter of time before he was apprehended. But behind the scenes he was methodically formulating a plan. Police began receiving reports about a man who presented himself at nine supermarkets – including locations in Brighton, Irondequoit, Gates and Henrietta, and two in Rochester – where he cashed cheques from the bank account of Marine Midland Trust Company. The man cashing those cheques produced a registration for a red Ford Mustang as identification: a registration attributed to a car that Joe Maloney had purchased before June's death. The signature on the cheques matched Joe's signature. The cheques bounced.

'At one county supermarket,' reported the *Democrat & Chronicle* on 12 November, 'the man who said he was Maloney stepped to one side when an identification camera snapped a picture of his face. The photo showed only the lower half of the face – with a moustache. Maloney had been clean shaven.' The man made off with $1,600 – enough perhaps to start again somewhere else. Joe's attorneys, Thomas Presutti and William Power, placed an appeal in the pages of the same newspaper appealing to their client to return so that 'a decent life may be possible for your children'. The only way Joe was going to prove his innocence would be 'in court and nowhere else', they pleaded, and 'if Joe gives himself up now, we can assure him his case will be tried during the November term'.

But Joe was gone, and nothing more was heard from him in Rochester. For months afterwards, families on Eastmoreland Drive kept their lights on at night and told their children not to play in the streets in case the wife murderer was prowling. Joe Maloney had become a spectre, a phantom lurking somewhere just out of reach.

5.

Never-Never Man

The seaside town of Dún Laoghaire was only eight miles from Dublin, but it may as well have been 80. By 1968, the town on Ireland's east coast had been a haven for the respectably retired for over half a century. Dún Laoghaire was a place 'of gentility and Victorian charm', a 'twilight zone for the well-to-do', as one TV news report described it. On a warm day, elderly residents of Dún Laoghaire's seafront hotels could be seen meandering along the promenade or loitering in People's Park, a traditional Victorian-style park to the east of George's Street, with its fountains, playground and bandstand. The Pavilion cinema on Marine Road drew big crowds and (if you knew the right people) black-market tickets could be acquired for cheap seats to popular matinee features.

Dún Laoghaire was door-stopped by a harbour built in the first half of the 1800s that featured long granite piers. The 3,500-foot-long East Pier had been walked by Ireland's literary greats – Oscar Wilde, Samuel Beckett, Bram Stoker – and by the 1960s it was a popular retreat for day-trippers from Dublin. Across the harbour, the lesser-frequented 4,950-foot-long West Pier offered views of Dublin Bay and Howth to the north.

Some Dubliners described Dún Laoghaire as a British colony because of the wealthy people from across the Irish Sea who came here to retire. Local travel agencies played up this reputation with promotional drives in Britain, offering deals on senior citizen holidays. 'Why wait for summer? Take a holiday in spring in Dún Laoghaire!' read one brochure from the late 1960s. Thousands of people flocked to the town for its annual horse shows and international bowling competitions. In the summer of 1968, a gala water carnival was held in Scotsman's Bay next to the East Pier. Visitors ogled the canoe demonstrations, water skiing, air-sea rescues and speedboat races featuring competitors from France and Cyprus.

The Britain–Ireland mail boat carrying foot passengers across the Irish Sea was Dún Laoghaire's lifeline to the outside world, and in 1965 a new roll-on roll-off ferry service was introduced from Holyhead in Wales that allowed people to bring their cars to Ireland. By 1968, 37,000 cars were being carried through the port: a number that increased with the construction of a £1 million car ferry terminal at St Michael's Wharf.

It was in this watery Irish suburb that, at some point in 1968, a tall, red-haired and bearded stranger appeared. The man was destitute and dishevelled, and, to the fishermen who worked out of boats in Coal Harbour, he introduced himself as 'Michael'. Although Dún Laoghaire was on the surface an affluent middle-class locale, it had a working-class fraternity who laboured on boats out of a fishing port between the East and West Piers. Michael seemed willing and strong and unafraid of a hard day's work, and skipper Noel Curran agreed to give him a job on the *Provider*, his 58-foot trawler. Curran and his crew, Michael included, travelled out to sea, cast out their net and brought home herring, pollock, coalfish or mackerel, which the fishermen stored and sold from a cold house on the pier.

Dún Laoghaire fishing evolved in tandem with tourism. Between 1967 and 1968, the fleet of trawlers grew so rapidly that the fishermen formed trading associations that organised transport to take fish to Dublin markets, organise export markets and purchase oil in bulk. By 1968, Dún Laoghaire was providing Dublin with 1,000 boxes of fish every day, and as fishing and tourism expanded so too did the harbour.

Michael found more work at Traders Wharf, where a team of Dutch civil engineers had been contracted to dredge the bay. The stranger seemed enamoured with their use of explosives in clearing the rock and sediment from the sea bed. Charismatic and a dramatic storyteller, Michael had limited means, but he was resourceful. He used his fishing and dredging earnings to buy a small car trailer, and he persuaded a local bricklayer to hoist it into his back garden in Dún Laoghaire. Michael handed the bricklayer a few Irish punts in rent and lived out of this trailer. Things were going well until an old injury came back to haunt him.

Brian Hanlon was a young doctor taking his internship at St Michael's Hospital in Dún Laoghaire, a few minutes' walk from the harbour, when a tall red-headed man was admitted expressing pain from an old wound in his abdomen. Hanlon was the doctor on call. He had a consultant look at Michael, but there was little they could do aside from offer pain medication. Michael had no insurance, and he didn't want any records to be kept of his stay. He also wanted to pay for everything up front and in cash, and he was in a rush to get discharged as soon as he was given medication.

Despite the man's unusual behaviour, Hanlon found him affable: 'I liked him as a person. A very sociable person. He had the gift of the gab, so to speak.'

Hanlon and Michael got to know each other and sometimes went to a pub opposite St Michael's Hospital for a drink. Michael told the young doctor he came from a family of Englishmen, landed gentry in fact, and that he had been born in County Kerry on the west coast of Ireland. 'He said his forebears had made good and he had inherited quite a lot of money. He always said he was Irish. Anglo-Irish was his spiel. That was his story. We all accepted that. There was no problem.'

Michael started to reveal a little more about himself over pints in the pub. And what a story it was. He was a military engineer who had served with the British Army in the west Asian country of Aden, a former British colony today known as Yemen. Following the independence of Cyprus in 1960, Aden became the base for Britain's Middle Eastern Land Forces – and one of the last bastions of a crumbling Empire. A permanent British garrison was established there in 1962, only to come under sustained assault by nationalist groups that included the National Liberation Front and the Front for the Liberation of Occupied South Yemen. Michael told Hanlon how insurgents had wounded him in action, hence the injury on his abdomen, before the British retreated from their colony in 1967.

Michael relayed the same story at the same time – late 1968, early 1969 – to a man who was looking for a salesman for his engineering company in Ballyfermot, a suburb in west Dublin. Michael told him he'd been in the Royal Engineer corps of the British Army. He was a multi-skilled solider, combat engineer and tradesperson, and he was made for this job.

'That was the story,' said Pat Fitzsimons, son of the company owner. 'Of course my father believed it – my father had no reason not to believe it.'

Pat heard the same story first hand, at the age of 17, when he was dropping a car to Kildare outside Dublin and his father sent a new employee to pick him up.

'I've just started,' Michael told Pat when he got into the car. 'I'm in sales now for your dad.'

During the 40-mile trip back to the factory in Ballyfermot, Michael was gregarious and full of spiel. He told Pat about his exploits in Aden and pulled up his shirt to reveal the scar on his abdomen: a memento from the battlefield.

Michael had the ability to fit in with whomever he happened to be talking to, noted Brian Hanlon: 'He was good at integrating in conversation with strangers'. His knowledge on a depth of subjects, pharmacology in particular, surprised Hanlon. 'He knew a lot about medical drugs. I don't know what his background was in that.'

The doctor brought Michael to meetings of medical representatives that took place in prestigious venues like Stillorgan Hotel, a few miles outside Dún Laoghaire. Michael freely conversed about medicine and drugs over dinner, and Hanlon's associates were impressed with his knowledge. 'He had one of these attractive personalities,' said Hanlon. 'He was great at putting you at ease and he was great at talking.'

Through odd jobs and a growing circle of connections, Michael was earning enough money to move out of his trailer in the bricklayer's garden and into a flat in Dún Laoghaire near St Michael's Hospital, which he shared with another man and two women. Around the same time, Michael met Pat McMahon, an artist who moonlighted as a movie set armourer (who in later years worked on movies like *The Devil's Own* with Brad Pitt) and they bonded over pints in the pub. There was a constant stream of parties at Michael's new apartment.

Michael drank but 'he wasn't a drunkard', Hanlon told me. He had the unusual habit of cultivating police officers as friends, and there were often off-duty Garda, members of the Irish police force, in attendance at his parties. Tall and erudite, Michael was not short of female admirers, and he found a steady girlfriend, Anne, who came from the Cabra region of Dublin and worked in a hair salon on Dorset Street in the north part of the city.

Despite his popularity, people who spent time with Michael noticed oddities about the man. Like the way he peppered his Anglo-Irish accent with funny little Americanisms – words like 'trunk' instead of 'boot' or 'yard' instead of 'garden'. In certain situations he was guarded, and he clammed up if someone asked too many questions. And some people couldn't help but notice Michael's pathological aversion to having his photograph taken.

'If you put a camera on him,' said one associate, 'he'd fucking shoot you.'

As 1969 gave way to 1970, Ireland was a country emerging from the weeds. The economic stagnation and mass emigration of the 1950s had been succeeded by a country reaping the fruits of a modern industrial society. Emigration had been reduced, population decline arrested and traditional ideologies were giving way to more progressive attitudes (in the Dublin region, at least). Ireland, still not yet 50 years old as a nation, was finding its feet.

Michael had graduated to become Michael O'Shea, a man with a surname, and he was rising with Ireland's tide. After leaving his sales job with the engineering company in Ballyfermot he struck up company with a couple of fellow outsiders running a car repair business out of a squat in Dún Laoghaire. When the three were threatened with eviction O'Shea allegedly convinced the redevelopers that the land had been owned by the Christian Brothers, an order within the Catholic Church, and they gave him permission to be there. The redevelopers accepted this story and gave O'Shea a few thousand Irish punts to go away. O'Shea used the earnings to purchase another Dún Laoghaire garage in a laneway off Marine Road, next to the side entrance of Royal Marine Hotel. O'Shea was the salesman at this car repair business. The property was not particularly valuable, but it allowed O'Shea to widen his social network.

Dún Laoghaire's sedate life and relative affluence was in contrast to events north of the border in Ireland. The previous summer of rioting in 1969 – in response to a crackdown against the Civil Rights movement and its demands for equality between Catholics and Protestants – had spiralled into chaos and violence. Catholics were burned out of their homes and the newly formed Provisional Irish Republican Army was fomenting armed resistance.

O'Shea, despite his charismatic can-do attitude, brought darkness of his own accord to the south county Dublin suburb. Tom Carty, whose joinery business stood opposite O'Shea's garage, had an ongoing feud with O'Shea and claimed the redhead 'tried to kill him'. A local writer who crashed his van and left it in the garage to be repaired was among O'Shea's many disgruntled customers. When he picked it up 'they'd made a mess of a job' and he refused to pay. The writer and O'Shea launched into a scuffle during which O'Shea kicked the van so hard he almost took off its door. The writer never forgot O'Shea's 'uncontrolled rage'. When the fight was over a part-time mechanic who worked in the garage walked out and, exasperated, told the writer: 'This happens *all* the time.'

O'Shea was by now arousing the suspicion of the Gardaí – even the officers who'd got up close and personal with the man at his house parties. Nobody could figure out what his game was, who he was, but the cops smelled something fishy about him. When I spoke to John Mulderrig, a detective inspector in Dún Laoghaire, for the podcast series *Runaway Joe*, he described O'Shea as a mystery man. 'Anyone that spoke with him got a different story. I often wondered which was the true story. Very few believed him. He worked at so many different jobs and trades that no one could be sure anything he said.'

Alongside his stewardship of the garage, O'Shea worked on and off for a furniture store in Dolphin's Barn Street opposite the Coombe Hospital in south inner city Dublin. Frank Doran owned the store (his name was on the sign), Matt O'Reilly was manager and there was a couple of staff. In 1970, credit and loans were hard to come by in Ireland, and shops like Frank Doran sold items like furniture and washing machines on hire purchase. Customers paid part of the cost upon collection and made small regular payments until the debt was settled. Agents for the store, known as 'Never-Never Men', visited the homes of customers to collect the debt, often on Friday nights or Saturdays, when people were more likely to be in. Michael O'Shea was one such Never-Never Man.

Rosie Morgan (I've changed her name at her request) worked for Frank Doran in the shop and she dealt with customers. The agents congregated in the store a couple of mornings each week to talk to her boss, and O'Shea was among them. Rosie remembered him as a large, scruffy individual. 'The jeans seemed to be all crumpled and big on him. In the shop he would have worn a suit but he still wasn't right. You'd still like to tidy him up a bit. And the big face with the big beard on it.' Rosie thought he looked a lot like Ned Beatty, the actor from the movie *Deliverance*.

O'Shea was forever telling Rosie and the other workers in the shop about his adventures.

'He told all these outlandish stories. There were planes. There were cars. There was everything. And the way he was all full of glee when he'd be telling you his ridiculous stories.'

O'Shea, she said, was an absolute maniac. On one occasion he told her about a time he was on a mission during his army service and a dog attacked him.

'Well,' O'Shea announced, 'when it jumped up at me, I grabbed its two front paws and did this.'

O'Shea spread his arms wide like Jesus on the cross.

'I pulled the bastard so far apart that its heart burst and its stomach ripped open and its intestines poured out around my feet.'

Rosie was horrified.

'Oh my God, I was faint. I was thinking about our poor little dog at home.'

Whenever O'Shea came into shop she would hide in the toilet just to avoid him.

'I didn't want to be around him. He'd make you very uncomfortable.'

One time she was standing at the back door of the shop, where a room divider separated her from the activity inside. She looked at the Never-Never Man as he held court and told his stories inside. A strange, uncomfortable feeling washed over her. And that sensation never left her, not even 50 years later, because she has never felt it about anyone before or since.

'It felt,' she said, 'like a sewer.'

By 1970, the Irish movie industry was progressing in fits and starts. The country was home to a handful of big productions over the previous decade, like 1967's *The Playboy of the Western World*.

In the summer of 1969, maestro auteur David Lean arrived in County Kerry on the west coast to make his epic period drama *Ryan's Daughter*. Gerry Johnston was a special effects supervisor a few years into his career. In 1966 he made his debut on *The Blue Max*, an action movie starring George Peppard, James Mason and Ursula Andress, about a German fighter pilot on the Western Front during the First World War. *The Blue Max* was partly shot in County Wicklow's Ardmore Studios, Ireland's ground zero for filmmaking. Ardmore was in financial dire straits by 1970 due to the lack of indigenous business; the state was forever bailing it out. But for Johnston, whose career was in the ascent after he worked with Lean on *Ryan's Daughter*, the studio lot provided a base for his special effects workshop.

One day Johnston received a call from his friend Pat McMahon, who had crewed on movies with him. 'Gerry,' McMahon said, eagerly. 'There's a guy I met, a friend of mine. He'd love to get into the movie business. Maybe have a chat with him?'

A day or two later, that friend knocked on the door of Johnston's workshop in Ardmore. Johnston was struck by the man's presence: broad, tall, ginger-haired and, in Johnston's mind, 'rough-looking'.

'You Gerry Johnston? My name is Michael O'Shea.'

O'Shea took out his passport and showed him the name on it: Michael O'Shea. Johnston's inner bullshit detector went off the scale. This wasn't normal behaviour. He wondered if the man might be involved with subversives.

'Pat sent me,' Michael told him. 'He said you could give me some work.'

'Pat's an armourer, what would he know,' replied Johnston. 'No, I don't have any work for you at the moment.'

O'Shea refused to take no for an answer. He kept asking Johnston questions and fishing for information about the Irish film industry. Johnston took an instant dislike to this character standing before him. 'He was not a nice man,' he later recalled. Johnston phoned McMahon as soon as Michael left to ask why he had sent this strange man to his door.

'Gerry, this guy's a con man,' McMahon complained. 'He's telling me stories.'

'So what are you sending him out to me in Ardmore to pick my brains for then?' Johnston shot back. 'That could get me in trouble.'

McMahon told his friend a story about Michael O'Shea – a story O'Shea had told him. He was an American who'd stowed away on a German merchant ship out of New York State. Three quarters of the way across the Atlantic he was discovered and transferred to a second, smaller ship, which dropped him off on the coast of Cork at the southern end of Ireland. From there he made his way up to Dublin. Michael had had an accident on the second boat, he'd told McMahon after they met in hospital, which resulted in a deep flesh wound on his abdomen.

Gerry Johnston wanted nothing more to do with this character, but Michael O'Shea was relentless. He kept phoning and asking Johnston if they could meet for a coffee.

'No,' Johnston, told him. 'I'm busy.'

Sometimes O'Shea turned up at his Ardmore workshop without invitation.

'I don't suffer from bullshit, and I asked him a lot of questions and he didn't answer them,' remarked Johnston. When Johnston asked if it was true he was American, O'Shea shrugged and confessed that he was. And that is how Gerry Johnston became one of the few people in Ireland to be aware of Michael O'Shea's port of origin.

* * *

In 1971, O'Shea broke up with his girlfriend Anne and moved into a house in Glenageary, a suburban area of Dublin that bordered Dún Laoghaire. Arkendale Road was a quiet neighbourhood of brick and stucco houses, sheltered from the street by walls and hedges. Generations of families lived in the locale, and many of the homes had nameplates hanging on wrought-iron gates that opened up to driveways and garages. Michael O'Shea's home was a two-storey building with a name of its own: Marylands. O'Shea, fresh from his job as a debt collector for Frank Doran's furniture shop in Dolphin's Barn, was now moonlighting as an independent antiques expert for Buckley's Galleries in nearby Sandycove, which had been established by John Buckley in 1947 and was now operated by his sons, Michael and Sean. The Buckley brothers facilitated property sales and held weekly furniture auctions.

Arkendale Road was mostly populated by government contractors, lawyers and other professionals. Children played out on the street when it wasn't raining, and they hero-worshipped the outgoing, adventurous, storytelling O'Shea. After one violent storm a tree fell across the road, and O'Shea was first outside, carving it up with his chainsaw. He brought glamour to an otherwise dull neighbourhood. In little over two years this outsider had graduated from a trailer in someone's garden to upper-middle-class Dublin, and it was here that Michael O'Shea met Sheila Mary Chandler: literally the girl next door.

Sheila grew up in a house called Glenmorris next to Marylands. Born in 1945, Sheila was one of four sisters. One sister was seven years older, another four years older and when Sheila was eight her mother had another child. Sheila, on account of these large gaps in ages, learned to enjoy her own company. She was studious and spent hours in her room with her extensive stamp collection or at the bottom of her garden, where she read books and recited

Shakespeare with a friend. As a teenager, Sheila attended Loreto Abbey on the southern shore of Dublin Bay. With its turrets and miniature mock battlements, this Gothic pile constructed from brown quarried granite looked more like a castle than a secondary school. The site was spread over 150 acres and had been built in the 1800s as a headquarters for the Loreto Sisters order of nuns.

The school was only a couple of kilometres from Arkendale Road, and Sheila cycled back and forth every day with a friend. The friend lived closer to the school, but Sheila insisted her friend cycle out of her way so they could make the journey together. Sheila liked being in charge; she was bossy that way. In her early teenage years, Sheila also cycled to school with her older sister and her sister's friends. Hanging out with these girls was rivetingly exciting for her, and she spent hours engrossed in her sister's magazines. Sheila was something of a loner, and she didn't have many friends. This was probably on account of her nature; she could be haughty and sometimes lacked empathy.

One of Sheila's few friends recalled her asking a question when she was 14: 'Do you like Dirk Bogarde?'

What seemed like a simple question about a Hollywood actor was loaded with implicit disdain. 'I thought if I said "Yes", she'd say "Oh my God, I can't believe it,"' recalled the friend. 'If I said "No", she'd say "You have no taste".' When that friend began dating when she was 16, Sheila was left alone with only her imagination for company.

Sheila Chandler was, in some respects, already an outsider in Ireland. Her parents had been born in Britain. Her father Vincent (Vinny to his friends) came from Hereford in England. Her mother was born Catherine Grimson in Scotland. Catherine retained a slight Scottish twang to her accent and her father,

Sheila's grandfather, Puffy, was a common sight on Arkendale Road. Isabel Grimson, Sheila's unmarried aunt on her mother's side, visited Glenmorris on Sundays. By the time Sheila turned 18 in 1963, Ireland was changing with the times. Young women were adopting fashion trends from England: long, straight hair, miniskirts and low heels. Sheila thought herself too sophisticated for all that. 'She preferred to keep the persona of the sophisticated and mysterious femme fatale,' said her friend.

Sheila had high expectations for herself and swore blindly she'd never become a secretary like so many women her age. From childhood, she was inclined towards learning other languages and after graduating from school in the summer of 1963 travelled to France to work as an au pair. Upon her return to Ireland she took a German language course at the Goethe-Institut in Dublin, moved back in with her parents in Glenageary and worked at a shop called Totterdells in Dún Laoghaire that rented TV sets. Then she got a job as a receptionist in the hairdressing department of Switzer's, a fancy department store on Dublin's upmarket Grafton Street. Some people thought Sheila was quiet. Those who knew her well, family for example, described her as supercilious; she had a superiority complex, they thought. She hadn't much experience of love and her very occasional boyfriends were dubious. One suitor, according to Chandler family lore, stole her father's cheque book and tried to cash the cheques in it before he was caught. By 1971, Sheila Chandler was 26 years old and at a dead end. Despite her high opinions of herself, her life was shaping up to be very ordinary indeed.

That was until she met Michael O'Shea.

O'Shea, with his stories of espionage and warfare, was everything Sheila was not. She talked about him with an adoring expression; she found him gorgeous and exciting. She told her family how 'Michael' had called into Switzer's to see her and her co-workers were swooning over her tall, charismatic boyfriend. Then Sheila started saying things out of character, like, 'It's nice to smoke a joint and listen to jazz.' That shocked everyone. She moved out of Glenmorris and into the house next door with O'Shea. This wasn't socially acceptable in the religiously austere Ireland of the 1970s – even in a liberal and bohemian enclave of Dublin. But Sheila didn't care. And O'Shea? He definitely didn't care.

*　*　*

Buckley's Galleries was more than just an auction house where visitors could pick up a bedside cabinet, a Victorian treasure, or a heap of junk they might later regret. This was a social haunt for a large cast of characters around south Dublin, and Michael O'Shea was amongst them. It was in Buckley's that O'Shea met Desmond Fenning, the owner of a record shop on Marine Road in Dún Laoghaire, around the corner from O'Shea's garage, next to the 59 bus stop. Desmond was steeped in the arts. He attended plays at the Abbey, Ireland's national theatre, and was friends with Hilton Edwards and Micheál Mac Liammóir, the Gate theatre's founders. He knew top musical artists of the time through his shop, like balladeer Christy Moore and British pop singer Dickie Valentine (although his personal taste was for classical). Every Christmas, Desmond put his family to work in the shop: daughters Vanessa, Olga and Pamela, and sons Roderic (Rod) and Patrick. Patrick loved being surrounded by 45s and LPs and interacting with the customers coming in to buy records from the Top 30 charts. In 1973, Patrick was 12 years old. It was when he first met Michael and Sheila, he told me, when they visited the Fenning home.

'They were there [at my house] more often than not,' said Patrick. 'You wouldn't be surprised to see them there for a couple of hours. They'd have a good old chat with Mam and Dad. They were exceptionally nice and typical of the people of that time back then. Everybody was a chancer. Everybody was trying to make a buck. I always liked Sheila. She was very calm and peaceful. She never really got bent out of shape. Michael was flamboyant but very casual and very cool. He wasn't the kind of guy I would have hung around with, but at the same time we always got on very well together.'

Pamela remembers Michael as big with reddish hair: 'Dirty-looking. Really scruffy. I wouldn't have found him attractive at all – he was just somebody that was a friend of my father's and mother's.' Michael seduced a lot of women before he and Sheila got serious, she recalled. 'We always knew Michael: he was in and out of the house and he had different girlfriends. I don't think he had settled with Sheila, but he had other girls and he was a bit of a lad. My mother used to tease him about the couple of girls he had on the go at the same time.'

Desmond was the conduit to Michael O'Shea's dramatic change in fortune. In early 1973, the record store owner was shown plans for a local council development: a £4.5 million shopping centre spread across eight levels, consisting of three floors of retail, a three-storey car park, a two-storey office block, and a basement, planned for a two-acre site at the intersection of Upper George's Street and the Royal Marine Road. Michael O'Shea's garage was slap bang in the middle of the planned development, Desmond realised. O'Shea was pivotal to the shopping centre going ahead.

Desmond rushed across the road to the garage. 'Michael,' he said. 'They can't proceed if you say no. You're entitled to a better price!'

O'Shea played hardball and the council offered him £20,000, which was then a lot of money, to sell them the garage. Planning permission was granted in March 1973 and O'Shea relocated his business a few miles up the coast to the seaside village of Dalkey. O'Shea now had more money than he knew what to do with. He had a business, friends and a loyal partner in Sheila. You would've forgiven him for thinking the past was behind him. But a few months after the garage sale, an incident occurred that opened up a new fork in the road.

*   *   *

Press reports from the time described the incident as a burglary. This myth perpetuated: an untruth that grew wings over the months and years that followed. In reality, according to the Federal Bureau of Investigation (FBI), what occurred at the home of one of Michael O'Shea's business colleagues in the summer of 1973 was something far darker. John Mulderrig, a detective inspector for the Irish Gardaí, described it as a 'business dispute between themselves and someone in business with him'. The FBI claimed it was a confidence racket.

Detective Sergeant John O'Rourke, a local Garda who had kept an eye on O'Shea since 1969, outlined details of the incident in a written report. O'Shea was at his colleague's cottage in Killiney, a seafront community south of Dún Laoghaire, when two men arrived at the door. One of them, an American, threatened O'Shea, claiming he was in possession a voice recording of O'Shea talking about something that could ruin O'Shea's life. Details of this voice recording were not revealed in O'Rourke's report – the police did not have the alleged recording in their possession – but there was speculation it was something to do with O'Shea's background and identity. A scuffle ensued. Weapons were involved: an antique sword, not firearms. Nobody was hurt, but the two men fled and in the ruckus the police were called.

O'Shea had no criminal record in Ireland, but the Gardaí knew this was their opportunity to learn more about the mysterious Michael O'Shea. O'Rourke and another local officer, Frank Mullen, went to the cottage, where they technically examined the area for fingerprints. They took Michael O'Shea's prints while they were at it: 'So we can eliminate you from the enquiries,' they told him. The officers took the prints to the Garda Technical Bureau, where copies were made. O'Rourke ordered that a copy be send to Interpol, the international police organisation. A few weeks later, Interpol's forensic team got back in touch. The prints were a match for a man wanted in upstate New York on a charge of murdering his wife: Joseph Michael Maloney.

* * *

Authorities in the Western District of New York were caught by surprise. Ireland had not been on their radar as a suspected destination for their fugitive (although it perhaps should have been, considering Joe's heritage and the fact that he had visited Ireland a few months before June's death). After searching the Rochester, Canandaigua and Buffalo areas, law enforcement, following the tip-off from the Monroe County Jail inmate who talked to Joe during their captivity together, focused their attention on Canada and Australia. Police in those countries had been involved in the hunt for the fugitive, but had reached a dead end. These fingerprints suggested he'd been hiding in Ireland under another identity this whole time.

On 21 August 1973, the story leaked to the press in New York. 'Irish Nab City Murder Suspect: 6-Year Hunt Ends' read a headline on the front page of the *Times-Union*. 'Escapee May Be In Ireland', read another report in Rochester's *Democrat & Chronicle*. According to the latter article, 'Federal agents claimed Dublin police called the bureau's New York office to say they were questioning a man whose fingerprints matched those of Maloney.' Philip Smith, head of the FBI for western New York, confirmed to the same newspaper that local police had arrested Michael O'Shea after they matched his fingerprints following an investigation into a 'confidence racket'.

The FBI's decision to inform the media was a huge error of judgement. Since 1965, when the law had changed, Ireland was precluded from extraditing people to the United States. Michael was not arrested. In fact, he wasn't even informed that his fingerprints had been found to match Maloney's. The Gardaí in Ireland kept their discovery secret out of fear that their suspect might flee the country. When Irish police were contacted by local news media in Rochester, they told them they'd never heard of Michael O'Shea or Joseph Maloney.

A fresh set of headlines then appeared in Rochester newspapers, like 'Irish Not Holding City Murder Suspect'. The FBI backed down, saying they 'didn't know' how the capture report originated. Behind the scenes, though, political negotiations between Ireland and the United States to widen extradition arrangements had begun. The Gardaí told the FBI that a new treaty was imminent and likely to be implemented within the next six to eight months.

Meanwhile, the Gardaí did some digging into the origins of Michael O'Shea. They made enquiries at Dublin's Registry of Births and Deaths and found he'd changed his name from Michael Grace, born on 3 December 1941, as an illegitimate child to an English woman.

'It would appear,' wrote an officer in a report, 'that Maloney on arrival in Ireland visited the Registry of Births and Deaths, observed the registration of Michael Grace and then took on his identity, possibly assuming that the real Michael Grace had been taken back to England by his mother or was adopted.' The suspect then changed his name by deed poll to O'Shea. It was an identity fraud popularised by Frederick Forsyth's novel *The Day of the Jackal*, in which the central character assumes a new identity by taking the name of a dead infant. Not that there was any suggestion that O'Shea might have been inspired by this fiction – his alleged name change took place two years before Forsyth's book was published in 1971.

Garda Frank Mullen placed Michael O'Shea's fingerprints, the documents detailing the incident at his colleague's house and the information detailing the alleged identity fraud into a filing cabinet at Dún Laoghaire Garda Station, where they would remain until O'Shea could be arrested. The FBI too was willing to play the waiting game.

None of them imagined they would have to wait another 12 years.

6.

Master of the Manor

August 2025

MY CAR ROUNDED A CORNER ONTO A QUIET COUNTRY ROAD, BORDERED WITH HIGH HEDGES AND SHOWING SCANT SIGN OF HABITATION ASIDE FROM A DILAPIDATED FARMHOUSE. A few hundred metres along this path in the townland of Raheen, County Laois, was my destination: a long two-storey house built of grey, rough-hewn stones, with rectangular, white-framed windows fitted into red-brick surrounds. I parked at the entrance and walked to the back of the house, where a modern sliding-glass door was installed into the ancient brick. A dog was ferociously barking from somewhere on the property. Behind a locked door or in a kennel, I hoped.

This was my third time visiting the site of Winfred Maloney's ancestral home in a hope to find more information about Joe's Irish ancestry, but on each occasion nobody had been at home. Joe Maloney's mother had grown up here before migrating to

Rochester, where she died in 1962. Near the house were the graves of her parents, Joe's maternal grandparents, James Doyle and Mary Quinlan. A few miles further west, across the Tipperary border in Roscrea, was the birthplace of Joe's late father, Joseph Senior.

I sat in the car and considered leaving another note for the occupant as I had done a year and a half previously while making the *Runaway Joe* podcast. After 15 minutes of procrastination, I was about to leave when a car pulled up. A man emerged, eyeballed me suspiciously and asked me my business. I told him I was trying to find information about the ancestral inhabitants of the building. I showed him a photograph of James and Mary's grave and he warmed up. He was the owner of the house now, he explained, and had lived here for 20 or so years. He didn't know anything about the Doyle family, but he was intrigued.

'What's the story you're telling?'

It's about someone who used to own Capard House I said, in reference to a stately home located 22 miles southwest of here in the village of Rosenallis.

'Michael O'Shea?'

'Yes, him!'

He laughed and clamped his hands on my shoulders. 'I knew Michael O'Shea.'

Decades beforehand, he had worked for the Irish Land Commission, he explained, and had had dealings with O'Shea. However, he knew nothing about Joe Maloney, nor his connection to this property, which had passed through many owners before him.

Joe visited the Laois area a few months before his alleged murder of June Fisk in 1967, I told the home owner. He knew this land well and maybe stayed at this very abode.

'Do you want to buy it?'

I looked at the man, surprised. 'Buy what?'

'The house. Do you want to buy it?'

He told me his family had experienced two terrible tragic events while living here, and now he wanted rid of the place.

He sighed and looked at the ground. 'I think it's cursed.'

* * *

The wedding of Michael O'Shea to Sheila Chandler was a low-key affair. These neighbours-turned-lovers announced their vows in the Catholic Church in Dalkey not far from O'Shea's new garage on 29 June 1974. He listed his occupation on the wedding certificate as motor engineer; she described herself as assistant manager of a salon. O'Shea's date of birth was recorded as 3 December 1941: the same date on the birth certificate of Michael Grace, which Garda unearthed as part of their investigation into O'Shea's identity. Sheila's parents Vincent and Catherine attended the wedding, but none of O'Shea's family was there, just a few friends, and nobody questioned O'Shea's reluctance to have wedding photographs taken. Neither did anyone notice the possible acknowledgement to a past life on his wedding certificate. O'Shea's absent parents were listed as Terrence O'Shea and Winifred Southgate. Winifred also happened to be the name of Joe Maloney's late mother.

O'Shea's fortunes were rapidly escalating. The confrontation at his colleague's house the previous summer was now forgotten, and a combination of good fortune, his new garage in Dalkey, odd jobs through the auction house and his marital status into a respectable local family gave the outsider roots in the community. Rosie Morgan, the woman who worked with O'Shea at the furniture shop in Dolphin's Barn a few years beforehand, remembered seeing O'Shea on a gorgeous sunny day in Dún Laoghaire in the summer of 1974 or 1975.

'I must have been out for the day with friends. I'm standing at a bus stop and he comes along with a much younger girl. I presumed it was his wife. She had this pram, a huge big pram from another era with a sun canopy on it. She was all smiling, wheeling the pram. He was beside her and he still had that smug swagger about him, you know, going down the street. I just had to look away. I couldn't look at him.'

Was the woman Sheila? Maybe. Was the child theirs? No. Michael and Sheila didn't have children. The story he told Sheila's mother was that he had an operation and was infertile; the story Sheila told people was that he'd had 'the snip'. Sheila would have loved children, her mother told people, but that was OK, because her daughter was infatuated with Michael.

In 1975, O'Shea's profile went into ascent. He was looking in the window of Buckley's Galleries in Sandycove when he saw a listing for a stately home, Capard House, in County Laois in the midlands of Ireland. Michael assembled a group of business associates and, upon convincing a bank to give them a loan, the consortium purchased the property for £42,000 (Irish punts). They paid £30,000 for the house, including 123 acres of land, and £12,000 for the contents of the property. In today's prices, with inflation in mind, it would be valued at $400,000: a bargain for an estate this size.

The estate was adjacent to Rosenallis, a small village of Quaker origin on the foothills of the Slieve Bloom Mountains. In 1803, a few years after Capard was built, the travel writer William Wilson described Capard as 'one of the most extensive in the kingdom', with a 'magnificent appearance'. A long avenue led from the gates to the two-storey property, built from cut stone in the Greek revival style. The building, with its single Doric portico entrance, looked out onto terraced lawns and walled gardens, a long pond and lake. A separate block housed the servant's quarters, which were attached to the main house by a corridor and were disproportionately large in comparison to the house because (according to lore) they were constructed before the main residence was completed. At the back of the house, there was a stable yard, accessible by the servants' quarters and an exterior laneway.

A black-and-white sheepdog roamed the estate, but the true security guard was a 20-year-old goose who lived in the yard and assaulted visitors. The minute a car went over the cattle grid at the entrance to the estate, the goose went crazy in the yard.

'That goose was massive,' said one local. 'He ruled the roost – he was the boss. I was terrified of him. Even the dog was scared of him.'

£42,000 didn't just buy O'Shea the house, its history and a goose. Capard came with a housekeeper and staff. Eddie and Maggie were two siblings born, raised and educated on the property. Their father had worked there as a butler, and now they lived in two rooms at the front of the house and tended to the property and its land. Maggie was elderly, glam, always with a bit of makeup – lipstick and earrings – and her brother was eccentric, wandering the grounds muttering to himself, 'Oh lord, oh lord. Lordy lord.'

Erika Lotze was the German housekeeper, the daughter of an orchestra conductor who grew up in Berlin, where she trained as a nurse before the Second World War. Lotze had been recruited into the Hitler Youth at the age of 12 or 13. An amateur gymnast, she was involved (but did not compete) in the 1936 Olympics in Berlin, a show of Nazi propaganda that attempted to legitimise Adolf Hitler's regime. (In later years, when anyone asked about Lotze's membership of the Hitler Youth, she shrugged and replied, 'We didn't know what it was. We just joined because everybody else did.') During the Second World War, Lotze worked as a nurse for the German Army. She told stories of her narrow escape from death in Dresden, when Allied forces bombed the city from the sky in 1945 with high-explosive bombs and incendiary devices. Lotze boarded a tram that day to work. When she reached the city centre, everything was on fire. The bombing had caused a conflagration, a chimney effect that drew flames from the periphery of the city towards the centre. She took a tram back to the suburbs, where she encountered more devastation. An estimated 25,000 people perished in the bombing of Dresden, but Erika Lotze survived.

Lotze was in Berlin during the Airlift of 1948 and 1949, when the US, United Kingdom and France flew vital supplies, including food, medicine and fuel, into the western part of the city after Soviet forces blocked land and river traffic to the area. It was in Berlin that she met Charles de Jenner, a former Swiss Minister posted to Bulgaria. During those post-war years, de Jenner worked for Berlin's International Red Cross, inspecting prisons holding convicted war criminals. Lotze was working as a nurse in one such institution.

Stories about their relationship vary. Lotze had been married previously and had a son, Dieter. Whether the initial bond between her and de Jenner was entirely professional or partly romantic, she left Berlin with him for his native Switzerland. De Jenner was a Swiss national, and he had a deep connection to Ireland. Mary Ellen de Jenner, his mother, was a sister of Robert Pigott, the former owner of Capard House, who died in 1917. As Robert was unmarried and had no children, the estate was passed on to Mary Ellen and then to Charles de Jenner when his mother died in 1928. Capard was uninhabited while de Jenner carried out his diplomatic duties and work with the Red Cross, but after the war he visited his estate every year for shooting season until 1961, when he retired and returned to live full-time here.

He brought with him Erika Lotze, his nurse-turned-housekeeper: the lady of the mansion.

*   *   *

Lotze took on a huge property that was run down following decades of neglect. Through her austere command and relentless cleaning and scouring, and with help from the retainers Maggie and Eddie Kenny, the place was eventually made to her liking. Rosenallis was a rural, working-class Irish community, but Capard played a part in the lives of locals. Villagers walked through its grounds and had picnics in its fields on weekends. Lotze wasn't a big part of the community, but she attended the occasional event.

'She was very dignified and lent a little bit of tone to the local society,' said one local.

Once a week, Lotze drove the four miles to the nearest town, Mountmellick, to buy groceries for the house and give a lift to any locals who needed one. Capard was cold even during the summer months. On these trips to town she collected reels of yarn and spent her free time in the estate deciphering knitting patterns and making jumpers for de Jenner. Lotze fell in love with Capard, its history and architectural eccentricities; she became indelibly entwined with daily operations. De Jenner, according to a later owner of the house, was in love with her. He asked her several times to marry him, and even though this would have made her baroness and an inheritor of the estate, she rejected his proposals.

In 1970, Charles de Jenner died and was buried under a tree on the avenue leading up to the house. Although he'd left authority of the estate to Lotze, the boundaries of her inheritance were vague, and his family opted to sell the lot to Robert Noonan, a Dublin-based property developer. Noonan was not impressed by the presence of Lotze or the Kenny siblings. One local mused that Noonan might have been spooked by the alleged (and probably false) rumour that Erika's son could have been de Jenner's child and therefore rightful heir to the estate. Tom Dobson, a jeweller who had lived in Capard years later, alleged that Noonan had refused her use of a car, forcing her to make her weekly journey from Capard to Mountmellick by foot. 'A loaf of bread, a pound of butter and a carton of milk: that's what she survived on for the week,' said Dobson. 'She told me if it wasn't for her experience in the war she would have never been able to survive it.'

In the end, Noonan departed. Five years after the passing of Charles de Jenner, news reached Capard that the house was sold to a new owner. Lotze was anxious, and Maggie and Eddie Kenny, who had no experience of life outside Capard, feared for their future. One local recalled of their anxieties: 'This new guy is coming along. Will he kick us out?'

But when Michael O'Shea stepped through Capard's portico, their worries dissipated.

* * *

O'Shea loved the idea of having a housekeeper and two servants. It appealed to his ego. Plus he needed help with the place. Capard was run down after years of neglect and didn't generate much money. Noonan, Lotze alleged, had stripped the place of some of its prized possessions, including Pigott-branded cutlery, coats of arms and glasses. Paintings of the Pigott clan that had previously adorned the walls were missing. The mansion's original period features were crumbling, and the gardens were overgrown and misshapen.

But all O'Shea could see was potential. He walked the formal terraces and explored the walled garden with its orchards of rhododendrons and roses. He surveyed the streams that ran through the garden and the woods with their blankets of wild bluebells. He threw his arms open wide and told anyone who was listening about his big plans and how he was going to renovate this and rediscover that. The property included a long pond and a lake that were overgrown with rushes and in need of serious drainage work.

'I'm going to restore those lakes,' O'Shea announced, 'and put a bridge across them!'

O'Shea contacted Peter Collins, a local builder who he'd encountered through his car repair business in Dublin. Collins and his brother-in-law Frans Jansen had spent the previous couple of years working for a company in France and Holland restoring old buildings and churches. Their background in period property restoration made them ideal for Capard's needs.

'Capard needed a lot of work,' said Collins. 'Michael must have got wind that we were there, and he asked me if I'd do something for him. He had all these enterprises going on. The first summer of his ownership I was putting roofs on outbuildings and sheds and potato storage houses. I worked on and off for him for about six months before Frans joined me.'

Paddy Gilfoyle from Mountmellick was one of the dozens of workers contracted to spruce up the estate. He started working there as a mechanic in 1975 and brought along his three sons. Tony Gilfoyle recalled painting the interior walls gold and dark purple. At various points in the day, Maggie Kenny made tea and baked buns for the workers in the kitchen.

The new master of the manor appeared sensitive to the history of the property. When the Irish Republican Army (IRA) seized the house in 1922 during the Irish Civil War there was a standoff between them and the Free State army, who assaulted the house from the front, firing on the building from two Lancia armoured cars – and from the rear with a phalanx of officers with rifles. One IRA man, Denis Dwyer, bolted from the house and was shot. The bullet detonated the ammunition he carried in his pocket, killing him 50 metres from the back door. O'Shea, entranced by the bullet holes visible in parts of the building, erected a small iron cross and a memorial stone to mark the spot where Dwyer fell, and he invited Dwyer's relatives to see them.

O'Shea and his wife Sheila tended to drive from Dublin to Capard in one of their two Vauxhall Cavaliers on Thursday evenings, returning to Dublin at the end of the weekend. 'I can never remember tax, insurance or nothing in the windows of either of the cars he had,' recalled Tony Gilfoyle. The couple stayed in an upstairs bedroom suite with a four-poster bed that overlooked the surrounding countryside.

Capard was O'Shea's playground. Tony remembered him building a bomb one day and strapping it to a tree on the lawn. 'He had a fuse on the lid and he walked back and blew a lump out of the tree.' He also fixed up a tripod near the front door, attached a rifle and shot wild deer that wandered onto the estate, packing their carcasses into freezers.

Neville James, a local car dealer and a vintage car enthusiast from Mountmellick, shared some of Joe's passions, including membership of the local gun club. Fiona, James's daughter, visited Capard with her father for the first time in the 1970s, when she was 11 or 12. O'Shea had set up a clay pigeon machine with help from Tony Gilfoyle and Eddie Kenny. Eddie Kenny loaded up the discs and let them loose while her dad and O'Shea fired shotguns. O'Shea was a good aim, and there was a lot of competition between the two men. Whenever her dad visited

O'Shea, the men talked about guns or cars, and O'Shea waxed lyrical about his war stories and his plans for Capard. Fiona would grow tired of their adult conversation and wander off to explore the estate. Even at that young age, she recognised O'Shea's magnetism. With his shock of red hair and big beard, he had the bearing of a movie star.

'Maybe he wasn't the best looking but he carried himself like he was Paul Newman,' said Fiona. 'You would know when he was in a room. The American parting on his hair and the height. There aren't very many Irish men that grow to be the height he was: six foot two or more. And also the way he dressed in jeans. A man in his 30s or 40s wouldn't have been wearing jeans back then. I don't think my dad ever did. He talked about life in a very can-do way. "I've had these great experiences and I'm going to make lots more experiences." So he's very positive about it, but it was very egotistical as well. There was a show element to it. My dad always liked that kind of life. He liked history. My dad liked artefacts, so they would go rummaging around in the house looking for old bits of furniture.'

O'Shea had a CB radio in his car, a short-distance communication system popularised in American movies like *Smokey and the Bandit* and *Convoy*, and this made him even more exciting for some locals. People noticed his unusual mannerisms, like his tendency to stand hunched with his head down into his chest. He didn't look forward during conversation but sunk his head low and gave you a side-eye with his arms folded. Then there was his habit of drinking Tabasco, a hot sauce made from vinegar, peppers and salt. He'd fill a spoonful from a bottle into a cup of boiling water, stir it and drink it right up.

* * *

Nobody threw a party quite like Michael O'Shea. At weekends there were loads of cars in the avenue outside the house. O'Shea greeted guests through the portico and ushered them into one of the reception rooms that led from the main hall: generously proportioned rooms with ornate ceilings and large open fireplaces. He had lunch parties and dinner parties where he mixed drinks and made cocktails. Fiona remembered having lunch at Capard with her parents and tasting cheesecake for the first time. ('That was a mind-blowing experience for me.') Her parents had never before experienced the idea of drinking wine at lunchtime, but they were happy to hold out their glasses while O'Shea kept pouring.

O'Shea served his food and drinks using the traditional china and glasses that came with Capard.

'He mixed all the drinks very American style: on the side with the fancy little glasses,' remembered Fiona. 'Things that you wouldn't have in the normal house in Mountmellick, for sure. Bourbon. The soda siphon. My mom loved all that.'

Sean Wisely ran a local haulage business and visited the house for parties on weekend evenings, where he played his accordion for guests. '[O'Shea] was a great man for parties,' said Wisely. 'You'd have big old crowds in and all the neighbours would be up there drinking to no end.'

Another invitee was Pat Fitzsimons, whose father employed O'Shea at his engineering firm in the late 1960s, who came to Capard for dinner with his wife Margaret. Over pre-dinner cocktails, O'Shea regaled Fitzsimons and the other guests with stories about the ghost that haunted the corridors of the mansion, and how Rosenallis got its name.

'He told me that there were two children, one called Rose the other Alice,' said Fitzsimons. 'They fell into the lake beside Capard House, and that's how Rosenallis got its name.'

The story was bunkum. Rosenallis was named by early ecclesiastical writers after *Ros Finnghlaise*, a phrase in Irish meaning 'The wood of the clear stream'. Fitzsimons laughed it off. He liked O'Shea and found him interesting. His host took him on a tour of the mansion, showing him the billiard room at the back of the house and his wartime ephemera: an African spear, a Nepalese Gurkha kukri knife and a flintlock pistol. O'Shea was an authority on guns. He had six-shooters that Fitzsimons had only seen in Westerns and a selection of rifles. O'Shea bragged that he made his own guns too. After the tour, O'Shea took Fitzsimons into the dining hall for dinner. The room's antique clock soundtracked O'Shea's monologues, and the night wore on. Halfway through dinner, O'Shea suddenly leapt up, energised. Cattle from neighbouring farmland had wandered into the garden and he ran off to get his shotgun and shoot them all. He wasn't in the least bit annoyed. Quite the opposite: he was thrilled to have the opportunity to annihilate a herd of cattle. When Pat and Margaret Fitzsimons left it was dark and Margaret was spooked. She had no desire to return.

'I just remember this madman,' she told me for the podcast *Runaway Joe*. 'A person that I wouldn't like to be around, you know. A person I did get a bad feeling about: a very wild sort of character. He gave me an uncomfortable feeling. A very uncomfortable feeling.'

O'Shea introduced other old friends to Capard. Pat McMahon, the film set armourer, decorated the house with portraits. Brian Hanlon, O'Shea's doctor friend, had migrated to Canada to manage a 100-bed hospital in Wingham, Ontario, and in the mid-1970s returned to Ireland to visit his old friend for a week over Christmas. Hanlon was impressed with the mansion, its housekeeper and servants, horses and barns. Before becoming a doctor, Hanlon had joined the Fórsa Cosanta Áitiúil (FCA), the reserve component of the Irish Defence Forces, and he and O'Shea and everyone else in attendance dressed up in army uniforms for Christmas dinner. O'Shea loved to rope others into his military fantasies. Afterwards, a drunken O'Shea rode around the estate in an Engineering Corps uniform on a thoroughbred horse firing his gun into the sky.

There was no shortage of horses in the stables. O'Shea had befriended Garda in the local area, and whenever they were given a stray horse they brought it to him. By 1978, he had eight of them. One was called Paddy Boy, another Capard Boy. O'Shea bought a Wild West-style saddle, stuck his rifle into a scabbard, and occasionally rode the four miles into Mountmellick for a pint in Moloney's Pub.

'He had guns on him every time, no matter where he went,' said Tony. 'One time he was at Moloney's and a fellow sat on his chair when he was outside.' O'Shea told the man to get up; the man told him to get out of his face. 'O'Shea put a gun to his forehead and he said, "I'll shoot you." The man stood up and got out of there.'

O'Shea thought of himself as an incredible horseman, but the reality was different. On one occasion, O'Shea turned up at the door of Peter Collins, who lived a mile from the gates of Capard, on the back of his favourite thoroughbred. O'Shea dismounted and proudly told Collins, 'This horse will stand there as long as I tell him.'

The animal promptly turned on its feet and trotted back to Capard without O'Shea.

He adored that horse, even if the affection was not reciprocated. When O'Shea arrived at Capard on Thursday evenings, Eddie had the horse saddled up in the stables and ready for him to ride around the estate. The name O'Shea gave the horse? Joey.

The same name as June and Joe Maloney's son: the boy Joe abandoned in Rochester in 1967.

* * *

Sheila Chandler, who now called herself Chandler-O'Shea, was rarely afraid to speak her mind. She turned up at the houses of friends, and if children were around would loudly opine, 'In my day, we didn't do that!' Family members described her as well-read, opinionated and not confrontational but able to fight her corner. People in Michael O'Shea's orbit in Capard have few memories of Sheila from that time, even though she joined her husband on his weekend trips to the estate.

'A soft face; mousy,' said one local.

'Better dressed than the average person around Mountmellick,' offered another.

'She was lovely and her mother was lovely,' offered Kitty Gilfoyle, Tony's sister, who did odd jobs on the estate with her sibling. Michael O'Shea, according to Kitty, 'was an awful-looking yoke. He was raggedy, never cleaned up.'

Villagers from Rosenallis, when asked for their memories of O'Shea's wife, were just as likely to say, 'I don't recall her at all.' Beside his roaring flame, her light dimmed. She was quiet in his presence, withdrawn even. O'Shea did all the talking, and friends don't remember her opening her mouth much in his company. The couple were wildly different said Peter Collins, who knew Sheila from when she was a young woman growing up in Glenageary.

'Michael couldn't see deer walking across the fields without thinking about how he was going to bring it down and put it in the freezer,' Collins told me for *Runaway Joe*. 'Sheila was more enamoured by the idea they would remain in the wild.' Collins found their relationship difficult to fathom, 'because they were so utterly different personality-wise. She was shy, introverted, an incredibly reliable person, whereas Michael was all dreams and "It'll be all be grand on the day" and bluff your way through it.'

Sheila maintained her job as a receptionist in the hairdressing department of Switzer's department store on Dublin's Grafton Street, but her life outside work had transformed. 'It changed beyond all the possible recognition when she met Michael,' Collins said.

Sheila enjoyed her time in the countryside. She loved gardening and cultivated garlic and other herbs in the gardens of Capard, and she read books in the property's ornate library in the company of taxidermied birds and foxes.

Sheila and O'Shea both had a good relationship with Erika Lotze, the German caretaker. O'Shea didn't treat Lotze like a servant and called her by her first name. Observers saw no demarcation between the master of the manor and his loyal chatelaine. She knew every nook and cranny of the property, and O'Shea recognised her as a valuable asset. Occasionally he infuriated her. O'Shea liked to bring dubious antiques to the house, which Lotze, who'd lived around antiques for decades, knew a lot about.

'These are not in keeping with house,' she complained, mostly behind his back. 'He keeps bringing Victorian things here. This house is not Victorian!'

Lotze could be prickly. 'It was like having a pet hedgehog,' said Esther Collins, Peter's daughter. 'You weren't going to come away without injuries.'

Although Lotze was argumentative, formidable and occasionally mean, locals liked her. She was soft beneath the surface, and her achievements during de Jenner and Noonan's time – managing a farm without experience and a house without money – did not go unnoticed. Lotze could be kind-hearted, and she loved animals and children. During her trips to Mountmellick she stopped to chat with locals in the street, openly admired what they were wearing and asked about their families. Lotze's English was not that great, but she made an effort. When she was angry, though, she lapsed back into German, to the bafflement of English speakers around her.

'The only time I remember Erika speaking German,' recalled Fiona James, 'was when a Dutch friend of mine had a go at her for invading Holland.'

*   *   *

Michael O'Shea wasn't in Capard House long before he realised what previous owners knew before him: this place was a money pit. As estate owner he needed to pay salaries for Lotze and the Kenny siblings. He had to feed the horses and fix and maintain everything else on the vast property. 'Unless somebody was funding them,' mused his doctor friend Brian Hanlon, 'I don't know where he would have gotten all that money.'

O'Shea surveyed his land and wondered how he might profit from his investment. There was discussion about turning Capard into a five-star hotel, but that level of investment was beyond his reach. There were suggestions Capard might help regenerate the Slieve Bloom Mountain region for tourism purposes, but public funding wasn't available. Instead, O'Shea and his investors turned their attention to the 60 semi-arable acres in Capard and tried to grow potato and turnip crops. The turnips were due to be purchased by a factory in Carlow, 35 miles southeast of the estate, but wild deer came down from the mountains at night and ate the crop. The potatoes didn't fare much better. When the first batch came into season, O'Shea charged a mechanic from a local garage to transport them to Dublin in an articulated lorry. The potatoes made it as far as the entrance to the estate when the lorry broke down. A local contractor later helped deliver the troubled spuds to Dublin, where the wholesaler rejected them on account of their poor quality.

Timing conspired against the project. When O'Shea became a farmer there had been three or four years of miserable potato harvest, and the price of potatoes went through the roof. Now O'Shea had a mountain of potatoes and nowhere to put them. A farmer in County Mayo offered to buy the potatoes to feed his pigs.

'O'Shea said, "There're no fucking pigs going to eat my potatoes",' recalled Conor, who drove tractors and did other odd jobs on the estate. 'So a huge pit was dug and hundreds upon hundreds of tonnes of potatoes were dumped in there.' The buried potatoes fermented beneath the ground and locals gossiped that the neighbourhood hadn't smelled like this since the famine of the 1840s.

Farming in Capard was a fool's errand, reckoned Larry Power, an agricultural consultant from Tipperary who O'Shea brought to the estate to get a valuation on the property. O'Shea wanted to give Power a tour in a vehicle.

'That's not the way to see what you're looking at,' the consultant told him. 'You have to walk the land.'

While they walked around the estate, Power surmised that, despite the land's arid soil and soft climate, it was not conducive to farming due to its altitude and location on the edge of the Slieve Bloom Mountains. He kept this assessment to himself. The land could have been as fertile as Mesopotamia and O'Shea still wouldn't have been up to the task. Farming was a skill learned over decades and inherited across generations – a skill O'Shea did not have.

Faced with endless bleak harvests, the master of the manor opted to make money through more nefarious means. He purchased a sawmill and had 20 men harvesting beech trees on the lawn in front of the house to sell off the timber. One winter he tasked Sean Wisely, the local haulier and quarry business owner, to transport a crop of fir trees from the estate to a supermarket in Dublin. When Wisely arrived with a truck full of trees, the supermarket owner refused to accept them on account of them being too big.

Wisely phoned O'Shea. 'What do I do now?'

O'Shea told him to drop half of them into his front garden on Arkendale Road in Dublin. The other half were to be fly-tipped elsewhere.

O'Shea faced legal threats from a local timber merchant, who claimed he'd arranged to purchase 38 oak, beech and timber trees from Capard and had given O'Shea a deposit. Two weeks later, alleged the merchant, he returned to the house and another contractor was working on the site. He didn't get his timber and O'Shea hadn't returned the deposit. O'Shea's timber business was stripping the estate of its natural habitat and doing nothing to stem his haemorrhaging income. In the opinion of some locals, it may have even hastened his misfortune. On the grounds of Capard there was a fairy fort. These circular earthen mountains were said to date back to hundreds of years BC in Ireland and were (according to Irish folklore) entrances to the worlds of mythical pre-Celtic beings.

Local legend in Rosenallis had it that O'Shea, in the process of deforesting Capard House, destroyed one such fairy fort. Some locals believed supernatural inhabitants enacted revenge, and this was the cause of the bad luck that plagued him over the years to come.

Others might argue that his misfortune was entirely of his own doing.

* * *

Michael O'Shea started accumulating debt around County Laois. Sean Wisely was one such contractor left out of pocket. O'Shea owed Wisely £1,000 (Irish punts) for his deliveries of stone and gravel to the estate. After weeks without payment, Wisely took a call from Capard's owner, who told him he didn't have the money but could give him a 1932 Model B Ford car in payment. Wisely accepted; others were not so fortunate. There was conspiratorial speculation amongst locals about O'Shea's high-profile associates, like the men who arrived in Mercedes cars, put on rubber boots and walked around the estate with O'Shea.

Eddie, Maggie and Mrs Lotze made the house look respectable and made food for the return of the visitors to the house. Eddie told Conor that Charlie Haughey, one of Ireland's most prominent and notorious politicians, had come to visit. At the time of Haughey's visit (1975 or 1976, according to the tractor driver), the politician was in the backbench wilderness of Ireland's government, having been dismissed as cabinet minister in 1970 over allegations he gave charitable funds to the IRA for the use of importing arms. In 1979, Haughey became leader of the political party Fianna Fáil and Taoiseach of the nation – a role he assumed on and off until 1992. Like O'Shea, the politician had delusions of grandeur, having purchased Abbeville, a stately home in Kinsealy, County Dublin.

Did Haughey really visit Michael O'Shea? It was never proven, but O'Shea certainly knew Charlie Flanagan, a local man from Mountmellick whose father was a Fine Gael politician and Minister for Defence in the Irish government. Flanagan was then attending University College Dublin and in training to become a solicitor. In later years he followed in his father's footsteps into politics and was appointed the country's Justice Minister. If these politicians knew the real Michael O'Shea, the man behind the beard, it's unlikely they would have given him their time.

Conor the tractor driver knew O'Shea as a 'big tall man with piercing eyes. He could be vicious but he could also be nice and sweet. Nice and so evil. There was a terrible bad streak in him. You wouldn't want to get on the wrong side of him. A Jekyll and Hyde character.'

There were periods in which O'Shea was in bad humour and people went out of their way to avoid him. Like the time in 1977 after he underwent extensive dental work in Dublin. 'I remember that going on for weeks and he was in fucking fierce pain and he wasn't talking,' said Conor. 'He'd always fold his arms when he'd be talking to you. But his face was swollen.'

A year later, O'Shea was being hounded by the ESB, Ireland's electrical board, over an unpaid bill. ESB sent an employee from the district office in Portlaoise to Capard to retrieve the debt or disconnect the house from the grid. The employee parked his van outside the steps of Capard, at which point O'Shea (who must have had a tip-off) emerged from the house with a rifle and fired two shots over the man's head.

'There's no fuckers going to turn off our power,' shouted O'Shea.

The man took off running, leaving his van behind him.

'I don't know how the man got back to the office in Portlaoise,' said Conor. 'It was a day, maybe a day and a half, before someone come to collect the van. But the power was never turned off.'

O'Shea employed a local contractor to dredge silt and weeds from the estate's pond and lake, and he too was not paid. A crew of six painters had been deployed to decorate inside the house around the same time. They were upstairs painting when they heard a ruckus and came downstairs to find Eddie, Maggie and Lotze in the kitchen tending to a man lying on the table and bleeding profusely from his nose and mouth. Lotze was pouring a fresh basin of water and Eddie was trying to clean up the injured man with a sponge. The man was a retired Garda who had come to collect the debt for the work carried out in the pond and the lake. This collector had confronted O'Shea in the stables yard that led into the back of the house, and O'Shea 'absolutely poleaxed him', according to a witness.

Police were called. It wasn't the only time they investigated skulduggery at Capard. There were unfounded rumours that O'Shea was growing cannabis on the property, which led to another raid, and darker allegations about O'Shea's sexual proclivities. Kitty, the daughter of the estate's mechanic, Paddy Gilfoyle, was then in her early twenties and helping her brother Tony with the horses in the stables. She was given strict instructions by her father: '"under no circumstances be on your own with O'Shea. Never go off riding with him on your own," Daddy used to say to me.'

Kitty knew of women, 'girls here in Mountmellick that were up with Michael regular and that's why Daddy said he wouldn't trust them'.

Did Sheila know what her husband was up to, I asked Tony, Kitty's brother. He nodded. 'Sheila would be there out in the garden, sitting down, while he entertained women in the house.'

Kitty concurred. 'She turned a blind eye.'

There was also a local rumour that O'Shea allegedly sexually assaulted a local girl who was horse-riding on the estate. This story, like other rumours that circulated about the mysterious property owner, was never substantiated.

* * *

O'Shea's admirers in County Laois were starting to question his character. O'Shea told Peter Collins and Collins's brother-in-law Frans Jansen stories about his past. Like how he'd 'spent six years at college' qualifying to become a doctor, and how he trained to be an engineer, which took another five years of study. O'Shea bragged about his escapades in the British Army, serving in Aden and elsewhere, and his engineering feats, including the construction of the Kish Bank lighthouse (which began in Dún Laoghaire in 1963, and which O'Shea claimed to have towed into position on a sandbank seven miles from the coast in 1965).

'This was Michael O'Shea's own account,' remarked Peter Collins. 'Frans and myself sat down one day and we reckoned he had the appearance of a 45-year-old man. But if you added up all the things he had done, he had to be 136. Michael made up his life as he went along. I genuinely believe it. He was completely sincere in his beliefs, but he never let the truth stand in the way of a good story.'

That story changed depending on who he was talking to. For some people he liked to be called Michael and loathed being called Mick. Others were advised to call him Mick. Maybe Capard allowed him to revert to his true self . . . or a true someone else. While some people thought of him as Irish or Anglo-Irish or maybe even English, the young Fiona James – who sat and listened while O'Shea gabbled with her father over canapés and cocktails in the dining room or fawned over vintage cars in the avenue – was in no doubt as to his true origin.

'I distinctly remember his accent being American,' she said. 'There's absolutely no way he could have faked an Irish accent unless he was in America, where Americans might fall for it. He just didn't come across as Irish in any way.'

Tony Gilfoyle added: 'When he had a few drinks in him he used to get real loud. He wouldn't be rowdy, but he'd get really loud.

And then you'd know he was American, because he'd start talking in an American accent.'

Then there was O'Shea's perpetual retelling and evolving story about his war wound. Sean Wisely one afternoon drove a lorry-load of sand to the estate, where he found its owner standing on the steps beneath the portico entrance. 'It was a fierce, warm, hot day in summer and Michael had no shirt on him,' said Sean. 'I got out to talk to him for a minute and he had a mark there on the stomach. He said, "A lad stuck a bayonet into me there".'

O'Shea told Conor, the tractor driver, he got the wound when he was in Africa hunting elephants. He was seducing the wife of an African native when her husband came home and attacked him.

'Look what the bastard done to me,' O'Shea announced, pulling up his shirt to reveal the two-inch-wide scar on his abdomen. The scar was in the same spot where Joe Maloney had, in an effort to garner sympathy from his wife June (in the estimation of Joe's best friend Neal Dunkleberg), stabbed himself with a screwdriver.

7.

The Children

Joey Maloney was only five when his mother June was killed and his father Joe fled Rochester, and he built a mental drawbridge between his pre-1967 existence and everything that followed. Memories of his time with June and Joe were never far from the surface, though. Some were sensory recollections; others were vivid and tinged with the innocence of a small boy. The house on Eastmoreland Drive was mapped onto his mind: his bed with its brown headboard and round ball posts; the tree swing in the front yard, which Joe built for him and once swung back and hit the boy in the face, knocking out a front tooth. Other memories: a terrifying blizzard and three feet of snow outside the front of the house. Utter fear as a snow plough bellowed down the sidewalk and Joe pulled three-year-old Joey out of its path. His dog: Barry. His parents' cars: June's olive-green Chevrolet Corvair, Joe's red Ford Mustang. He remembered the neighbours but not their faces.

Family members were more defined. There was Joseph Senior, Joe's dad: a friendly bald man. And June's parents: Ward and Marie. Joey could recall Ward's weathered old rural farmhouse in Albion, and how he gained another grandparent when the Wards divorced and Marie remarried. Joey had a distinct memory of meeting for the first time Gladys, the girlfriend and soon-to-be wife of June's brother. It was 1966, and they had just started dating. She had 'blondish, curly hair'. Dale? 'A thin guy, dark hair and wore glasses.'

Then there was his baby sister, Patricia Ann. Joey was three years old when June brought Patti home from the hospital in a baby carrier, and Joey thought she looked like a little doll. Like most little boys, Joey could be naughty and on one occasion tried to flush Patti's diaper down the toilet, which resulted in a flooded bathroom and his parents frantically calling a plumber.

Joey remembered June as a good mother. She fed him, cared for him, cuddled him when he was upset, took him places. Joe spent a lot of time down in the basement of the house on Eastmoreland. Joey wasn't supposed to go there, but on one occasion he went down with a friend. Joe opened a box to show them what appeared to be a severed hand. Joey was shocked, although in later years he imagined it must have been a theatre prop. Joe could be strict. One time Joey snuck into his father's bedroom when he was asleep and woke him up while looking for a toy and Joe freaked out. Another time he was playing Captain America and jumping off the staircase and Joe got enraged and ordered him to knock it off.

'But he was never violent towards me,' said Joey.

Joe and June kept their unravelling domestic life largely hidden from the children, although Joey recalled arguments about which church they should attend, because Joe was Catholic and June was a Protestant. When Joe left for Ireland in early 1967, Joey remembered his mother driving back to the house on Eastmoreland Road and frantically looking through drawers and cupboards. He suspected she was looking for money. 'She was digging through everything and she couldn't find it and she just sat down and started crying.'

Even when June was experiencing her darkest days, she kept her children content. Joey fondly recalled playing outside the back door of their new apartment at LeChase Manor, where June and her new best friend Wanda had taken materials from the neighbouring construction site and built a makeshift wooden fort for the kids to play in.

Joey adored Wanda. 'I remember her well. But if I saw her on the street, I would never recognise her. I remember the person, not the face, if that makes sense.'

The same might be said for Lee DiClemente. Joey, in those pre-1967 days, didn't know DiClemente as June's boyfriend – just somebody who was in his life and a friend of June's who visited their apartment.

Then there was Joey's road trip with his father across Midwestern states, which most likely occurred in April 1967, six or seven weeks before June's death. Holiday Inn receipts, which Joey and I unearthed in the package of Joe's materials, reveal a record of their journey from Ohio to Staunton, Virginia, and on to Williamsport, Pennsylvania, before coming back to Rochester. Joey had no idea what the trip was about, but he had one vivid memory: being alone in a motel room. The TV was on and *Batman* was playing. On the table next to the bed there was a handgun. He remembered picking up the gun and jumping off the bed, firing imaginary bullets at imaginary bad guys while Batman dished out justice on the TV.

Joey never forgot his fateful fifth birthday and his mother's immediate illness afterwards. 'I can't remember who told me she had passed away,' he said. But it was in a car. (According to Wanda Mordenga, it was his grandmother, June's mother, Marie.) 'Truthfully, I was a newly minted five-year-old, so I probably didn't have a concept of death at that time.'

When June died and social services took him, on the way to the foster family in Canandaigua their car got a flat on Route 96 and they spent the afternoon in a tyre repair centre. For Joey, who was mad about automobiles, it was a small distraction from the terrible events that befell him and his sister. When they eventually arrived at the house in Canandaigua he gripped his teddy bear tight and told his adoptive family: 'I'm not staying'. Patti-Ann was one and a half, so she didn't know any better.

'I want to go home,' Joey told them.

Those early days were difficult, but his adoptive parents were prepared and patient. They had someone return to June's apartment to retrieve Joey's bicycle and his Tonka truck. They understood they needed to give Joey space to grieve; they knew this would take time.

* * *

Joey and Patti-Ann only had a few weeks at their new home when Joe escaped from the hospital in Rochester and went on the run. To the family's horror, he was sighted in the Canandaigua area. Did Joe have a tip-off that the kids were there? Did he plan to abduct them? The family took Joey and his sister to the home of their adoptive grandparents in Rochester, and the story Joey heard from the adults was there was 'a prowler in the neighbourhood'.

Even after the search for Joe died down and he appeared to have left the state, the family remained cautious. They had a close friend who was a police officer in Canandaigua, and he kept an eye on their property and sometimes followed Joey's school bus to school. Joe Maloney was still out there somewhere, and so rules and boundaries were put in place. Joey was instructed never to get into a car with anyone, even people from his pre-1967 life. No one was to pick him up from school other than his foster parents. He later equated it to being in a self-imposed witness protection programme. He and Patti were advised not to tell their story to anybody, because Joe was still a fugitive.

In those early years of fostering, the Canandaigua family kept in contact with some people who knew June. They took Joey and Patti-Ann to visit Dale and Gladys, June's brother and sister-in-law, who had a baby, Joey's cousin Amy, born in 1969. June's father Ward occasionally travelled from Albion to visit the kids, and Joey remembered being taken to see June's friend Catherine Blair, who'd played an instrumental role in testifying about Joe's alleged declaration to kill June (and raising baby Joey while June was at nursing school). When he got older, Joey didn't remember who Blair was or how she fitted into the puzzle of his former family.

Lee DiClemente also returned to the periphery of Joey's life. Joey's foster family occasionally took the boy to Bristol Mountain ski resort, a short drive south of Rochester, where DiClemente was a competitive skier. Neither Joey nor the family knew then, but DiClemente lived in fear after the fallout from June's murder and Joe's escape. People close to him wondered why he always carried a gun and kept other firearms on his nightstand, next to his bed, and another in his car. When DiClemente went to hospital for an angioplasty, his daughter, who he never told about his relationship with June and his conflict with Joe, was surprised to find a gun hidden beneath the sheets of his hospital bed.

Joe was gone, but in his absence he weighed heavily on the minds of those left behind. In August 1972, a Monroe County social service worker placed a notice into the Rochester *Democrat & Chronicle*, alleging Joseph Scott Maloney and Patricia Ann Maloney had 'been neglected and abandoned by their father'. She summoned Joe to appear before a family court to consent to the children's adoption. The kids had been in limbo until now – fostered but not adopted due to their father's dereliction of duty. Joe, of course, didn't turn up to the hearing, and the family in Canandaigua were allowed to proceed with a full adoption.

When the papers were signed, they cut all ties with the children's pre-1967 life. Regular visits with June's side of the family and with Catherine Blair ended. The family left Canandaigua and moved south of Rochester to a small rural dairy town with a population of less than a thousand people. This clean break was perhaps best for the kids, who would no longer be overshadowed by the terrible events of the past.

'There we were able to hide,' said Joey. 'Nobody really knew what was going on; nobody knew the story. It was a totally different life growing up down there.'

Joey and his baby sister had stability. It was a family made up of seven siblings.

'I've got three brothers and three sisters, and it was just a large, fun family, and they took care of us,' said Joey. 'We stayed together. We always ate together.'

They didn't have a lot of money, but they were happy and vacationed every summer in Maine or Virginia. 'We were the kids with Kmart sneakers in school gym class – but we had sneakers. We weren't wanting for anything.'

When Joey started high school, he dropped the 'Joey' moniker and came to be known as Joe. He moved on with his post-1967 life, compartmentalising everything that came before. But he sometimes wondered what had become of Dale and Gladys's baby, cousin Amy, who he last saw in 1973, before his adoptive family cut off contact with the Fisks.

'Amy,' he said. 'She was the cousin I wish I knew more.'

* * *

June's death weighed heavily on Dale and Gladys. Their trauma was accentuated by guilt around Joe's manipulations and how in the aftermath of June's hospitalisation he'd convinced them and others that she was suicidal. The couple consequently never spoke of June. Their daughter Amy only found out what happened by accident, when she was in her early teens and found a photograph of June in her nursing uniform.

'Who's this?

'That's my sister,' her father replied.

'So where is she?'

'She passed away.'

Amy presented the photos of Joey and Patti-Ann to her dad. 'These two little red-headed kids. Who are they?'

'They're my sister's children.'

That was all Amy was able to glean at first. Her father, she said, 'was a quiet person. I can only guess how terrible it was, losing his sister. They did not openly talk about it at all. It seemed like they were really trying hard to put it behind them, if they could.'

But Amy was young and curious, and she asked questions. When she was 16 her father told her the whole story of June and Joe. She wished she knew more about her cousins, but they had been swept off into new lives, perhaps even new identities.

'All I know is they were adopted,' Amy told me and Tim Desmond from RTÉ's *Documentary on One* team when we visited her in 2023. 'I don't know who adopted them. I think my mom knew, and she tried to keep in touch with the adoptive parents, but they declined to have any further contact, which I'm assuming was for the children. Not because they didn't like my parents, but probably to separate the kids. I doubt very much I will ever find them. I don't even know their names. Those poor children. They're the real victims. Not having a mother.'

Amy never met Joe Maloney; he'd fled two years before her birth, yet his actions sabotaged her family's future as well as their past.

'He took away family members. He robbed me of that time with my aunt. He robbed me of meeting my cousins. He took three family members away from me.'

* * *

Joey and Patti-Ann were not aware of the existence of Karen Maloney when they were growing up. Karen, born in 1957 as a child of Joe Maloney's first marriage with Joan Howland, had her own unfortunate circumstances to deal with. Karen's earliest memory of Joe was when she was five years old in 1962 and Joe came to see Joan to tell her his mother Winifred had died. Karen remembered a big dog in a box, Joe's dog Barry perhaps, who jumped up on her. She remembered Joe and her mother shooing the dog away. A year or two later, Joe came to her house, where she was washing dishes. He looked through the window and said 'boo' to her and came into the house to see Joan but didn't stay long. Karen didn't know then as a little girl that Joe Maloney was her father. It was not until she was 10, by which time her family had moved to Rutland, Vermont, that she learned the truth.

Karen was staying at her aunt's house in Connecticut when she fell off her bicycle and hit a tree and had a severe concussion. Karen overheard her aunt outside the hospital room describing her as Karen Maloney, which confused her. She thought she was the daughter of William Firth, the ex-con who Joan married after fleeing Joe. Her mother travelled from Rutland to Connecticut and told Karen the story of her real identity.

'I can remember sitting at a picnic table and she tells me the story of what happened – that Joe was my father. Of course, here I was at 10 years old, just elated.'

Karen did not have a happy relationship with Firth, who beat her when she was a child for reading a book about sex education at school. 'I stayed home that whole year because he took me out of school. I didn't go to school the rest of the year.'

She changed her name from Firth to Maloney, which distanced herself from her family. Her mother told her the truth about Joe but did not tell her that Deborah was also Joe's daughter. Karen loved her sister, but in her mind they were half-siblings. 'I was treated differently,' said Karen. 'My stepfather was very cruel to me, mentally and physically.'

Joan and Firth kept Joe's alleged murder of June from the children, although this was perhaps in their best interests. 'I think that my mother and stepfather kept everything hush, hush. Not saying a word.'

With an unhappy home life, Karen idolised her absent birth father, Joe. 'I would cry at night,' she told me. 'My stepfather belittled me and sent me to bed early – like it was seven o'clock at night and my mum would come in and she knew I was crying. I would look out the window and just daydream. It was like waiting for somebody on a white horse.'

When she was 16 in 1973, Firth attacked her after accusing her of cussing at him. 'He came after me and chased me into the bathroom and my mom's screaming, "Bill don't, don't." And he tried to put my head through a bathroom wall. I ducked and the fist went through the bathroom wall.' Karen had had enough and ran away from home. She stayed out all day long and lost her shoes in a river. When it got dark she was hitchhiking on a road when a cop car pulled over and took her to the station. Her parents arrived to collect her and they were furious. Firth yelled at her, and Joan showed her the newspaper clippings about how her father Joe was indicted by a grand jury for the murder of his wife June. In an instant, Karen's fantasies about Joe coming to her rescue were shattered.

'It was like my whole life cratered. They showed me those press reports and all my dreams crumbled in a heartbeat when I realised who he was. It was horrible.'

Karen's next few years were a cornucopia of issues. She ran away from home and slept by railroad tracks and found respite from her stepfather in foster homes. At 18 she came back home and started to feel greater agency over her life. She'd heard about Joe Maloney's brother, her uncle Jim, and decided she wanted to see him. She got her hands on a Rochester phone book, found his number and took a bus from Vermont. When she stepped off the bus Jim took her in his arms and hugged her tightly.

'You look like my grandmother, Winifred,' said Jim.

Jim didn't share his brother's reckless, violent genes, or his predilection for con artistry. He maintained a steady job as a manager at Xerox's international headquarters and had a stable marriage with children. Karen stayed with him for four days. She sat on the floor at Jim's feet, listening to him speak and gazing at photographs of Joan and Joe's wedding. Jim didn't divulge whether or not Joe had contacted him while on the run, but he'd clearly been damaged by events; here was more collateral damage from Joe Maloney's behaviour.

The following year, Jim travelled to Vermont for Karen's high school graduation. For Karen, this interaction was a glimpse of a life that might have been. But it was a life that was never feasible given the chaos that surrounded Joe, the coercive way in which he approached relationships and his dereliction of duty when it came to his children. Besides, he was gone – where, nobody knew – and he had no intention to return home to face justice.

After the graduation, Jim got in his car and returned to Rochester, and Karen never saw him again.

8.

Shooting from the Hip

Michael O'Shea was still keen to get involved in Ireland's film industry, and he hounded special effects supervisor Gerry Johnston for work. Johnston told him to get lost but gave him a tip about two camera tracking vehicles that Ardmore Studios was auctioning off. Camera rigs could be mounted in any position on the vehicles, allowing film and TV productions to shoot footage alongside or in front of other cars. These were box-like vans painted light silver with a fat front grill, big tyres and large windscreens. They looked like fishing trawler wheelhouses or the Peerless armoured vehicles used by the British Army in the First World War. But they weren't built for aesthetics; they were built for function and sported six-cylinder Rolls-Royce engines.

O'Shea resold one of the vehicles and tried to keep the second at Ardmore.

'You're not leaving it here, you don't work for me. This is my premises,' Johnston snapped. Johnston never had time for

Michael O'Shea. 'He was an imposter. He used to tell me he was a colonel in the army and he was in charge of the engineers – cannons and all that – but he wasn't. He was a spoofer from day one.'

O'Shea had finally hit upon a returnable investment. He was one of the few people in Ireland who owned a tracking vehicle, and he started renting it out to commercial producers. And even though Gerry Johnston refused to entertain O'Shea, their pal the armourer Pat McMahon started sneaking him onto movie sets. The first major production that O'Shea showed up in was *Excalibur*, an epic fantasy feature about King Arthur filmed at Ardmore Studios and on location around Wicklow, Tipperary and Kerry. The director was John Boorman, known for movies like *Point Blank* and *Deliverance*, and the film featured a young cadre of cast and crew that included Liam Neeson, Gabriel Byrne, Helen Mirren, Jim Sheridan, Neil Jordan and Ciarán Hinds. This was a colossal production, and it required a huge armoury team to make and repair the armour, weapons, swords and shields.

Pat McMahon was an uncredited crew member who helped out on the project in 1980, and Michael O'Shea came with him. O'Shea's wife Sheila helped out, sourcing halberd ribbons for jousting spears. Alan Walsh, a stuntman who worked on *Excalibur*, recalled O'Shea and McMahon as a kind of double act. McMahon was respected in the industry and gave O'Shea a seal of approval.

Maurice O'Callaghan, a novelist, lawyer and businessman, moonlighted as a stunt horse rider on *Excalibur* and met O'Shea on the set. O'Callaghan and O'Shea hit it off and would meet in south Dublin, usually at lunchtime in Dalkey or Stillorgan or closer to the city centre.

'Michael was always extremely friendly,' remembered O'Callaghan. 'He was a guy who stood out because he was tall and rangy. He looked like Buffalo Bill. He had long hair and a beard. You wouldn't call him handsome, but he was very striking, and he had a fantastic presence about him. If he walked into a room, you'd wonder "Who's that guy?" He had a swagger. He had very deep, penetrating eyes, but he would always speak to you slightly sideways and stand slightly to the side of you so he would never look at you straight on. He'd look over and give you the sideways treatment. That was slightly odd. It was a mannerism.'

O'Shea was not generous with money. In fact, he was positively tight. He sometimes phoned O'Callaghan in the late morning. 'Come on, Maurice,' he'd say. 'I'll buy you lunch.' O'Callaghan assumed the owner of a stately home might take him to the posh Shelbourne Hotel on St Stephen's Green or another establishment of similar calibre.

'Instead we'd go to the local McDonald's and he'd buy me a chicken sandwich.'

These encounters were rarely frivolous. Michael O'Shea was always fishing for information or advice or opportunity. Gerry Johnston was, by the time of *Excalibur* in 1980, a renowned special effects supervisor, having worked with Stanley Kubrick on *Barry Lyndon*, John Boorman on *Zardoz* and Michael Crichton on *The Great Train Robbery*. O'Shea name-dropped their tenuous connection at every opportunity. This infuriated Johnston.

'He started telling people he was an armourer,' said the filmmaker. 'Was he a proper armourer? He wasn't. He told one of my friends he was a pilot. I mean, was he a pilot? I don't think so. O'Shea could convince people to burn down a forest just to keep the house warm.'

O'Shea kept wrangling his way onto projects that Johnston worked on. After *Excalibur* it was *The Manions of America*: the first major role for Pierce Brosnan, the actor who later became James Bond. In *The Manions of America*, Brosnan played an Irish stable boy in the 1800s who falls for the daughter of an English lord, joins an Irish militia, then absconds to the United States, where he gets swept up in the American Civil War.

Johnston had started pre-production on the TV mini-series in Ardmore Studios when a production manager approached him one day.

'There's a guy here with guns and I don't trust him,' he said.

'What's his name?' asked Johnston.

'Michael O'Shea.'

'Jesus Christ,' Johnston sighed. 'Bring him up to me.'

O'Shea gleefully approached the special effects supervisor with a proposition.

'I hear you're making a film about the American Civil War! I have a lot of guns.'

Johnston looked at him incredulously.

'I have *a lot* of guns. Meet me later in the week in Dublin.'

The special effects supervisor decided to humour O'Shea and went to meet him in the city. O'Shea parked his car in a quiet spot on the quays next to the river Liffey and opened the boot of the car to reveal four or five cases filled with handguns and machine guns and rifles, most of which were unsuitable for a drama set in the 1800s.

Johnston's first thought was, 'Where did he get these?'

His second was, 'I bet he's not licensed.'

But he decided to invite O'Shea back to the studio to test his antique muskets. The production manager raised a polystyrene sheet 20 feet away from where O'Shea stood. O'Shea raised the rifle and began firing at the sheet. As lumps of polystyrene flew around the studio, Johnston scratched his chin. This was the real deal.

* * *

O'Shea certainly talked up his celebrity connections. He lured the British actor Peter Bowles to Capard after O'Shea rented the property's antique furniture, porcelain and china to *The Irish R.M.*, a TV series that starred Bowles. Peter Collins, O'Shea's builder, recalled seeing a photograph of Sean Connery sitting in Capard's dining room. Some of O'Shea's show business stories, like a longwinded tale about how he was personally acquainted with Clint Eastwood, were fanciful. But Barry Blackmore, a film producer and director working at the top rung of the Irish film industry, certainly had time for this unusual character.

'He was outgoing, interesting, albeit a lot of his interesting stories were lies,' said Blackmore. 'My memory of him was fair to ruddy-looking. A ruddy face from being outdoors. He was exuberant. Not boisterous. If he was in your space, you'd be aware of it because he'd be part of any conversation. He would be pushing himself to the fore. He was no shrinking violet.'

A career high for O'Shea was working on *Angel*, Neil Jordan's directorial debut that told the story of a showband saxophonist, played by Stephen Rea, who witnesses the murder of his band manager in South Armagh during Northern Ireland's Troubles. The film was shot in Dublin and the countryside around Bray, a town south of Dún Laoghaire where Jordan grew up and which doubled for Northern Ireland's bandit country. O'Shea provided pistols, rifles and a submachine gun which Rea's character assembles and shoots.

'I knew this man,' said Jordan, who went on the make *Interview With a Vampire* and *Michael Collins* and won an Academy Award for *The Crying Game*. 'He supplied the weapons on *Angel*. In fact, he revealed to me that if anyone' – and by anyone, O'Shea meant the Irish Republican Army or police – 'came to seize those weapons on set he would shoot it out with them.' After the film was completed, recalled Jordan, 'for some strange reason he would offer me graphite weapons that could be carried through customs'.

Blackmore was O'Shea's conduit for *Angel* and the *Irish R.M.* But the producer had concerns about O'Shea's volatility and his eagerness to blow shit up. In one production that required an explosion, the normal recourse would have been to use the magic of special effects. Instead, O'Shea petitioned the producers to use real dynamite and blow the hell out of the set – which they of course ignored. Johnston recalled another production in which O'Shea's actions led to a crew member being injured. They were making a crime drama in Sally Gap, an east-to-west pass across the Wicklow Mountains, when Johnston heard two gunshots. 'I turned around and I saw a body crossing the road. O'Shea shot someone off the camera dolly with a blank. He had fake bullets in his guns that were made out of balsa wood, which was normal. But he was putting in double the gunpowder, which made them dangerous.'

O'Shea was promptly expelled from the production.

*   *   *

Under normal circumstances, O'Shea's behaviour on film sets would have alerted the authorities. But these were not normal circumstances. The police were watching him closely after his fingerprints had been found to match the fugitive Joe Maloney. In the absence of an extradition treaty between Ireland and the US, they didn't want to book him over a misdemeanour and risk his potential escape from the jurisdiction. Until the extradition paperwork was signed, there was not much law enforcement on either side of the Atlantic could do other than watch and wait.

In 1978, Detective Inspector John Mulderrig moved into the ranks of the Gardaí in Dún Laoghaire. Mulderrig had worked in the Irish police force since 1962, previously at stations in Donnybrook, Irishtown and Harcourt Street in Dublin's city centre. He was not in Dún Laoghaire for long before Detective Sergeant John O'Rourke and Garda Frank Mullen gave Mulderrig a potted history of their unusual local resident. Whenever Mullen passed O'Shea in the street there was a strange frisson between them. O'Shea knew the local police had his fingerprints, but if it was a concern he was not acting on it for now.

John Mulderrig was drawn into this strange unspoken pact with their suspect.

'I got to know O'Shea by sight,' Mulderrig recounted. 'I met him on many occasions. He would always salute you and give you the impression, "I know who you are". I did speak with a few people that knew him who would say, "You can't believe anything he says".'

Mulderrig described O'Shea as tall, slim-built, with reddish hair going grey.

'I only say his accent was nondescript. His parents had come, as far as I know, from either Cork or Kerry. A few people that knew him quite well would always say there was some mystery about him. He was into many different trades. He was supposed to be an expert on explosives and he was in the car business. He was farming down in Laois. From the few short conversations I had with him, he would appear to be quite intelligent.'

Mulderrig was given access to O'Shea-Maloney's files and fingerprint identification, which were locked in a filing cabinet at Dún Laoghaire's Garda station. Mulderrig's task was to keep this information safe until such time as an extradition treaty was ratified between Ireland and the US.

In Rochester, authorities were also playing the waiting game. In 1977, shortly after his promotion to the position of first assistant district attorney in Monroe County, Donald Chesworth received notification from the FBI that Joseph Maloney was still residing in Ireland under an assumed name. Every couple of years, the FBI sent Chesworth updates. Their warrant for Joe Maloney's arrest was still outstanding, they told the DA, and they were still prepared to bring him back to America. Investigators at the DA's office were able to shed more light on the origins of Michael O'Shea, the name their suspect used after changing it from Michael Grace by deed poll in 1969.

They found record of another Michael O'Shea, born in Ireland in 1892 who migrated to Rochester, New York, as an adult. This Michael O'Shea and his wife Elizabeth lived less than a mile away from the Maloney family residence. The O'Sheas attended mass with Joe's parents at the Church of the Blessed Sacrament, and Michael's funeral was held here when he died in 1963. Michael O'Shea worked as a patrolman and a security manager at Rochester State Hospital: the same institution Joe Maloney had escaped from in 1967. Michael O'Shea had been, the DA's office in Rochester discovered, the boss of Joe Maloney's father.

* * *

Eamon J. Martin, a businessman from Dublin, first encountered the second, resurrected Michael O'Shea in the late 1970s. Martin was a collector of military regalia, 'old swords and that type of thing' related to Irish history. Collectors of historical items operated in small groups in Ireland, and most of them knew each other. One day one of these collectors told Martin: 'There's this interesting guy in Glenageary. You've got to meet him.'

Martin drove to O'Shea's home in Glenageary and knocked on the door. A 'big guy with a big beard on him, dressed in denims, long hair, looked liked a hippy' ushered him inside and introduced him to his wife, Sheila. O'Shea showed Martin a container full of small weapons. Martin was surprised. Antique weapons like these were not easy to come by. Where did he get a collection like this in Ireland? O'Shea wasn't telling. Martin picked out an old duelling pistol that used a flint-striking ignition mechanism.

'I'd love to fire one of these,' said Martin.

'Would you?' replied O'Shea and went straight to his phone to make a call. 'I've got a friend here,' he barked, 'and he wants us all to meet and to do some shooting.'

O'Shea hung up and turned to Martin.

'Come on, get into your car. Follow us. We're going to the old quarry.'

O'Shea and Sheila locked up the house, jumped into their car and took off. Martin was amazed by the suddenness of all this, but he buckled up and followed. When they arrived at the quarry a number of people were already there. O'Shea pulled out an antique revolver and loaded the chamber with black powder. This mixture of potassium nitrate, charcoal and sulphur (which when ignited created the pressure to propel a projectile from the gun barrel) was not available anywhere on the market in Ireland or the United Kingdom.

O'Shea put a lead ball into the barrel and wiped Vaseline on the cylinder.

'You have to do this,' explained O'Shea. 'If you didn't you could misfire and the thing would blow up in your hand. A spark could set the whole thing off.'

O'Shea assumed a firing stance and unloaded his bullet into a pile of scrap.

Next he opened a case and pulled out an old John Rigby rifle. John Rigby was an Irish gun-making firm that produced rifles, carbines, shotguns, pistols, spring guns, muskets and blunderbusses in Dublin between 1775 and 1897. His firearms were rare beyond belief.

'I'd love to fire that,' Martin said.

O'Shea loaded it up and handed him the rifle, and Martin fired at the heap of scrap.

Eamon Martin met O'Shea a number of times after that shoot-out in the quarry and, like most people who encountered him, he questioned O'Shea's relationship with the truth. In the antiques trade, the reputation of dealers was built on their honesty. O'Shea's propensity for extraordinary storytelling, on the other hand, was off the charts. He told Martin a story about the time he was in the army on a train in North Africa. The train stopped and the men got out to take a piss in the desert. O'Shea walked over a hill, where he saw a dozen upturned rifles buried in the sand, muzzle-first, with helmets hanging from the butts.

'They were graves,' O'Shea announced dramatically.

Martin wasn't buying any of it. 'As soon as I heard that, I said to myself, "This is pure fantasy. I'm listening to a compulsive liar."'

O'Shea boasted to Martin that he was a qualified doctor who used to work at the Royal College of Surgeons in Dublin. 'At the back of the building there was a cold room which we used to preserve human bodies with formaldehyde,' he said. 'We'd hang them up on hooks like a meat locker. Then students would take them away and dissect them.'

'Jesus,' thought Martin. 'Is the guy off his head or what?'

Martin cut off communication with O'Shea after his friend John Donovan told him about an encounter he'd had with O'Shea. Donovan kept a small yacht in Clontarf Yacht Club on Dublin's north side and mentioned to O'Shea that he'd love a berth for his boat in Dún Laoghaire. 'Pick whatever one you want,' O'Shea announced. 'Seriously, pick a site. I'm a personal friend of the harbour master. Just pick it yourself.'

'When he said that,' Donovan told Martin, 'I realised he was a compulsive liar. There's a long waiting list of people to get a berth in Dún Laoghaire harbour.'

* * *

A small toilet was tucked at the base of the main staircase in Capard. One day in 1977, the estate's retainer, Eddie Kenny, approached a couple of labourers to tell them that the toilet wasn't flushing and asked if they could repair it. The workers, while trying to figure out how to get water into the toilet's cistern, noticed a small trapdoor at the top of the cubicle. They got a stepladder, looked inside, and found a pile of antique paintings that had been taken out of their frames and stashed in gauze. They unravelled one package to find an elaborate, ornate and apparently genuine Chinese mosaic. They put back the trove, closed the trapdoor and mentioned nothing of it to O'Shea. The paintings were, they assumed, stolen property.

According to people who worked at Capard in the 1970s, O'Shea led a small circle of thieves – four men, including him – who plundered the local area at night. One worker said it was a 'regular occurrence, especially in wintertime' that the clandestine party convened in Capard around seven or eight o'clock in the evening. Maggie or Eddie would have tea and food ready for them and they departed, returning at three or four in the morning with their spoils. The gang might drink whiskey for an hour or two and then disperse by daylight.

'The first thing they took out that we were aware of,' said one labourer who worked for O'Shea at Capard, 'was the bell from the old chapel in Rosenallis.'

The labourer described the theft, which was witnessed by another local, as a 'fair achievement'. O'Shea and his three colleagues climbed into the belfry and lowered the bell down with ropes, put it in the back of a jeep and hid it in a farmyard. Church gates from another local chapel went missing, and they too ended up in Capard.

Until the mid-1970s, Capard had no central heating and residents used the fireplaces to keep themselves warm. O'Shea found an old boiler he wanted to convert so he could burn timber to heat the building. A contractor from Dublin and a local worker from Rosenallis set about preparing the plumbing and removed floorboards throughout the house to fit the piping. When they took up flooring in the billiard room at the back of the building they discovered another treasure trove. Wrapped up beneath the floorboards was the processional canopy from the chapel in Rosenallis: a huge rectangular frame of rich cloth, decorated with a gold inlay, used for ceremonies of the Blessed Sacrament. The canopy was clearly worth a lot to the right buyer. The local plumber went to O'Shea to tell him about their discovery. O'Shea's response was: 'How the fuck did that get there?'

'O'Shea knew only too well,' said somebody who worked on the estate.

After keeping the stolen bell in the farmyard near Rosenallis for three or four weeks he transported it to the capital city in the back of a BMW. There he cut it up, melted it down, and used the bronze to craft Viking daggers that he flogged to antiques dealers complete with period-correct engravings under the pretence they were the real deal.

Eamon J. Martin had cut ties with O'Shea, but he kept running into his trail of con artistry. Martin purchased an ornate military powder flask in a small shop off Grafton Street in Dublin. The flask had been used to carry gunpowder and was made from a cow horn. Its engraving referenced a gun maker who had a workshop in Dublin Castle in the 1700s. Martin knew a gun from the same workshop was kept on display in the Tower of London.

'It's a magnificent weapon, extremely well made, with beautifully intricate gold on it,' said Martin. 'As soon as I saw the engraving, immediately I associated it with this maker.'

On a visit to England, Martin took the powder flask to the Tower of London. The curator there took one look at the flask and described it as a fake. Martin was not upset – the item had only cost him a few pounds – but he was curious as to the fake flask's origins. A few weeks later, Martin took an item to be engraved at a specialist shop in Dublin and he showed the proprietor his powder flask.

'We did that,' said the engraver. 'That's our work.'

Martin was taken aback. 'Are you serious?'

'Oh yes, I'd know it anywhere.'

The engraver described the man who commissioned it.

'He described Michael perfectly,' said Martin. 'Michael O'Shea faked this powder flask. Even I thought it was the real thing. He was smart enough to know about a little-known gun maker in Dublin and he'd engraved their name on it to enhance the value.'

The engraver told Martin other stories about O'Shea, like the time he came in to his workshop with an old sword. He wanted to get the name of Robert Emmet, the Irish Republican who tried to overthrow the British Crown after the 1798 Rebellion, etched onto the blade, and the engraver was happy to oblige.

'So there's a fake sword out there somewhere with the name Robert Emmet on it,' said Martin.

On another occasion, O'Shea came bounding up the stairs and into the workshop. 'I need help,' announced O'Shea. 'Could you come and help me?'

The engraver's assistant followed him downstairs, where O'Shea showed him a wrought-iron cannon – a genuine historic cannon – laid across the backseat of his car.

'Do you want it?'

The son looked at the cannon and then at O'Shea. 'Er . . . No.'

Michael O'Shea got back in the car, slammed his door and drove away.

Gerry Johnston, the movie special effects supervisor, heard about how O'Shea happened to come into possession of the cannon: he allegedly stole it from Powerscourt, a country estate in County Wicklow that was decimated by fire in 1974. When he couldn't sell it, said Johnston, 'he melted it down'. O'Shea melted down a lot of items and flooded the antiques market with forgeries.

'In his mind,' recounted Johnston, 'that was the normal thing to do.'

* * *

Michael O'Shea's trade in illicit military paraphernalia went hand in hand with his bogus tales of wartime adventure. He saved his darkest stories for Lawrence Power, the agricultural consultant hired to survey Capard. During his visits to Power's house, O'Shea bragged about his spectacular means of interrogating people during his service in the British Special Forces – he took them up in airplanes and told them to start talking or he'd throw them out the door.

'There are guys who will tell you things 15,000 feet up in the air that they won't tell you on the ground,' O'Shea said with a grin.

That's a pretty dark story, thought Power.

O'Shea also gave Larry a tip about murder, should the necessity arise. 'Get sand, put it in a pair of tights, roll it up tight into a ball, and use it as a cosh. Beat them to death. Then afterwards undo the tights, empty out the sand and the murder weapon is gone.'

Jesus, thought Power. Why would he tell me something like that?

O'Shea's prized possession was a Royal Engineer's uniform, the same get-up he wore at his Christmas military dinner at Capard. Sheila, his wife, must have been dubious about his stories, because an uncle of hers had been in the Marines and told her the regalia on O'Shea's jacket was thrift store claptrap. But she played along and happily ironed it for him.

O'Shea even turned up at the door of an exasperated Gerry Johnston in Ardmore Studios in the uniform. Johnston told him to piss off.

Once a year, O'Shea pranced off in his uniform to London, where he attended a Royal Engineer's reunion. This wasn't the only time he left Ireland. O'Shea tended to purchase his antique firearms from auctions in England, travelling to and fro on the ferry from Dún Laoghaire, and he roped hapless locals into assisting him on these missions. On one trip home, he was on the ferry with a retired man who'd come over with him (and has preferred to remain anonymous in the telling of this story). As the boat was approaching Dún Laoghaire, O'Shea announced he had something to do.

'Here are the car keys,' O'Shea said. 'You take the car. I'll meet you in Dublin.'

O'Shea walked off, leaving his friend holding the keys. The man was baffled and then broke out in a cold sweat when he realised O'Shea had left him with a car full of weapons and ammunition. Northern Ireland was imploding with violence and mayhem. He had no paperwork. If customs stopped him and inspected the car would they really believe this weaponry was intended for movie props? The man made it off the boat and to shore. He wasn't questioned or apprehended, but he swore never to fraternise with O'Shea again. He also concluded that O'Shea must have had some kind of handshake deal with the IRA in order to bring arms, even antique ones, into the country en masse.

*   *   *

O'Shea's travels were not limited to weekend jaunts across the Irish Sea. In 1976, he flew to Canada to visit his doctor friend Brian Hanlon in Wingham, Ontario. (One of Sheila's sisters had also relocated to Canada, although Sheila did not accompany her husband on his trip.) O'Shea and a business partner bunked up in Hanlon's house and spent a few days indulging themselves in the basement, where Hanlon rigged up beer kegs and a makeshift pub. Hanlon's neighbour, a huge fellow called Roger Kaye who owned two nursing homes, was present at these impromptu sessions, and he and O'Shea arm-wrestled for everyone's entertainment. After a week of partying, O'Shea announced he wanted to see Canada.

'I had a Corvette, an American sports car, and I loaned him that,' said Hanlon. O'Shea and his business partner took off east towards Ottawa and Montreal. O'Shea had barely left Wingham when police pulled him over for doing 100 miles an hour on Highway 7. The speed limit was practically half that. O'Shea sweet-talked the officer.

'I'm sorry. I thought the speed limit was in miles and not kilometres. I'm so sorry.'

The officer bought his spiel and let him go. When they arrived in Ottawa they discovered there were no hotel rooms available because a function was on, and so they slept in the car.

In the middle of the night three policemen banged on the window and asked what they were doing. O'Shea explained they'd looked for a hotel but couldn't find one. Once again he used his charm and within minutes the police were gone. Following his road trip, O'Shea returned to Wingham and stayed with Hanlon a couple more days before flying home.

Rochester was just on the other side of the Canadian border. Both the UK and Canada had extradition treaties with the United States during the 1970s. If O'Shea had been identified and apprehended travelling to these jurisdictions, he could have been extradited. FBI officials, following O'Shea's fingerprint identification in 1973, routinely checked in on his movements through the Gardaí in Ireland and their legal attaché in London. Tom Bush, a former officer for the FBI's fugitive unit, said Interpol likely issued a red notice international arrest warrant at border control posts next to the names Joseph Maloney and Michael O'Shea. Yet neither name was flagged during his trip to Canada. This could have been due to systemic failures in a pre-digital era: a time of primitive manual checks and analogue data collection.

I was able to ascertain that Michael O'Shea had a passport in his own name – he showed it to the special effects supervisor Gerry Johnston. But was this his only passport?

FBI agent Bush believed he must have used another identity. 'I'd have to assume his visa applications or his travel documents were falsified and he had somehow obtained a passport,' said Bush. 'I don't know to what level of sophistication it was, but it was probably in a different name.'

Gene Harding, another FBI agent who worked the Joseph Maloney case out of the Rochester office, reached the same conclusions. 'His travels outside Ireland would tell me he had an alias other than Michael O'Shea that was unknown to any authority, law enforcement authority. That could be the only way he was getting through customs.'

The Gardaí concluded that Joe Maloney obtained his identity in Ireland by taking the birth certificate of an illegitimate child who was born in 1941 and used that to create a new identity.

Is it feasible he could repeat that process multiple times with multiple names?

Harding didn't hesitate: 'Absolutely.'

9.

Forgive Us Our Debts

Over her five years riding horses at Capard between 1978 and 1983 as part of Erika Lotze's pony trekking centre, Fiona James, daughter of the car dealer from Mountmellick, witnessed the devolution of O'Shea's grand rural project. Sure, he renovated and painted the estate, but most of his ambitions, like his idea to build a bridge over the pond and lake in the garden, never went beyond concept stage.

'He never did any of the stuff that he said he was going to do,' she said.

A report in a local newspaper from 1980 described O'Shea's venture into potato farming as being 'peculiarly ill-timed', although 'his timber raids into the fine oak forests [of Capard]' can't have left him 'completely without cash'. With little knowledge of farming or the practicalities of managing a country house, he amassed considerable debt. In 1981, Allied Irish Bank, who provided O'Shea with the initial loan to purchase the estate, won a judgement against him and his business partners, declaring he owed the bank £514,418.27: a staggering amount for an estate valued in 1981 at £170,000. But if Michael O'Shea was bothered by half a million pounds of debt, he wasn't showing it.

'Michael would never recognise a deadline that was over there when his life was right here,' said the builder Peter Collins. 'Debts? That's only a number in the bank. It was the bank manager's problem, not his.'

As much as O'Shea could ignore the barrage of bills and debt collection letters, there was no doubt about it. Capard was a ball and chain. It just wasn't fun anymore. So he began visiting his estate more infrequently and spent his weekends in Dublin, where he socialised with people like Desmond Fenning, the man who owned the record store in Dún Laoghaire close to O'Shea's former garage. Desmond's three daughters, Pamela, Vanessa and Olga, remember Michael as being friendly and willing to drop everything to come to their dad's rescue whenever he had car trouble.

'I'll be there. I'll come and get you. No problem,' O'Shea would bark down the phone.

On one occasion, Desmond received a worrying letter from the tax man. 'You leave it with me. I'll sort him out,' announced O'Shea.

'He was always on your side,' explained Vanessa.

O'Shea also became close to Desmond's son Roderic. Born in 1953, Rod was much younger than the tall, bearded redhead who by the early 1980s was balding and going grey. Rod's tenure as an aircraft mechanic on HMS *Ark Royal*, a Royal Naval aircraft carrier, appealed to O'Shea's military fetishes. Rod was cut from a similar cloth. He was mysterious and prone to stretching the truth – 'a bit of a Walter Mitty', according to someone close to him.

'My brother was the most secretive person you'd ever meet in your life,' said Patrick, Rod's brother. 'My brother was a bit weird. I got on well with him but I wouldn't have hung around with him either.' Rod started spending time with O'Shea when he got out of the Navy. He was unemployed but had odd jobs and fancied himself as a salesman. Sheila kept to herself and had few friends, but she trusted Rod. She could see how much he admired – worshipped even – her husband. He hung onto Michael's every word and was the couple's staunchest ally.

O'Shea cultivated another unusual friend in the early 1980s. Michael Cox was a freelance priest living in Monkstown, Dublin, who visited people's houses to administer on-demand baptisms and confirmations. He drove around in a 27-foot-long Ford A series Luton body van acquired from Swastika Laundry (the unfortunately named Irish linen service), which he used to redistribute household items to the poor and needy. Chris Wren, a mutual friend from Northern Ireland, introduced Cox to O'Shea.

'From the moment I met Michael, he recognised my clergyman status and we became friendly. His wife as well,' said Cox. 'I used to go to his house and visit him. I was that way with a lot of people.'

Cox was an unconventional priest – notorious, some might argue. He was born in Mitchelstown, County Cork in 1945 and educated by the Christian Brothers in Birr, County Offaly. In 1961, aged 16, he joined the Irish Army and remained there until he was discharged for medical reasons, a wound in his stomach, at the age of 28. After working a few years as a harbour policeman in Dún Laoghaire, Cox pledged to fight for the Lord. He travelled to El Palmar de Troya in Spain, where a splinter Roman Catholic sect called the Palmarian Catholic Church had built a lavish basilica to house their breakaway pope.

In 1978 Cox was ordained a priest at Bourg-Saint-Pierre in Switzerland. He was unorthodox, a maverick, and one of the few Catholic priests in Ireland to have been married before donning clerical garb. He was wedded to Bridie Hansbury in 1971. Divorce was illegal in Ireland at the time, but the couple had an annulment five years later, declaring their nuptials invalid 'and according to the Roman Catholic Church, once a marriage is annulled, it never existed,' Cox declared.

As a Tridentine priest, Cox did not accept Rome's regulations as gospel. The Tridentine sect decreed the Second Vatican Council, a newly reformed version of the Church known as Vatican II, to be unlawful. The Tridentines' conflict with Vatican II included criticism of the Church for neglecting its duties around exorcism, and Cox considered himself an exorcist whose powers were granted as part of his Holy Orders.

'I am experienced enough to exorcise people or places or things of a satanic nature,' he said. He preferred exorcising places. 'I generally don't like exorcising and would [exorcise a person] only if medical experts were present.'

Around the time when he met O'Shea, Cox conducted a live-on-air exorcism on a pirate radio station because of its 'blasphemic' music. He recalled: 'I was mocked and jeered and I got up off my knees and I held up the crucifix and I pointed at the turntable and said, "If you don't stop blaspheming Almighty God and the Blessed Virgin, this evil place will burst into flames and burn to the ground".' The radio station subsequently burned down 'and no one could determine how that happened'. At least, this is how he recounted the story.

When Cox wasn't exorcising radio stations or dishing out divine healings, charity and advice, he enjoyed having cups and tea and chats with Michael and Sheila O'Shea. The couple introduced him to Erika Lotze, whom he got along well with.

Cox had spent two years in Germany and had a good grasp of the German language. He used to visit Lotze at the estate, where they would chat in her native language. Cox found O'Shea a 'highly intelligent individual. He was friendly and helpful and co-operative. He was a friend.'

Cox was five feet in height, and O'Shea, at six feet two inches, towered above him. 'I nearly got a crick in the neck looking up at him,' the priest said. 'I wouldn't say he was religious, but he took to this little character here and he recognised my clergyman status. And, you know, I helped him out along the way as well.'

* * *

When O'Shea returned on rare occasion to debt-addled Capard in the early 1980s, he would often find an unusual number of off-duty policemen loitering around the estate. Garda from the local towns of Mountmellick and Clonaslee would visit to play cards and drink poitín with O'Shea in the evenings. He enjoyed the company of cops (and had done so since the parties at his apartment in Dún Laoghaire in the late 1960s), but local builder Peter Collins wondered if something else was going on here. Was O'Shea cultivating friends within law enforcement to get a helping hand should he fall foul of the law? Or was it the police who were cultivating O'Shea?

'The police watched him assiduously, and they did that by befriending him,' explained Collins. 'They were keeping a very close eye on him.' If O'Shea suspected they were watching him, he didn't make a fuss about it. Instead, he accepted their friendship.

'He slipped into this parallel universe that he created for himself,' explained Collins. 'Nothing could go wrong as long as it didn't go wrong.'

But in the background, the events set in motion in 1973 when O'Shea's fingerprints were identified as belonging to Joe Maloney were catching up with him. On 14 July 1983, an article appeared in the *Irish Press* newspaper with the headline 'Ireland and US Sign Extradition Treaty'. The article detailed how, the day beforehand, the Irish attorney general and his US counterpart formally signed a treaty in Washington to permit law enforcement in either country to arrest and extradite fugitives. The treaty was primarily intended to stop the exodus of IRA volunteers who sought safe harbour in the US, but it would also apply to other crimes, ranging from fraud to murder. 'It covers offences committed before as well as after the treaty comes into force,' the article outlined, although arrests would not be imminent, because 'yesterday's signing is subject to ratification'.

News must have reached police in Mountmellick, because the local sergeant took Neville James into the barracks one evening and showed him a file that declared Michael O'Shea and Joseph Maloney, an alleged wife-murderer from upstate New York, to be one and the same. James gazed with horror at Joe's mug shot, photographed in the aftermath of June's death in 1967. The sergeant and James were lifelong friends, and when Fiona James was a child she played in the barracks with the sergeant's children. There was a mutual trust between James and the sergeant, and although the latter may have been breaking regulations, he told James all this for the safety of he and his family. He was concerned the car salesman was getting too involved with Michael and Sheila O'Shea.

Before James left the barracks, the sergeant gave him a final piece of advice: 'Keep quiet about this. Don't tell anyone. We don't want to spook O'Shea before we have a chance to arrest him.'

Fiona James turned 17 in 1983. She obtained her driver's licence, ditched her bicycle and took the family car from

Mountmellick to Capard for her weekly riding excursions. One of her last encounters with O'Shea was a lunch with her family in the estate on a warm summer's day, followed by a walk around the grounds. A few days later, everything changed. Neville James ordered Fiona and her sisters not to visit Capard again. He didn't explain his reasons and asked them not to ask any questions.

'We were told we were not going up there again,' said Fiona. 'And that was it.'

* * *

Did O'Shea that know Ireland and the US had signed up to a new treaty? Was he aware that authorities suspected he was Joseph Maloney? Was he planning an exit strategy? Investigating this story, I was unable to find out. But we do know that O'Shea engaged in a flurry of investments around this time, apparently designed to turn a quick buck.

Peter Collins received a call from O'Shea asking if he and his brother-in-law Frans Jansen could renovate a house that O'Shea said he'd bought in Castletown, a village 13 miles south of Capard. This was an elegant, traditionally designed home, described by realtors as a 'gentleman's residence', next to a church in the heart of the village. The building included a dining room, a sitting room and three bedrooms, and it was in dire need of renovation, according to Collins. A lot of work needed done, and the builders began reviving the interior and exterior and constructed an extension at the back of the house.

William Telford and his brother ran a builder's providers and hardware business in Mountrath, a 10-minute drive from Castletown. One day O'Shea arrived explaining he was renovating a house and wanted to open an account to purchase building materials.

'At that time, it was bad economically and we were very glad of extra business,' remembered Telford.

O'Shea told him he owned Capard House in Rosenallis and Telford asked to see the estate. 'He showed me around like he was lord of the manor. I got the impression he reckoned we should feel privileged to be doing business with him rather than him doing business with us.' Early on in their business relationship, O'Shea's monthly account was overdue. Telford phoned him at his landline in Capard.

Tony Gilfoyle answered the phone and handed it to O'Shea.

'What the fuck does he want?' muttered O'Shea.

'Mr O'Shea, could you call in and see me at your convenience?'

'Yeah, I'll be there in 20 minutes,' replied O'Shea. He hung up and turned to Tony. 'Do you want to go for a spin?'

'No, sir, I don't,' said Tony, anticipating violence.

Sure enough, O'Shea threw a handgun into the glove compartment of his Cavalier and took off down the lane at a hundred miles an hour.

O'Shea arrived at Telford's office in Mountrath. 'What's this about?'

Telford explained his account was overdue.

'Oh. I thought it was something serious.'

O'Shea produced a vertical wallet which he opened up like an accordion, revealing what appeared to be ten different credit cards. People rarely paid bills with credit cards at the time – it was either cash or check – but O'Shea picked out one of the cards and apologised.

'This is no problem whatsoever,' O'Shea said. 'I overlooked the matter.'

Although that payment went through (and although Telford unknowingly avoided the contents of O'Shea's glove compartment), payments over subsequent months bounced. O'Shea ordered a sophisticated solid-fuel cooker that Telford imported from Switzerland. 'I remember our people had a very tough job getting it into the house. It would be quite expensive even in today's terms.'

Telford was starting to wonder about this man's relationship with the truth. O'Shea told the shopkeeper and his staff that he had a herd of pedigree cattle on the farm at Capard. A Telford's employee who was a part-time farmer and interested in cattle and farming matters drove up to Capard one Sunday to inspect this prized livestock. On Monday morning, he arrived back at the shop looking nonplussed. There had been no herd of pedigree cattle, he reported back, just a single poor cow sheltering under a tree.

'So this again raised suspicions,' said Telford.

By the time O'Shea was finished with the property in Castletown, he was in major debt to the builder's providers (on top of the hundreds of thousands he owed to the bank for Capard House loans). Exactly how much, Telford wouldn't divulge to me.

In 1983, Castletown House was sold to a restaurant owner from neighbouring Portlaoise town called Annette Sullivan. Sullivan's husband had just died and she purchased the property for 'between £50,000 and £60,000'. The auctioneer told Sullivan that Michael O'Shea of Capard House was the owner. However, as soon as the deal was closed and she got possession of the deeds she called her solicitor. O'Shea's name was not on the deeds.

'The name here is Isabel Grimson,' she told her solicitor.

Grimson was Sheila's unmarried aunt on her mother's side – the same aunt who visited the Chandler household in Glenageary on Sundays when Sheila was growing up. Grimson had built up a nest egg of property through a lucrative sideline working for the Irish Sweepstakes, an Irish lottery launched in 1930 and authorised by the Irish government as the Irish Free State Hospitals' Sweepstake. The Sweep, as it was commonly known, allowed ticket purchasers to gamble on the outcome of horse races in Ireland and the United Kingdom. It played a major role in Irish people's lives. Children were given shares as a gift for Christmas and on birthdays, and adults daydreamed about how their lives would transform if they bought a winning ticket.

The Sweepstakes, which at its height employed 4,000 people in Ireland including Grimson, derived the bulk of its business in the United States, where the lottery was known as the Irish Sweepstakes and prizes could amount to $500,000 if you bought a ticket that matched the winner of a big horse race like the Irish Derby.

The Irish Sweepstakes became engrained in American popular culture and was referenced in TV shows like *Boardwalk Empire* and *Breaking Bad*, and novels like Stephen King's *The Stand*. They were illegal in the US due to a ban on lottery gambling, but that did not stop millions of tickets being sold there every year. Some Sweepstakes employees had a sideline selling tickets to Americans, and Isabel Grimson was one such go-between. During the day, like other single or widowed women at the time, Grimson worked at the Irish Sweepstakes office in Ballsbridge, Dublin, close to her home on Pembroke Road. Outside work hours she topped up her salary by posting tickets to Americans, who reciprocated with cash and checks in the mail.

The details of Michael and Sheila's financial arrangement with Grimson over the renovation and sale of her house in Castletown are murky, but O'Shea was able to skim money from the property in other ways. After Annette Sullivan's purchase of the property she met a local historian, who pointed out a hole in the wall at the back. The hole, he told her, once housed a sheela na gig: an ancient pagan Irish carving that depicted a crudely fashioned naked female figure displaying intimate body parts. These sculptures dated as far back as the 12th century and could be found on castles and churches; the particular one in Castletown was likely here due to the house's vicinity to the church, or whatever religious structure preceded it.

'I wrote about your sheela na gig for the local papers,' said the historian. 'In fact, I took a photograph of it. Where's it gone?'

'I have no idea,' she said.

It wasn't until 10 years later that she found out what became of this near-priceless antique, which was protected in Ireland as part of the country's national heritage. Sullivan was at a party in Portlaoise, where she encountered a local tradesman.

'Are you local?' he asked.

'Yes, I live in Castletown.'

'Oh, I know Castletown. I worked there for a fellow called O'Shea and there was a sheela na gig in the shed.'

'I heard about that,' said Sullivan. 'We found a hole in the wall where it was taken.'

The tradesman nodded. 'I climbed up and dug it out. O'Shea and myself, we wrapped it up in newspaper, put it under the seat of the car, drove to England and sold it.'

* * *

After offloading Castletown House in 1983, O'Shea turned his attention to another property. Dalkey was a leafy suburban enclave in south county Dublin next to the coast (which in later years counted Bono and the Edge from U2, Enya, and film director Neil Jordan among its neighbouring residents). Wealthy settlers were drawn here by the affordable house prices and idyllic location next to the sea, overlooking Dalkey Island and on the boundary of Dalkey Hill. Nowadays Dalkey is a prime location – one of the most affluent areas in Ireland – but in the early 1980s villagers kept the place to themselves and the only interlopers were the scouts and scuba divers who arrived to explore the watery environs come summertime.

O'Shea's car repair business was located around the corner from Bullock Harbour, a small fishing port where local fishermen sold fresh catch on the quay and a ferry took visitors to the island. O'Shea had sold off his garage by 1983, but he remained part of the local community, and he purchased a three-storey house on Kent Terrace, a picturesque street of four identical Tudor-style houses designed and built by the architect William Edward Porter and his son in 1836. The Porters hailed from Kent, hence the name of the terrace, and they displayed their architectural prowess across the three-storey gable-fronted houses, each decorated with cast-iron railings and granite steps leading to Gothic entrance doors.

Sheila's aunt was again the instigator behind O'Shea's involvement at Kent Terrace. Isabel Grimson owned the third house in the row, perhaps purchased from her earnings from the Irish Sweepstakes. According to the property deeds, Grimson sold the home to Sheila Mary Chandler, O'Shea's wife, on 4 November 1983, for £15,000. It was a bargain. Further south, in County Wicklow, much smaller bungalows were on sale for £30,000. O'Shea moved out of his rented abode next to the Chandler family home on Arkendale Road in Glenageary and into 3 Kent Terrace, and he set about renovating the property with help from local labourers. Employment was scarce during the mid-1980s – a generation was migrating en masse to the United States – and so the decorators and builders appreciated the work.

O'Shea's red hair had by now gone grey, and he wore a long beard, prompting the workers to nickname him Santa Claus. Mick O'Shea was 'easy-going and the money was good,' according to one worker. 'A character who wasn't aloof with the guys.

He felt like he was one of them.' O'Shea allowed the builders to drink beer and smoke marijuana on site.

Brian Porter, great-great-great-grandson of Kent Terrace's original architect, heard all the stories: 'He was great to work for because everyone was allowed to be themselves as opposed to being under some strict regime.'

There was a lane at the back of Kent Terrace where O'Shea wanted to store his camera tracking vehicle. One of his first tasks was to knock down a decorative arch over the lane and rebuild it to make it wider. He also built a workshop at the back of the house. Tony O'Toole, a local welder, helped renovate railings and gates at the property and was impressed with the workshop. 'Mick was going to show me how to do some casting in that workshop but he never got around to it,' recalled O'Toole. 'He was a fairly average-looking chap, but he had this heavy, heavy beard on him. He was well hidden by it, you know.'

O'Shea didn't just integrate with the locals; he socialised with influential local figures like Jim Delaney, a local entrepreneur and owner of the grand Dalkey Island Hotel who counted members of the rock band U2 among his friends. Delaney was known locally as the King of Dalkey. Such was O'Shea's expanding spread of influence in the area that some locals referred to him as 'the next King of Dalkey', according to Power.

O'Shea boasted that the Irish sculptor Eddie Delaney, whose work includes a statue of Wolfe Tone and a famine memorial that stands today at the northeastern corner of St Stephen's Green in Dublin, was amongst his friends. Barry Blackmore, the filmmaker who worked with O'Shea on *Excalibur* and *Angel*, visited O'Shea and his wife for dinner at Kent Terrace, and O'Shea presented him with a supposed Delaney wooden carving. Blackmore appreciated the gesture but wasn't blind to O'Shea's ambitions. 'Because I was a film producer, it would have been in his interests to cultivate me as a person. I could give him work.'

Despite his sociability, O'Shea was showing signs of a deepening paranoia. The doctor Brian Hanlon, on a rare return to Ireland from Canada, visited O'Shea and his wife at Kent Terrace. It was daytime and the curtains were drawn. Hanlon rang the doorbell but there was no answer. He started to walk back to the car when the door opened. It was Sheila.

'Brian. You can come in,' she said.

Hanlon went inside and found the couple sitting in darkness. He could just about make out their silhouettes and no more.

'He wouldn't trust anybody,' Hanlon believed. 'But he did trust me, because I had no axe to grind.'

Matt Dunne was the foreman at Capard House. On one of O'Shea's infrequent visits to his mansion in 1984, Dunne had a measure of his capacity for wrath. O'Shea had been drinking whiskey for hours. They were in the library and O'Shea was ranting about people who were out to get him.

O'Shea pulled out a pistol and shouted: 'If anyone crosses me!' And he fired three shots into a bookcase in the corner.

Dunne was terrified, but that seemed to be the end of the matter.

O'Shea's spiralling paranoia was accompanied by a mad scramble for money by any means necessary. Yet all along he was oblivious to a fortune beneath his feet. When O'Shea purchased Capard House from Robert Noonan in 1975, the sibling retainers Eddie and Maggie Kenny lived in two large rooms at the front of the house. Eventually, the servants' quarters were restored and they prepared to move into smaller rooms at the back of the property. O'Shea asked three local workmen to help Eddie move his belongings, but when they arrived there wasn't much to do. Eddie and Maggie had spent the night beforehand moving their own possessions, and now Eddie was out taking the estate's sheepdog for a walk. While the workmen were loitering in Eddie's bedroom waiting for his return, they noticed a trapdoor in the floor. They looked inside and their eyes widened.

'Oh God, Eddie had a serious amount of money,' one worker alleged. There were thousands upon thousands of Irish pounds in cash hidden under the floorboards.

The worker considered with horror how differently events might have played out.

'If O'Shea had known what Eddie had in his room, then Eddie wouldn't have lived.'

10

Meet Me on Killiney Heath

BY 1984, MAURICE O'CALLAGHAN WAS MAKING A NAME FOR HIMSELF. The part-time actor who met Michael O'Shea as a stunt horse rider on *Excalibur* had set up a law practice. He had a barrister and a secretary on his books and took on a client a month, which gave him time to explore artistic endeavours on the side. O'Callaghan wrote a screenplay for a story set during the War of Independence and got some funding from the Irish Film Board to make a short pilot for the proposed full-length feature. At the time he was sharing an apartment with Barry Blackmore, *Excalibur*'s producer. Blackmore knew O'Shea had amassed a large gun collection and suggested O'Callaghan ask him to help out. As soon as Michael O'Shea heard the pitch for the pilot, *Soldiers of Destiny*, he wanted to be involved and invited O'Callaghan and Alan Walsh, the film's stunt co-ordinator, to his house in Dalkey to check out his munitions.

When they got to Kent Terrace, O'Shea threw bags on the floor and said, 'Take a look'. They opened the bags to find Colt 45s, Lugers and Webleys. O'Callaghan was particularly interested in O'Shea's old Lee-Enfield rifles, which suited the story's time period. Walsh picked through the piles of ammunition, assuming they were blanks.

'Where did you get these?' O'Callaghan asked.

'England. Arms dealers. I paid for them. I've got the licenses, the certificates, if you want to see them?'

O'Callaghan didn't bother looking at the paperwork. The 1920s-era guns were in pristine condition. 'Jesus, these are all working,' exclaimed O'Callaghan.

O'Shea grinned. 'My estate in Laois is available if you want to shoot down there?'

While O'Shea was talking, Walsh looked at the fireplace and saw what appeared to be a human skull on the mantelpiece. O'Shea also showed him a hole he'd dug under the stairs that led to the back garden. A handmade escape tunnel? That's strange, thought the stuntman.

Weeks later, Maurice O'Callaghan and 20 cast and crew – including soundmen, technicians, actors and actresses – assembled at Capard House for a shoot that lasted four days. Among them was Seamus Deasy, a cameraman who later worked on *Vikings* and *Reign of Fire*, and the actors Peter Gowen (whose later work included the Neil Jordan movies *Ondine* and *Breakfast on Pluto*) and Nigel Mercier.

'Maurice had pulled out all the stops with all the equipment, the gear, the crew and everything,' recounted Mercier. 'It was a very professional setup.'

The director was taken aback by the beauty of the surroundings and set about filming scenes inside Capard and its surrounding gardens, stables and farmland. A collection of locals hung around the set each day. O'Callaghan assumed they were O'Shea's friends until he asked, 'Who are those people?'

'Garda Special Branch,' replied O'Shea.

O'Callaghan nodded. He understood. It was the height of the Troubles in Northern Ireland. People were being murdered on a weekly basis, and the Irish police were wary of anything involving guns. They obviously wanted to make sure everything was above board while remaining incognito. Portlaoise Prison, Ireland's high-security penitentiary that housed IRA prisoners, was close to Capard and Garda in this region were particularly jumpy.

O'Shea gave the filmmakers the use of his entire house, including the bedrooms for their stay. 'I can't remember now what he charged us, but it was very little,' said O'Callaghan. 'I paid him for his services, for his armoury business, and we bought our own food.'

On the first night one of the actors had a problem with his bedroom. He wrapped a sheet around himself and went door to door trying to find a spare bed. Nigel Mercier laughed at the memory. 'All the actors and crew could talk about at breakfast the next morning was, "This house is fucking haunted. I saw it." They thought it was a ghost and I'm nearly sure it was Peter Gowen wandering around in his sheets.'

In the evenings, Maggie, Eddie and Erika Lotze cooked and served dinner to the filmmakers. Officers from the Garda Special Branch were present too, and everyone ate around the huge table in Capard's dining room. They ran out of wine and O'Shea disappeared and came back with three bottles under each arm, which he raided from Capard's antique stock.

'It was the best wine I ever tasted,' said Mercier. 'We guzzled it down like cider.'

O'Shea had given O'Callaghan the use of six Lee-Enfield .303 rifles, which he nicknamed 'smellys' (referring to the

Short Magazine Lee-Enfield, or SMLE). The guns had been decommissioned, the firing pins removed, but they fired blanks. Stuntman Alan Walsh was 'worried because O'Shea was giving us bags of ammo for the Enfields and telling us to shoot away at each other'. There were period-specific pistols on set too.

At the end of the four days of filming, O'Callaghan was preparing a scene in which a man runs across a bog brandishing a pitchfork to save a girl being assaulted by Black and Tans (British soldiers brought in to quell the rebellion during the Irish War of Independence). In the script, a soldier unholsters a pistol and shoots the man dead. Before they filmed the scene, an actor playing a Black and Tan looked into the barrel of his revolver and announced, 'There's live ammunition in this!'

O'Shea snatched it off him. 'Jesus, give me that. Who did that?'

Over the months to come, O'Callaghan changed his assessment about the presence of the Special Branch at his film shoot. It wasn't for reasons of health and safety but because they were probably aware of the pending extradition treaty between Ireland and the US and wanted to monitor their suspect.

'For sure,' said O'Callaghan. 'They were keeping an eye on Mick O'Shea.'

*   *   *

On 18 April 1984, while O'Shea was deep into his renovations at Kent Terrace in Dalkey, the President of the United States signed off on a letter to Congress.

To the Senate of the United States:

With a view to receiving the advice and consent of the Senate to ratification, I transmit herewith the Treaty on

Extradition between the United States of America and Ireland, signed at Washington on July 13, 1983.

I transmit also, for the information of the Senate, the Report of the Department of State with respect to the Treaty.

The Treaty is the first law enforcement treaty directly negotiated between the United States and Ireland. It fills a gap resulting from a 1965 change in Irish law which precludes the implementation of any applicable extradition agreements between the United States and Great Britain. The Treaty follows generally the form and content of extradition treaties recently concluded by this Government.

This Treaty will make a significant contribution to international cooperation in law enforcement. I recommend that the Senate give early and favorable consideration to the Treaty and give its advice and consent to ratification.

Ronald Reagan
The White House,
April 18, 1984

Within days Thomas Snow, a trial lawyer in the Office of International Affairs at the Justice Department of Washington, contacted the Monroe County District Attorney's office. Seventeen years had passed since Joe absconded in 1967. Three DAs had filled the role since John Little's retirement in 1969. In 1984 the man in charge was Howard Relin, an upbeat, loquacious lawyer described by his friends as gregarious, honest and friendly. He had no Irish ancestry, but he visited Ireland often on vacation with his wife Betsy. Relin had been briefed about the Maloney case upon taking office and was all ears when Snow called.

'The president has passed the treaty with Ireland,' explained Snow. 'Do you still want to extradite Joe Maloney?'

'Let me get back to you,' said Relin.

Relin and his first assistant, Charles Siragusa, went to their storage room and took out the cardboard boxes containing Joe's case files, evidence, photographs, witness statements and testimonies. Relin was struck by the brutality of the killing. Methyl alcohol, the agent used in June's death, oxidises into formaldehyde, the main agent in embalming fluid. First it caused June to become violently ill, then it flung her into a coma, causing blindness and shutting down her internal organs, sending her body into paralysis and constricting her airwaves. This was a long, drawn-out, brutal death over 10 days, which Joe Maloney observed at close quarters while describing it as 'suicide'.

The district attorneys methodically went through each box, contacting witnesses who took part in the police investigation and indictment hearing of 1967. There was no statute of limitation on a murder case, but so much time had passed since the alleged crime that Relin wondered if they had sufficient evidence to prosecute and to convince a judge in Ireland to send their suspect back to the US to face justice.

As they progressed through the boxes, Relin and Siragusa became confident. Some witnesses had passed away over the previous 17 years, including two key police investigators, William Mahoney and Anthony Fantigrossi. But Gail Mann (who allegedly gave Joe a bottle of poison) and Cathy Blair (June's friend and babysitter who Joe allegedly told of his plans to kill June), Lee DiClemente (June's partner) and attendees at the birthday party where Joe fixed June the cocktail, including June's brother, were all alive, as were cops within the Rochester Police Department who investigated June's homicide. Relin and Siragusa counted over a dozen key witnesses, and they started to formulate a case.

Joe Maloney, 1936

Joe Maloney, age 20, August 1956

Joe Maloney with his first wife Joan Howland, Nov 15 1954

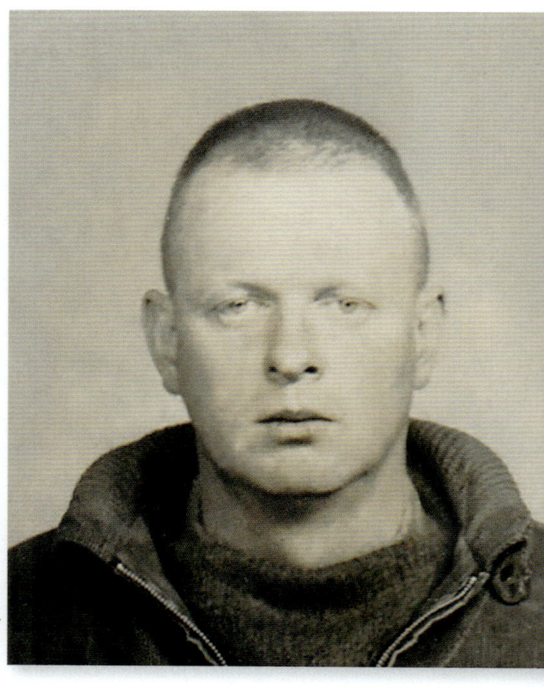

Joe Maloney, age 30, December 1965

June in nursing uniform

June and Joe's children
Joey and Patti-Ann
with their dog Barry,
Christmas 1966

Wendy and Gary Lehmann

Gene Harding, special agent in the FBI, Rochester division, who handled the Joe Maloney case in the 1980s and early 1990s

No. 1	Date of Marriage 2	Name and Surname 3	Date of Birth 4	Marital Condition 5	Occupation (in full detail) 6	Normal Residence before Marriage 7	Father's Name and Surname and Mother's Name and Maiden Surname 8	Intended Future Permanent Residence 9
268	29th June 1974	Michael O'Shea	3Rd Dec 1941	Bachelor	motor Engineer	Marylands Arkendale Road Glenageary	Terence O'Shea Winifred Southgate	Marylands Arkendale Rd Glenageary
		Sheila Mary Chandler	20th Jan. 1945	Spinster	assistant Manager Salon	Glenmorris Arkendale Road Glenageary	Vincent Chandler Catherine Grimson	

Marriage solemnized at the Catholic Church of Dalkey in the Registrar's District of Killiney in the Superintendent Registrar's District of Rathdown in the County of Dublin, Ireland

Married in Catholic Church of Dalkey according to the Rites and Ceremonies of the Catholic Church by me Michael Geaney C.C.

This Marriage was solemnized between us: Michael O'Shea, Sheila M. Chandler — in the Presence of us: Cameron Chandler, Kathy O'Boyle

Sheila Chandler and Michael O'Shea's marriage certificate, 1974. O'Shea's mother's name is listed as Winifred, the name of Joe Maloney's mother

Sheila Chandler. Early 1960s

Capard House

Michael O'Shea 1980's
AI photofit

Michael O'Shea dressed in military gear

Horse-riding at Capard House with Eddie Kenny, Capard's retainer, 1970s

Sean Wisely with a picture of a vintage car given to him by Michael O'Shea

© Pavel Barter

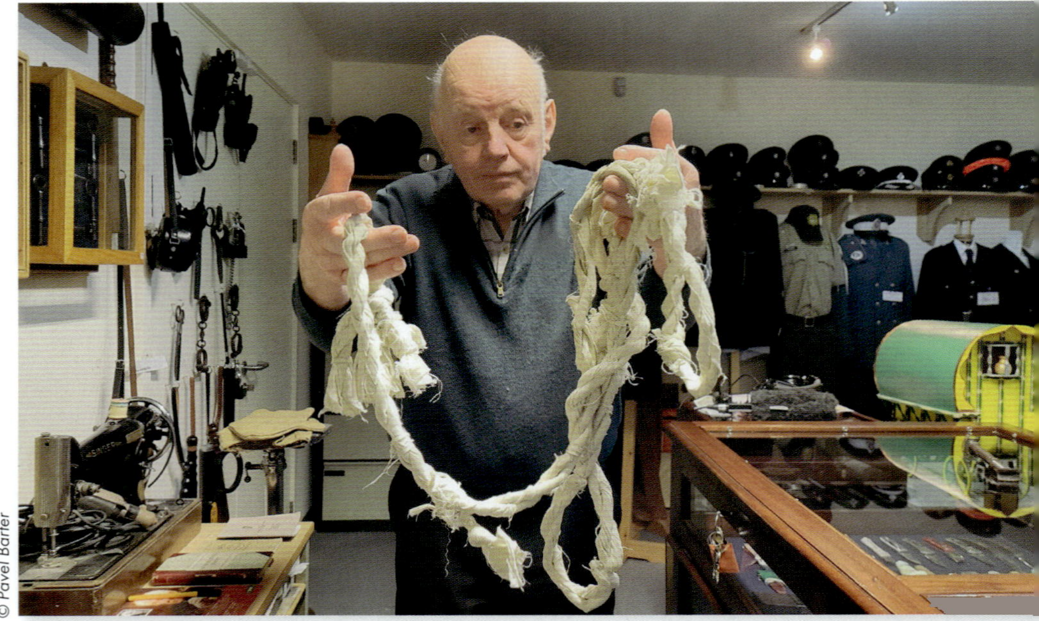

Seán Reynolds, Curator of Mountjoy Prison Museum, with a rope made from bedsheets which Michael O'Shea used in his 1986 escape attempt

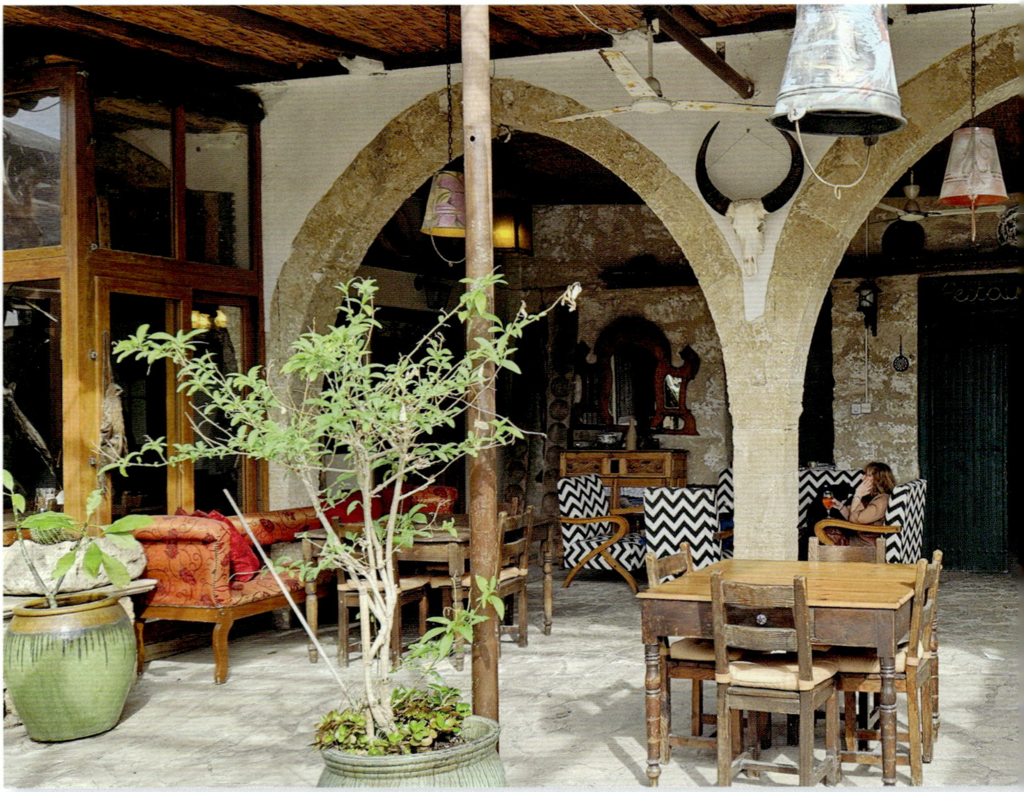

© Pavel Barter

The Old Grapevine restaurant in Girne, North Cyprus, which Joe and Sheila (under the guise of Mick O'Shea and Maria) frequented in the 1990s

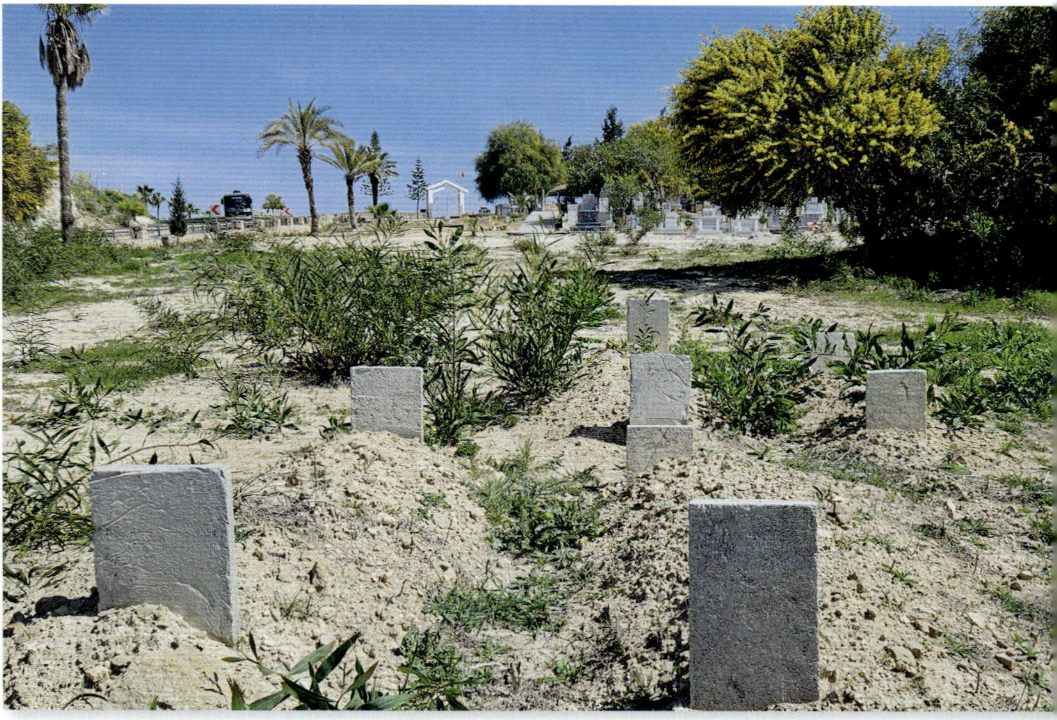

© Pavel Barter

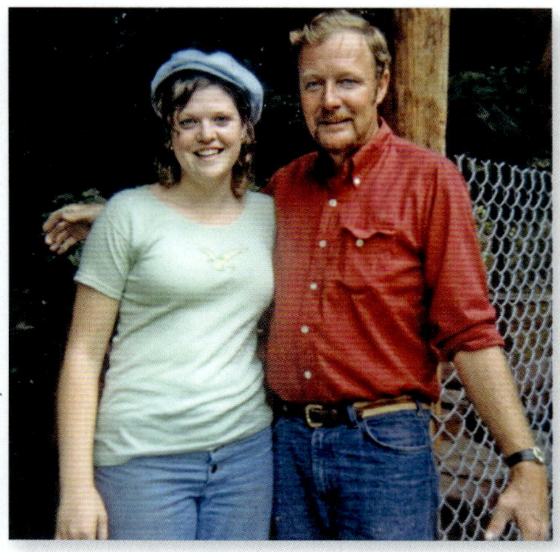

Unmarked graves in Dipkarpaz, North Cyprus

© Karen Maloney

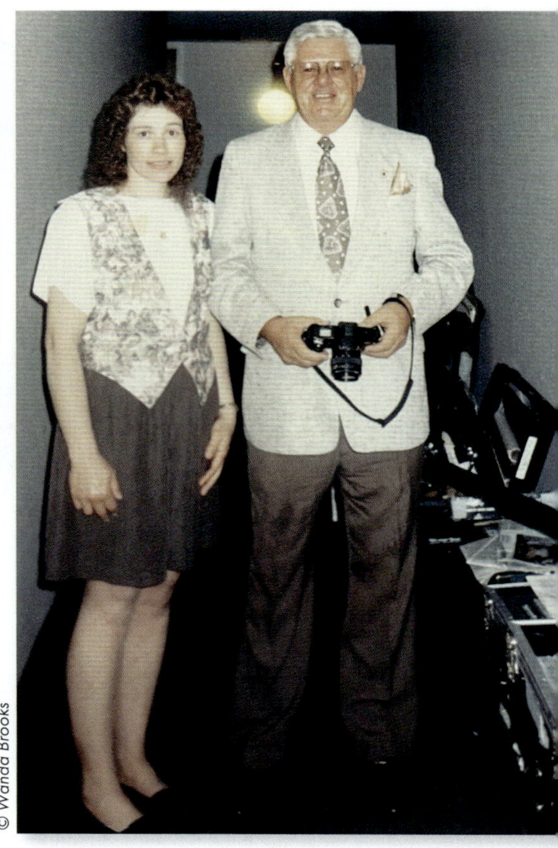

Above: Karen Maloney, Joe's daughter, and James Maloney, Joe's brother. 1975

Right: Wanda, June Maloney's friend, and George Reiss, the retired police detective who identified Michael O'Shea as Joe Maloney in Dublin's High Court. 1991, Boston, on the set of *Unsolved Mysteries*

© Wanda Brooks

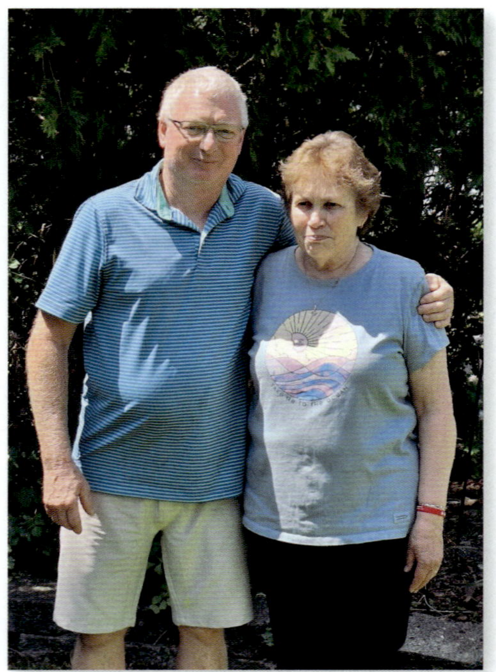

© Joey Scott

Joey and Wanda

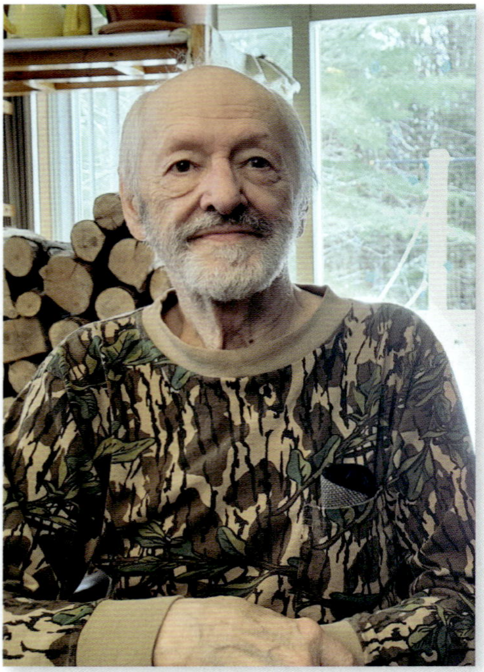

© Pavel Barter

Neal Dunkleberg

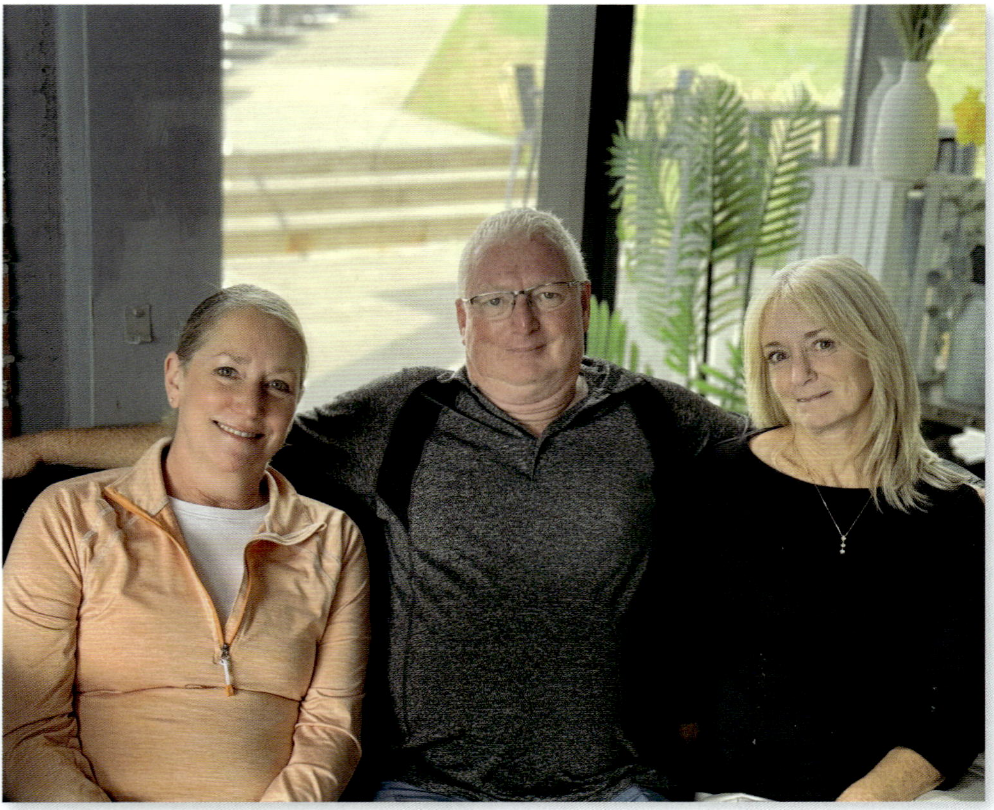

© Joey Scott

Amy (June's niece), Joey and Patti-Ann (June's children), 2025

'There is no statute of limitations on murder,' Relin said. 'The community expects that a murder case like this will be prosecuted fully. It's our responsibility. It's a tough process to pick up a case that's 17 years old and then review it to present for trial. Witnesses are scattered from Alaska to North Carolina.'

But Relin was convinced that his case was strong, and he jotted down four crucial points of testimony:

- That Maloney threatened his wife in the months before the party.
- Asking Neal Dunkleberg about killing an animal without a trace. Told wood alcohol would work, returning to borrow the wood alcohol from Neal's sister.
- Acting as bartender at Joey's fifth birthday party. June Maloney returning home, falling sick and telling Lee DiClemente she suspected Joe had poisoned her.
- Wood alcohol found in June's system and ascertained as the cause of her death.

Relin knew the prosecution would cost thousands of dollars. 'But the nature of the case, the nature of the charges and the fact he's escaped for 17 years . . . warrants the maximum effort on our part.' He contacted local FBI to make sure they were on board. The Bureau confirmed their unlawful flight to avoid prosecution warrant for Joe's arrest was still active. Special Agent Gene Harding, in charge of the case in Rochester, 'felt pretty secure in the fact that Maloney was still in Ireland' and was eager to proceed.

Relin phoned Tom Snow in Washington: 'Let's do it.'

O'Shea had one more adventure in filmmaking before the house of cards collapsed. In mid-1984 he worked with Pierce Brosnan for a second time on two episodes of the TV series *Remington Steele*, which were shot partly in Ireland and partly on the Mediterranean island of Malta. O'Shea again slipped under the radar of authorities when he drove his camera tracking vehicle from Ireland in the company of his confidante, Rod Fenning. Travelling the road south of Dublin to Rosslare in Wexford, the departure point for the ferry to Europe, the vehicle broke down. They fixed it up and took the ferry across the Bay of Biscay to France, then drove to the tip of Italy, where they took another ship to Malta. Gerry Johnston was working as special effects supervisor on the same production and was flabbergasted when O'Shea showed up on set. The so-called armourer was uninvited, he said.

After filming wrapped, O'Shea was done with his unreliable tracking vehicle. Unwilling to have it break down again on the long return trip to Ireland, he abandoned it in Malta and made his own way home. Returning to Ireland while a US extradition treaty was in the works was a critical error of judgement.

In Rochester, Assistant DA Wendy Lehmann hurriedly put together the paperwork for Joe Maloney's return to the US. Lehmann worked for Monroe County since 1981 as assistant head of the Appeals Bureau, the office that handled extraditions. She'd handled extraditions across state lines and several out of the country, including Canada and the Caribbean. Armed with the required documentation, she flew to Washington, where she handed Joe Maloney's dossier to Thomas Snow at the Office of International Affairs in the Justice Department; Snow in turn gave it to George Shultz, Ronald Reagan's secretary of state, for a final sign-off. At the beginning of November 1984, officials from the US Justice Department flew into in Dublin with the names and addresses of the alleged fugitives they wished to extradite.

The first extradition treaty between the US and Ireland went into effect on 15 December 1984. The following day, the police pounced on three suspects: Norman Douglas MacCaud, wanted for a mafia-style assassination in Buffalo, and Charles Joseph Walsh and James Hildage Gilliland, who were wanted for alleged white-collar crimes.

Michael O'Shea, however, was not arrested.

Howard Relin, the Monroe County DA, attributed this misstep to 'manpower shortages' and 'delays in the international channels'. Whatever the reason, he feared it could torpedo the case and send Joe Maloney back into hiding. After the treaty was announced on 15 December, and following the arrest of the three Americans the following week, there was a deluge of press coverage. Surely O'Shea knew he was next to be targeted?

'I'm surprised,' said Relin, 'he didn't move right out of the country.'

O'Shea instead continued life as usual. Maybe he had suspicions and they were allayed when the other men were arrested and he wasn't. But something was bugging him: the fingerprints that the Garda in Dún Laoghaire took from him after the incident in 1973. Those fingerprints were still out there somewhere. A few days after the new US-Ireland extradition treaty was announced, Frank Mullen, one of the investigating officers into the 1973 incident, was in Dún Laoghaire Garda Station making preparations for Michael O'Shea's arrest. Copies of O'Shea's fingerprints and Interpol's validation of their match for the prints of fugitive Joseph Maloney were locked in a filing cabinet at the station. Mullen harboured those fingerprints for over a decade, and he'd been anticipating this moment for a long time. Then the phone in the station rang. To Mullen's surprise, it was O'Shea.

'Can I help you?'

'You might remember me,' said O'Shea. 'We met in the past. I wanted to tell you about something very secretive that's going on at the moment.'

O'Shea described a drug deal that was about to go down. He'd been asked to take part in the deal but didn't want anything to do with it. He wanted to stay on the right side of the law and wanted Mullen to bust the criminal with his help.

'Go to Killiney Heath,' he told the cop. 'That's where the deal is going to happen.'

Killiney Heath was a coastal promontory a few miles south of Dalkey. The heath was on the boundaries of a relatively urban area, and in the 1980s it was wild and underdeveloped. O'Shea reaffirmed he wanted Mullen to meet him there to arrest the drug dealer as part of a sting operation.

Mullen's bullshit detector was tingling. This sounded too weird.

O'Shea continued: 'You need to come on your own, because if there are any other guards there, it'll frighten off the guy. It has to be just you.'

Mullen thought, this is completely suspicious. There's no way this is true. It sounds totally bizarre and it's clearly aligned with the fact that the law has just changed. O'Shea knows that I know, and he's going to do me harm.

Mullen told O'Shea none of this, of course. He just said, 'I'll meet you there.'

O'Shea gave him a time, in the evening after nightfall, at a location in a remote part of Killiney Heath. They ended the call.

Mullen arranged for two of his colleagues in the police force go to the arranged meeting point in advance and secretly stake out the place. When he arrived, O'Shea was looking shifty and uncomfortable. Mullen told him two officers were watching them to ensure their security when the drug deal went down, and this made O'Shea even more uncomfortable. The alleged drug dealer never showed up; O'Shea made excuses and left.

Afterwards Mullen and two officers searched the area. They discovered what Mullen described as a 'shallow grave' in the undergrowth and next to this apparently manmade hole was a gun and a sum of money. Mullen later told people he believed O'Shea was going to try to bribe him – perhaps to coerce him to destroy the fingerprints in his possession. Failing that, they feared he planned to shoot the policeman and put him in that shallow grave.

* * *

On Monday, 7 January 1985, Detective Inspector John Mulderrig finally got the news he and his fellow officers in Dún Laoghaire Garda Station had been waiting 12 years to hear. The request came through from Garda headquarters, who in turn had received a warrant from US officials to arrest Michael O'Shea. Mulderrig had rehearsed this moment in his head. He'd already made enquiries about the time of day his suspect was due to return to his house. O'Shea was out preparing for a film shoot and came back to his home on Kent Terrace every day around lunchtime, Mulderrig was told.

The officer sat in his car and waited, watching people coming and going on the street.

'It was a very upmarket place to live in,' recalled Mulderrig in the podcast *Runaway Joe*. 'There were all fine houses there. I wouldn't have known many of the people living in them. It was a quiet area – never any trouble or anything like that in it. A well-to-do and affluent area.'

Eventually O'Shea showed up with his wife Sheila.

Mulderrig stepped out of his vehicle. 'What's your name?' he ordered.

'Michael O'Shea.'

'Your real name.'

'Michael O'Shea.'

'I believe that it's not,' Mulderrig continued. 'I'm satisfied your true identity is Joseph Maloney. I'm arresting you, Mr Maloney, on a provisional warrant following a request from the Embassy of the United States of America.'

O'Shea calmly replied, 'You have the wrong man.'

Mulderrig ignored him. 'I'm taking you to Dún Laoghaire Garda Station, and you'll be appearing in the District Court in the afternoon.'

'What's the charge?'

'Killing your wife.'

Sheila observed all this and said nothing. If she had an emotional response to the accusation, she kept it well hidden. O'Shea gave Sheila the keys of the house and Mulderrig put handcuffs on O'Shea and sat him in the back of his squad car.

'I'm an Irish citizen,' said O'Shea from the back seat. He was composed and confident. 'I've been here so many years. I wouldn't have stayed in one area so long if I was running from someone.'

Mulderrig ignored his protests and drove the two miles along the coast from Dalkey to Dún Laoghaire. O'Shea gave up and looked out the window at the roads he knew well, the tributaries of Irish society he'd risen through – landmarks of his ascent from poverty and anonymity to status and recognition.

Michael O'Shea was returning to Dún Laoghaire, where life began for him in Ireland 17 years ago, where he worked on trawlers and lived in a back garden and ran a car repair business. The seaside town that offered him a fresh start in 1968 was now the crucible that would hold him to account for the sins of a past life. It was to be the site of his final reckoning.

11.

A Question of Identity

MAURICE O'CALLAGHAN LOOKED AT THE MAN HE HAD KNOWN
FOR THE PAST FOUR YEARS. O'Shea was calm and inscrutable,
like he always was. Not panicked in any way.

'What do you think of this?' said O'Shea. 'Complete nonsense.'

They were in a room at Dún Laoghaire Garda Station surrounded
by police officers. Following O'Shea's arrest, he had been allowed
to make one phone call, and he'd called O'Callaghan, the lawyer
and filmmaker who shot his pilot short film *Soldiers of Destiny* the
previous year at Capard House.

'Can I meet you?' O'Shea said. 'It's nothing to do with the film
business. It's a legal matter.'

'Sure,' O'Callaghan had said. 'Where are you?'

When O'Callaghan arrived at the police station O'Shea handed
him the charge sheet, which laid out the alleged crime of murdering
his wife June Fisk with a poisoned cocktail. The charges said he
was an American, Joseph Maloney, and living in Ireland under

173

a fake identity. O'Callaghan looked at the document again. This couldn't be right. It was such an outlandish charge, such a far-fetched idea. Then he remembered the strange business with the officers from the Garda Special Branch at Capard. Standing in the presence of O'Shea and a phalanx of law enforcement officers, a flurry of thoughts raced through his mind. O'Shea always had a fantastic ability to deflect conversation or not show any emotion or uncertainty. Could this be true?

O'Shea told him he needed representation. He knew O'Callaghan specialised in property and movie-related legal matters rather than criminal law, and so he said to him: 'I need you to find me a lawyer to get me out of this problem I'm in.'

O'Callaghan recommended a number of criminal defence barristers, and he left O'Shea to find someone to represent him at his hearing at the District Court in Dún Laoghaire.

* * *

Prior to O'Shea's arrest, Detective Inspector John Mulderrig visited the courthouse to inform the local judge about the unusual case about to come before her. He had some experience with extradition cases, albeit extraditions to the UK rather than the US. Judge Gillian Hussey was in the early stages of her career on the bench. She had started eight months beforehand, April 1984, in the socially deprived jurisdiction of Bridewell in Dublin's inner city before migrating to well-to-do Dún Laoghaire.

'Look,' Mulderrig told her, 'there's a prisoner coming before you in court this afternoon in relation to a provisional extradition warrant from the United States.' The cop wanted to forewarn Hussey, 'because there would be certain documents she would need at hand to make the order'. Hussey recalled of their meeting: 'John explained very briefly about this man who was alleged to have murdered his first wife in Rochester, New York, and then escaped custody from a hospital. I, in my innocence, didn't know anything about extradition. Clueless.'

Dún Laoghaire District Court was a small suburban courtroom that, in 1985, was attached to the Garda station. This courtroom showed its age. There was dignity in its design, but it was decrepit in function. A handful of electric heaters were scattered around the room – essential on a frosty January day like this but hardly enough to stave off the cold. On the afternoon of 9 January 1985, a few hours after his arrest in Dalkey, Michael O'Shea was brought before a special sitting of this court with his chosen barrister, Paul Walsh. Sheila rallied a few supporters to attend at the last minute. When Judge Gillian Hussey took her seat at the front of the room she recalled Garda Mulderrig's words to her that morning: 'The court will be full of people that you wouldn't expect to see.' He was correct, she thought. These were regular middle-class locals – not the type she'd seen before in a criminal courtroom.

Michael O'Shea sat in a space reserved for the accused. 'He was well enough away from me, but he wasn't a man you would feel you'd have to be well enough away from,' said Hussey, who in her previous year as a judge dealt with violent offenders and gangland kingpins. 'There were other lesser criminals that you'd have been terrified to be beside.' If it was suitable to infer a person's character by the company they keep, she thought, then O'Shea was a pillar of society.

The charges were read. Joseph Maloney was accused of the murder of his estranged wife June by poisoning her in 1967. He had been committed to Rochester State Hospital, New York, for psychiatric examination to determine if he was mentally fit to stand trial. On 25 September 1967, he escaped from the hospital.

Detective Inspector John Mulderrig provided the court with the details: 'The Garda at Dún Laoghaire became aware of Maloney's presence in the area in 1969. He was known as Michael O'Shea. In 1973 an incident at the home of [one of his associates in the motor business] gave the Garda an opportunity to fingerprint Joseph Maloney and as a result of this his true identity was established.' Mulderrig presented the court with a copy of the report detailing this incident, written by Detective Sergeant John O'Rourke in 1973. The fingerprints taken from Michael O'Shea were a match for the fugitive Joseph Maloney, Mulderrig explained.

'It would appear that Joseph Maloney used the name Michael Grace on his arrival in Ireland. In October 1969, he changed his name by deed poll to O'Shea.' Mulderrig presented the court with a copy of deed poll enrolment No. 3763, 2 October 1969. 'Michael O'Shea is a fiction,' Mulderrig told the judge. He explained how, when he arrested O'Shea, the suspect had protested: 'This is ridiculous. I am not Maloney.'

O'Shea, in his defence, listed his address not as Kent Terrace, the house Sheila had purchased from her aunt, but as Arkendale Road, the rented premises in Glenageary next to Sheila's family home. When the question of identity arose, his barrister told the court they had the wrong man. Michael O'Shea had lived in Ireland for 20 years and publication of his name would harm his business interests. Mulderrig countered by saying the Gardaí were in a position to definitively prove this man's true identity. In his arrest report, he included a copy of O'Shea's 1974 marriage certificate to Sheila Chandler.

'The parents of O'Shea as shown in my report are fictitious,' Mulderrig announced.

The judge's hammer hit the gavel. She remanded O'Shea in custody and ordered him to be taken to Mountjoy Prison in Dublin. Proceedings had concluded.

* * *

News of O'Shea's arrest reached Irish media the following day: 'Man Held on US Warrant', read a headline in the *Irish Independent*; 'Extradition Case Man Remanded', announced the *Irish Press*. Inhabitants of Kent Terrace in Dalkey opened their curtains to find reporters and news crews hovering outside O'Shea and Sheila's house.

The Fenning family was watching TV when they found out. 'The news came on and it said that Michael O'Shea had been arrested for murder,' said Pamela Fenning. 'We were blown away. Of course we couldn't believe it.'

Desmond Fenning, owner of the Dún Laoghaire music store, went straight to the Garda station with his son Rod to offer bail. He was listed on a bail affidavit alongside Sheila and her father, Vincent Chandler, which barrister Paul Walsh presented to Judge Gillian Hussey at a second hearing at Dún Laoghaire District Court later in the week. The District Court did not have jurisdiction to grant bail, Hussey told him. At the same hearing, Ireland's state prosecutor, Barry Donoghue, applied for a further remand in custody until the full extradition documents arrived from the US.

'O'Shea has not been charged with any indictable offence in Ireland and should be released,' protested O'Shea's barrister.

Hussey contested that the state's argument was valid and further remanded O'Shea in custody. Walsh vowed to appeal to the High Court for bail as his client was marched back to Mountjoy Prison.

In Rochester, news broke that Joseph Maloney, now 49 years old, had finally been apprehended. Howard Relin, the Monroe County DA, told local newspaper *Democrat & Chronicle* that he'd asked Irish authorities to hold their suspect without bail pending an extradition hearing. 'We need documentation and proof to satisfy an Irish court that this man is Joseph Michael Maloney and that he committed the crime of which he's accused,' he said.

Relin was confident of a conviction. The DA's office had kept Dale Fisk, June's brother, and his wife Gladys abreast of the situation since O'Shea's arrest. If Maloney was to be convicted of the murder in Monroe County, he could face a minimum penalty of 15 years to life and a maximum of 25 to life. The DA recommended the maximum sentence. 'I thought once he left Rochester, they'd never get him. It's good that they did,' Dale told local media. He confessed he was no longer in communication with June and Joe's children, Joey and Patti-Ann. 'Their adoptive family didn't want the tragedy to follow them through life. We've lost touch with them . . . It's probably just as well.'

* * *

Laura Meade was the epitome of a dogged reporter. When the Maloney story resurfaced in 1985, the 24-year-old had worked a couple of years for the *Democrat & Chronicle*, where she covered the police beat in Rochester. She was young but determined and unafraid to knock on every door required to get whatever story she covered. Her editors were impressed with her ability to get people to open up. Meade strove to humanise victims and give faces to individuals whose lives were tragically changed by events, and she brought empathy to the darkest stories.

The *Democrat & Chronicle* was part of the Gannett Company, a newspaper group that incorporated national publications like *USA Today*. Newspaper sales in the mid-1980s, before the Internet or social media, were robust and the *Democrat & Chronicle* had a large readership in Rochester, one of the largest cities in upstate New York.

The newspaper covered the entire region from the shores of Lake Ontario to Buffalo. News agencies in America were willing to spend money covering big stories of interest. But while Rochester was a big city, it was no Boston, New York or Chicago, and the paper rarely sent its reporters to other countries for scoops. Meade had crossed state lines on occasion but had never left the country, and she was surprised when her editor told her he wanted to fly her to Ireland to find out more about the man alleged to be Joseph Maloney.

'For them to make that investment tells you this was a very significant story in our area,' explained Meade. 'It had a lot of interest. They knew that if they sent me, I would probably get the story better than other people could.'

Meade landed in Dublin Airport a few days after O'Shea's arrest. She wanted to start her investigation with an official source and her first stop was Dún Laoghaire Garda Station to meet Detective Inspector John Mulderrig, whom she'd contacted before leaving Rochester. Meade was dealing with a government and a police force she knew nothing about. She had no idea how helpful the local authorities would be. Mulderrig, however, was accommodating. He impressed on her the degree to which O'Shea courted police in the local area during his time on the loose.

'He went out of his way to befriend them,' she said. 'It was almost like, "I'm going to be your buddy. You don't have a clue who you're with right now." It was cat and mouse for him. It gave him a sense of power to have a relationship with a cop, despite or maybe because of his background. It piqued my curiosity that he would go down this path and flirt with the other side. Of course, this didn't help him in the end.'

The policeman told her how, following the confrontation between O'Shea and two of his associates in 1973, O'Shea 'didn't even think twice' when officers asked if they could take his fingerprints. 'He just said blithely, "Go ahead",' said Meade.

'It never dawned on him that his own fingerprints would be checked and could be matched. That was his fatal mistake. He wasn't as smart as he thinks he is. The fact he was just so willing to give this information up proved to be his own undoing.'

O'Shea's attorney refused to grant Meade an interview with his client, and O'Shea was not accessible before or after the hearings in Dún Laoghaire – he came and went from court with a jacket over his head to prevent photographers from capturing his image. Realising she wasn't going to be able to speak to the suspect, the Rochester reporter instead scoured for information about him in Irish library newspaper archives and knocked on doors, following tips given to her by John Mulderrig and other sources.

'I compiled every address I could find for him and took out a map and tried to figure out where to go. I went to locations where he worked, where he lived, where he hung out, where people who knew him might be. I knocked on doors and got people to talk.'

Meade charted Michael O'Shea's chronological history in Ireland and began by visiting the fishing port at Dún Laoghaire harbour, where he had worked in the late 1960s. Before moving to Rochester she had worked for a newspaper in a fishing community in Gloucester, Massachusetts, and she was familiar with wharfs and dealing with fishermen. Walking through Coal Harbour, she struck up a conversation with a man, Brian Crummey, who was painting the hull of a boat in dry dock. Crummey remembered O'Shea working on the trawler *Provider* in the 1960s.

She travelled to Arkendale Road, home of the Chandler family and, with notebook and *Democrat and Chronicle* ID in hand, knocked on every door on the street. Most residents slammed their doors in her face. There was no answer when she knocked on the door of the Chandler household, but Meade got someone on the phone who was close to the family. Sheila, they told her, would grant an interview if she was paid $10,000 'to defray her husband's legal expenses'. At the time it was common for newspapers in the British Isles to pay for interviews, but this practice was not considered ethical in the US, and Meade turned down the offer.

She was relentless in her pursuit of the story: 'One of the things that I discovered as a reporter is there's always people who will talk.'

* * *

Meade wanted to see Capard House for herself. She rented a car and drove the 75 miles from Dublin to Rosenallis in Laois. 'I hadn't been to Ireland before, and this was an adventure on many levels,' she said. Part of the adventure was remembering to drive on the left side of the road: 'I almost got killed a couple of times!'

Erika Lotze welcomed Meade into the mansion. It appeared to be in a state of limbo. O'Shea and his associates were already under threat of bankruptcy due to their half a million Irish punt debt to Irish banks, and with O'Shea now in prison, vultures were circling. The German caretaker made Meade a cup of tea and described her emotions when she heard news of O'Shea's arrest on the radio: 'It's a terrible shock. I just wish it wasn't him. But you never really know today. Some people just disappoint you.'

Lotze told Meade that O'Shea had been trying to sell the property for the previous three years because it was losing money. He was a 'very nice man. He has always been good to me. I'm very, very sorry, you know. I'm really deeply hurting because I really can't believe it but this must be serious. They wouldn't arrest him without proof.'

As her investigation continued, Meade was surprised by the degree to which Michael O'Shea had infiltrated Irish society: from working as a fisherman to running a garage, filmmaking and selling props to movie productions and owning properties. 'It was incongruous to me that he was able to fit in at that level,' she said. Most people who knew him found the allegations impossible to believe. To them he was Michael O'Shea, a 43-year-old born in 1941 in County Kerry. There was no way he could be a 49-year-old fugitive American (despite the documental evidence and the fact that he looked a lot older than 43).

'Almost all of his relationships were absolutely confident that he was not Joseph Michael Maloney,' Meade said. 'He was Michael O'Shea. They talked about how smart he was, how personable he was, how he fit into every situation and how there was no possible way he was an American. He had them 100 per cent convinced. It speaks to who this person was: a true chameleon who could fit in all of these different places, all these complex relationships, and pull the wool over everybody's eyes.'

Sheila Chandler's family were among those who refused to accept the allegations. Rod Fenning, O'Shea's staunchest ally besides Sheila, was enraged by what he considered to be the victimisation of his friend. Rod, said his brother Patrick, 'was hugely supportive of Michael and had no feeling he would have killed anybody'. Rod's sister Vanessa felt much the same. 'Everybody we knew who met Michael said no way he could have killed his wife that way. He might have picked up a hammer and banged her on the head with it in a temper, but he would never have planned the poisoning that took place.'

Meade got the sense that Michael O'Shea had become so integrated into people's lives and the lives of their families over decades that to accept him as a fabrication would unravel their own experiences and identities. If O'Shea never existed, then what was real?

'I definitely got the sense that these people didn't want to believe he was capable of that,' said Meade. 'They really didn't want to believe it of him because they didn't want to believe they had been duped.'

But some people who knew him began to wonder. Pamela Fenning, one of Rod's sisters, had a close friend who was an Irish solicitor and was unsurprised by the arrest. 'Oh, Michael tried to kill my brother,' the solicitor announced to Pamela.

Apparently the brother had had a dispute with O'Shea and O'Shea had tried to run him over with a car, narrowly missing and avoiding killing him. When Desmond Fenning heard this story he said, 'Well, actually, yes. I can see Michael doing that all right, because he has a really bad temper. But he wouldn't have the maliciousness and the forethought and the conspiratorial thinking to commit murder.' Pamela, like the others, could not believe the allegations. 'Never for a minute did we think that he could have done it . . . although that might make us very gullible.'

One person in no doubt about O'Shea's guilt was Gerry Johnston, the special effects supervisor who in 1985 was on a hot streak in film after making *Educating Rita* with Michael Caine and *Lamb* with Liam Neeson. He already knew what he believed to be the truth about O'Shea from Pat McMahon, O'Shea's fellow movie armourer and confidante.

'Pat told me that O'Shea told him his real name: Maloney. It slipped out in the pub.'

Johnston said he presented this information to O'Shea, alongside the story Pat McMahon had told him about how he'd stowed away on a boat out of New York in 1968, and O'Shea confessed. 'He told me his wife in America died,' said Johnston.

'She died in a coma and she committed suicide. He told me that. I didn't believe him.'

Meade continued down the rabbit hole of O'Shea's enigmatic life over her two weeks in Ireland, and she became fascinated with the suspect. She saw parallels between what was happening in 1985 and what had occurred in 1967, when June fell into a coma and Joseph Maloney convinced hospital staff and friends of his innocence.

'That horrific crime in 1967,' said Meade. 'It took a while for the police to nail it down, because it was a slow death of poisoning. June did not die straight away and it took a while for them to figure it out. In researching that back story, I recognised the same disbelief among his neighbours and family members in Ireland as there was disbelief in Rochester following his arrest. His relationships in Ireland mirrored those relationships in Rochester.'

The *Democrat & Chronicle* ran Meade's report on its front page, featuring a sketch of Maloney's mugshot with two parallel stories: one about Joseph Maloney and the other about Michael O'Shea, illustrating his alleged split personality and the legal question around O'Shea's true identity.

After speaking to O'Shea's staunchest allies, did Meade wonder if Irish police had arrested an innocent man? 'Absolutely not. I am very fact-based, and the evidence was irrefutable. There is no way Joseph Michael Maloney's fingerprints landed in the home of Michael O'Shea's associate unless they were O'Shea's. The coincidence is too much of a stretch. I had no doubts.'

* * *

As the hearings at Dún Laoghaire District Court progressed, Judge Gillian Hussey wondered how O'Shea's wife was navigating the disturbing revelation about the man she thought she knew. 'It must be a surreal experience to have someone you love become an entirely unknown person before your eyes as their past unravels,' Hussey wrote in her memoir.

Sheila had given up her job in the hairdressing salon in the shopping centre on Dublin's Grafton Street and was making hand-woven cloth toys at home, which she sold to shops and markets. As news reports kept coming and the prosecution's case was laid out in court, her perspective about her husband's true identity wavered. Brian Hanlon, O'Shea's doctor friend in Canada, received a letter from Sheila a couple of weeks after the arrest. Hanlon, she was well aware, was one of her husband's oldest friends in Ireland.

'Can you tell me more about his background?' she wrote in the letter. 'When exactly did you meet him?' Hanlon got the sense that Sheila not only wanted to create an alibi for her husband's movements at the time of June's murder in 1967 but was genuinely uncertain about his past.

She also turned up at the door of the James family in Mountmellick, a few miles from Capard. Neville James had not seen O'Shea or Sheila for many months – ever since the local Garda superintendent warned him about the allegations against O'Shea and since Neville banned his teenage daughter Fiona from visiting the estate. Sheila arrived at their home in tears, distraught, telling them she was blindsided by her husband's arrest. She had no idea about Joe Maloney and believed everything Michael told her and was certain it was a case of mistaken identity. Fiona's mother felt sympathy for the woman sobbing at her table.

'Imagine if you found out your husband wasn't who he said he was,' said Fiona. 'You would probably wonder, "Am I legally married to this person? Am I going to be implicated in what he has done? How have I survived when he allegedly murdered his first wife?" Can you imagine what she was going through? I can't.'

Sheila eventually calmed down, stopped crying and got to the point. She was gathering money for her husband's legal representation. Would Fiona's father buy one of her Vauxhall Cavalier cars so she could get some cash? Furthermore, would the James family provide character witness statements to help secure her husband's release? As she talked to them across the kitchen table, Fiona's parents suspected she was doing the rounds and asking favours of everyone who knew Michael O'Shea. Fiona's father, however, had been privy to the allegations against O'Shea for months and wanted no association with a man accused of murder. So he turned down her requests and Sheila left.

While O'Shea was behind bars, Sheila and Rod Fenning were his eyes and ears to the outside world. Rod was Sheila's rock. He accompanied her on prison visits and took her to every court appearance. 'Rod couldn't have done more,' said Patrick Fenning. 'He looked after Sheila. He made sure she was all right. There wasn't anything he wouldn't have done.'

They were O'Shea's first line of defence. Sheila followed his commands, ran errands and barred any associates from visiting him in prison unless they were necessary for his needs, particularly in a financial capacity. Some business colleagues who had known him closely for a decade or more were summarily dumped because their usefulness had expired.

'I asked to see if I could go down and talk to him and word came back he didn't want to see anybody,' said one disgruntled former colleague. Some business partners were hurt by this rejection, because they thought he was a close friend. Perhaps Michael was too embarrassed to see them in prison: that must be it, they told themselves.

In reality, they were dumped while casual acquaintances that might be of service were summoned to the Mountjoy visiting room. Pat Fitzsimons, whose father employed O'Shea at the engineering company in Ballyfermot in the late 1960s, was one such invitee. Fitzsimons received a call from Rutherford and Co., the Dublin law firm who represented O'Shea in his dealings with Capard and were now fighting his extradition.

'Can you visit Michael in Mountjoy,' asked a lawyer. 'He wants to see you.'

Fitzsimons arrived at the prison and waited in a Portakabin beside the main entrance. An officer summoned him into the visitor's room and O'Shea came in and calmly asked if Fitzsimons could rely on his support for bail and if he could find any paperwork detailing his sales job at the engineering factory in Ballyfermot.

'I'll look,' said Fitzsimons, whose father died in the mid-1970s. Fitzsimons found an old wages book but it didn't have O'Shea's name on it. He phoned the solicitor at Rutherford and apologised. He couldn't help.

O'Shea's defence team seemed confident in their application for bail, which was to be heard at the High Court in Dublin. The application stressed that O'Shea was a businessman and a resident of the Dún Laoghaire and Dalkey areas for over a decade, and he was willing to give up his passport and honour conditions of bail. The application did not mention O'Shea's disputed identity.

O'Shea was privately confident, arrogant even, about his chances of release. Prosecutors in the US and Ireland were nervous about the prospect of bail. Howard Relin, Monroe County district attorney, said, 'I think anyone who tried to avoid a homicide case for 17 years would do anything in his power to try to avoid it now. If he admits he is the person who's being sought, then I think we've sent enough paperwork to convince an Irish court to set no bail or set very high bail.'

O'Shea was in no mind to admit anything. Since his arrest, he repeatedly claimed he was not Joe. The only linkage between him and Joseph Maloney was the fingerprints obtained in 1973, and they were bogus, he complained to his solicitor, Derek Greenlee of Rutherford. According to Greenlee, he was furious with the Garda who he'd trusted to dispose of his fingerprints following the 1973 incident. He wanted out of prison on point of principle. Barry Donoghue, prosecutor for the Irish state, was in no doubt what would occur if this man was prematurely released.

'If he's granted bail,' Donoghue said, 'based on his past history, he will abscond'.

* * *

The Four Courts, a bastion of the legal system in Ireland, had stood on the banks of the River Liffey in Dublin for over 200 years. It bore witness to major events in Irish history, including the Irish Civil War in 1922, in which it was occupied by rebels from the anti-Treaty Republican force. Within this majestic domed building was the High Court: the third tier of the Irish courts system which had jurisdiction over criminal and civil matters and the power to grant bail in extradition cases – including the one that came before it on 15 February 1985.

A who's who of Michael O'Shea's life was in the court that day. Sheila was there with her family and Rod Fenning. Pat Fitzsimons and O'Shea's business associates came too. But there was also space for his antagonists, including Detective Inspector John Mulderrig.

O'Shea was confident. There was no way the authorities could pin any of this on him. They were accusing him of being another person. An American! It was outlandish. Everyone knew it was nonsense. But this certitude was short-lived.

O'Shea was sitting at the back of the courtroom surrounded by police guards when a man entered the room. The man coolly walked the aisle between the benches then stopped, turned and looked O'Shea in the eyes. It was George Reiss, the detective and police captain from Rochester who lived a couple of blocks away from Joe Maloney on Eastmoreland Drive. Reiss, who had retired from Rochester Police Department the year beforehand, had known Joe for 10 years at the time of his disappearance. They had socialised together, attended neighbourhood barbeques, spent late nights drinking and chatting, and shared close quarters driving around Rochester while Joe sought construction work. Reiss had seen Joe only a day or two before his arrest on a charge of murdering June, and he was closely involved in the manhunt after Joe escaped.

He continued staring at Michael O'Shea. 'I just looked at him. I looked at him for a few minutes,' he later recounted. 'I wanted to make sure.' O'Shea held his gaze for a few seconds then looked down and fidgeted with his glasses, discomforted.

'This,' Reiss announced to the room, 'is Joseph Maloney.' O'Shea didn't respond. He seemed unable or unwilling to meet Reiss's eyes, and he whispered something to his attorney.

Reiss took a seat.

The Rochester district attorney thought the fingerprints obtained in 1973, which identified O'Shea as Maloney, were watertight. But they wanted something more, something that would make their case irrefutable. And here it was, the ace in their deck: George Reiss. As the formal proceedings began, Reiss continued to look across the room at O'Shea, and O'Shea continued to avoid his gaze.

'He'd look at me, looking at me sideways, but when I looked at him, he'd look down,' said Reiss. 'I recognised him, even though he's older and he's got a beard and his hair is white. That's Joe Maloney.'

O'Shea was not notified in advance that Reiss would be testifying at the bail hearing, according to Relin. 'It must have been a total shock to him. Maloney never expected to see George Reiss again in his life. All of a sudden he was confronted by the fact a person who knew him 10 years up until the crime was committed was going to identify him.'

A few minutes into the hearing, O'Shea's solicitors withdrew their bail request, cutting short the proceedings in order to avoid having Reiss testify. 'Obviously, he felt that having Reiss there was going to be devastating in terms of his defence that he was not Maloney,' recounted Relin.

In further insult to the pride of O'Shea and his supporters, the High Court judge ordered him to pay the $340 round trip flight that it cost to bring Reiss to Ireland to testify – a punishment for withdrawing his bail application at the last minute.

This was a watershed moment for Sheila Chandler, O'Shea's wife. Everything he had told her across the 12 years of their marriage was a fabrication. Michael O'Shea never existed. He was a front, a cover for Joe Maloney. A woman called June – his wife, the mother of his two children – was alleged to have died brutally at his hands.

Yet rather than react with shock or horror or use this moment to reassess her relationship, Sheila was angry and resilient. Pat Fitzsimons overheard her raging to her family members in the High Court lobby following the hearing, 'I don't care how many he's killed,' she spat. 'I still love him.'

Sheila's family members rallied around her. Vincent, her father, believed in O'Shea's innocence, even if his name was fabricated and Catherine, her mother, was overheard complaining to a friend: 'I don't care whether he did it or not. He's ruined my daughter's life.'

* * *

When Reiss returned to Rochester after the hearing, he told his children about the surreal experience of encountering Joseph Maloney again.

'Was he positive that this guy was Joseph Maloney? Yes, he was,' said Alice Fisher, the oldest daughter of George Reiss. 'He was positive it was him.' His son Ed Reiss added: '[My father] was in no doubt. When he came back I talked to him and he said it was Joe. He was impressed by Joe. Joe was a very smart person. Joe didn't have any reaction to him in the court but with the fingerprints and everything, Joe knew it was a done deal.'

One of O'Shea's lawyers confirmed to me that, behind the scenes, O'Shea gave up any question around his true identity from this point. He accepted he was Joe Maloney. While he continued to fight his extradition and his supporters continued to refer to him as 'Michael' or 'Mick', the veil was lifted and pretences were gone.

Joe Maloney, the man wanted on a charge of killing his wife June, had returned.

12.

Jailbreak

WENDY LEHMANN, MONROE COUNTY'S ASSISTANT DA, HAD HANDLED FOREIGN EXTRADITION CASES BEFORE, BUT SHE'D NEVER TRAVELLED TO OTHER COUNTRIES. County prosecutors didn't travel – they stayed in their own jurisdiction and prosecuted. In the case of Joe Maloney, however, her DA boss Howard Relin thought it best that somebody oversee proceedings in Ireland. There was a feeling in the Monroe office that parts of the Irish government and judicial system were not overly keen about this new extradition treaty. Relin thought it vital to have someone on the ground in Ireland to ensure everything was done by the book. Before leaving Rochester, Lehmann consulted over the phone with Barry Donoghue, the DA office's prosecutor for the Irish state, and he in turn introduced her to Michael Collins, the solicitor fighting their case.

'Intercontinental telephone calls were not a normal part of my job,' said Lehmann. 'This was my first experience with the Irish legal system, so that was all very interesting.'

In March 1985, Lehmann travelled to Ireland with her husband Gary, a real estate broker, for Joe Maloney's first extradition hearing, which was to take place on the 27th at Dún Laoghaire District Court. Gillian Hussey was presiding again. Wendy Lehmann knew of no female judges working in Monroe County at the time; this was another first for her.

The courtroom was full. Joe had many supporters there, and Lehmann was surprised to see the defendant sit in the back of the courtroom as part of the audience: a contrast to proceedings in the US, where the defendant sits at the front of the room with their attorney. Wendy was struck by his appearance. 'I remember thinking he looked like Father Time. He had a long straggly beard, as far as I recall it, and looked kind of diminished.'

His fingerprints were the focus of the day. John O'Shea, a detective sergeant in the fingerprint section of the Garda, told the court how he obtained O'Shea's prints in 1973 from detective Frank Mullen, and how Interpol found a match from FBI records with Joe Maloney. Barry Donoghue presented a copy of the matching prints to the court.

Patrick McEntee, Joe's counsel, told the court that police promised to destroy the prints following the 1973 incident once his client had been eliminated from enquiries. 'Why were they kept and not destroyed?' he demanded. Garda Mullen responded by saying the prints were kept in view of possible extradition proceedings at a later date.

Lehmann observed the proceedings while Donoghue and Collins did most of the talking. When Donoghue wanted information from the Rochester DA, he asked the judge for a moment and whispered to Collins, who in turn whispered to Lehmann. She whispered the information back to the barrister via Collins.

Meanwhile, her husband Gary was in the audience at the back of the room observing Joe. Gary was surprised that the defendant was not better guarded and was sitting freely next to his wife. Sheila's large purse was between them, and Gary couldn't take his eyes off them or the purse.

I asked Gary, during the making of *Runaway Joe*, if he was concerned there might be a weapon in it. 'Yes, absolutely. He was completely capable of that. This looked like a set-up.'

Gary, knowing all about Joe's escape from the psychiatric institution in Rochester, was concerned about Joe's proximity to a door that led out of the courthouse and onto the street. Nobody else seemed to be watching the defendant, and Gary raised this issue with officers of the court – but they brushed off his concerns.

Gary later remarked to Wendy: 'If I had just been reunited with my wife after some time in prison, I wouldn't put a purse between us. I was suspicious that she was doing that to pass something to him – either some information about how to get out or something else.'

The extradition hearing of 27 March concluded without a resolution, and another date was set for a week's time. The prosecution team – Wendy Lehmann, Barry Donoghue and Michael Collins – had a meeting afterwards and made the decision to present the court with more evidence of the defendant's identification.

Lehmann, in-between giving interviews over the phone to the media in Rochester, whose interest in the case continued unabated, wanted to figure out the extent of Joe Maloney's assets in Ireland. If he had money and property, it could impact his eligibility to use a public defender paid by the state once extradited to Rochester. Aside from Garda John Mulderrig's brief appraisal of Joe's life in Ireland that was detailed within his arrest report, little investigation had been undertaken into the defendant's assets.

Gary, with his experience as a Rochester realtor, volunteered to help his wife and visited the Registry of Deeds in Dublin, where the Irish land registry catalogue system was similar to that used in the United States. He uncovered information about Capard House without much trouble and made copies of Michael O'Shea's deeds, which detailed the transferral of the property from Robert Noonan in 1975 and included a description of the lands and a cadastral map illustrating the estate's geographical boundaries. O'Shea, they ascertained from these materials, was half a million Irish pounds in debt four years beforehand in 1981. What kind of hole was he in now?

Lehmann reported this information back to Howard Relin, the DA in Rochester, and asked an auctioneering firm in Laois near Capard House to provide an up-to-date assessment of the property. Hume Auctioneers subsequently wrote to Relin:

Dear Sir,

I've been instructed by your office to inspect the above estate and report as follows. I am a principal in the firm PJ Hume and Son Auctioneers and Estate Agents, having taken over from my late father who established the firm in 1940.

I consider [Capard Estate] to be unattractive in today's depressed market due mainly to its remoteness and poor state of repair. It is my opinion the value of the entire holding, if placed on the open market – free of all encumbrances and unusual outgoing would be £250,000 (Irish punts).

Ray Hume

The DA was satisfied Joe Maloney could avail of a public defender given the extent of his debt. In their investigation, Wendy and Gary did not unravel the financial dealings behind their property in Kent Terrace, which was registered to his wife Sheila Chandler, nor did they learn about Joe's recent sale of the house in Castletown. They had a few days to kill after finishing their research, though, and rented a car and drove around the midlands of Ireland from one bed and breakfast accommodation to the next. It was late March, cold and rainy. They stopped at a pub in a rural village in Laois, where locals, mostly young men, were sitting around a fireplace drinking beer. Wendy and Gary bought pints and joined them.

A villager overheard their American accents and asked: 'It's not tourist season. What are you doing here?'

'I'm an attorney in the States,' Wendy explained. 'I'm here trying to extradite a guy who tried to kill his wife a long time ago.'

The local stopped, looked around and muttered in her ear. 'If it's Michael O'Shea you're talking about, you oughtn't to be talking about him here. We're all IRA.'

Wendy and Gary finished their drinks and left.

* * *

On 2 April 1985, Dún Laoghaire District Court convened a final time for the case of Joseph Maloney. Joe hid his face beneath his coat upon arrival, ignoring pleas from the press to show himself. Inside the courtroom, he looked old and deflated – white-haired and bearded – and he held Sheila's hand as proceedings began. Prosecution decided to seal the deal by bringing over the son of Rochester detective George Reiss, George Junior, who had been a teenager when June's death occurred and mowed Joe Maloney's lawn on Eastmoreland Drive. George Junior had followed his father into the profession and worked as a detective in Rochester's police department. Like his father at the recent High Court hearing, he closely observed Maloney/O'Shea in the Dún Laoghaire courtroom.

'For three and a half years, I cut his grass at least once a week during the summer months,' George Junior told the court. He pointed at Joe: 'That's him.'

'I recognised him when I saw him this morning,' he told Rochester's *Democrat & Chronicle* later that day. 'His gait was similar and his complexion was the same. He still has freckles.'

Joe knew the game was up and did not testify. Judge Hussey ordered the extradition of Joseph Michael Maloney from Ireland to Rochester in the United States.

'Will you surrender yourself to the order?' she asked him.

'No,' he replied, bitterly.

Detective Inspector John Mulderrig was in court that day and, as Joe was led back to Mountjoy Prison under police guard, he was confident that justice had been done. He reflected on a conversation he'd had with Laura Meade, the journalist from Rochester, when she visited him a few months previously. 'She said, "What mistakes did Maloney make?" I told her, "He made the mistake of coming to Dún Laoghaire, where he brought himself under notice."'

Wendy and Gary Lehmann were also satisfied and left Ireland the following day. 'We were very happy we'd done our job,' said Wendy. 'I thought, "June is finally going to get justice." They're finally going to get him to bring him back to stand trial for what he did.'

In Rochester, the local FBI office began making plans for Joe's extradition. It was their task to notify the US marshals who would travel to Ireland with a Rochester police detective or another local law enforcement agency to transport Joe back to the Western District of New York. From there he would be confined in the Monroe County Jail, explained Gene Harding, special agent in charge of the case. 'At that point, the Monroe County District Attorney's Office and local police would take over, and the FBI would drop our unlawful flight to avoid prosecution warrant. That's normal procedure.'

This was by no means a done deal, though. The court had ordered Joe's extradition, but now he had to be held pending that extradition, and he had the right to appeal. Wendy Lehmann had done everything she could. But she also knew it wasn't over until Joe's feet were on US soil.

* * *

After being dealt what he considered to be a bad hand by the law, Joe Maloney sought help from religion. Michael Cox, the Tridentine priest he'd befriended years previously, was no stranger to Mountjoy Prison. In 1982, Cox had established his own religious order, a breakaway group from Rome, in which he adopted the title of Bishop Superior of the Irish Orthodox Catholic and Apostolic Church. Bishop Cox was a regular visitor to Irish prisons and hospitals. He would arrive dressed in his clerical robes and deliver divine healings to the inmates and patients. Sometimes he visited prisoners at Mountjoy upon request of their families, seeking their temporary or permanent release on spiritual grounds. The bishop had a good relationship with the prison governor and its social workers, and he was known as a man who could get things done.

Cox received word through two sources – Sheila, Joe's wife, and a mutual friend of his and Joe's called Desmond 'Dessie'

Monks, who lived in Dublin's north inner city close to the prison – that Joe wanted to see him. Joe did not profess to be religious, but he gave a confession of sorts to Bishop Cox at one of their first meetings in Mountjoy.

'He said he was American,' recalled Cox. Joe added that his wife June had perished, although his version of events differed to the historical record. 'My understanding was that him and his wife in America got drunk and one of them wound up dead.'

Cox visited Joe frequently after that. Joe, he knew, had a good grasp of the German language. 'Don't ask me where he learned it,' said Cox, adding that Erika Lotze, the German caretaker at Capard, was probably responsible. Cox spoke German too, and he and Joe often conversed in the language in the visitors' room, to the annoyance of the guards. Whether talking in English or German, Joe was crystal clear about his ambitions.

'He wanted to get out of that prison,' said Cox. 'Prison was not for him. I got the impression he felt like a locked-up bird in a cage, and out of prison he wanted.'

Joe's acknowledgement of his Rochester roots gave him an opportunity to get back in touch with people from his hometown. Neal Dunkleberg would never be on his Christmas card list again. Neal's sister, after all, blew the whistle on Joe's alleged procurement of methyl alcohol from Neal's home laboratory. But he had never fallen out with his other childhood best friend, Warren Daansen. He called Daansen and his old pal flew to Ireland to visit him at Mountjoy. Joe had another call to make. He wanted to secure a powerful legal defence attorney for his return to Rochester, and he found the right man (perhaps with Daansen's help).

Felix Lapine was one of Rochester's most famous defence attorneys. His record included defending alleged mobsters, killers and corrupt cops. One of Lapine's most recent cases was the defence of Thomas Torpey, a mafia bodyguard accused of a murder in 1981 outside a restaurant in Irondequoit. Wendy Lehmann was in Rochester when she had a tip-off that Lapine had flown to Ireland to do a preliminary interview with Joe to assess his feasibility as a client. She phoned Lapine's office to confirm this and was told he wasn't there.

'Well, when will he be back?'

'Er . . . He's not feeling well,' said a secretary. 'Might be a couple of days.'

A Garda called Wendy from Ireland and confirmed that Lapine visited Joe in May. Lapine wanted to keep his meeting with O'Shea under wraps, and the attorney didn't even offer details of his trip to Ireland to his wife, limiting his description of it to 'work-related', although he did bring one of his sons an Aer Lingus airline blanket from the journey home.

Details of the conversation between Joe and Lapine, who died in 2018, are unknown.

'I never heard anything more about that, and I never talked to Felix about why he had gone,' said Wendy Lehmann. But Joe Maloney clearly wanted the best for his defence in Rochester. 'And Felix,' she added, 'would have been the best.'

*   *   *

With his prospects of a successful appeal looking increasingly shaky, Joseph Maloney turned to more innovative methods of release from prison.

In his arrest report, Detective Inspector John Mulderrig expressed his satisfaction 'that Maloney is not in any position to finance any rescue operation of himself from Mountjoy Prison. Any such operation would have to be financed by some other person or organisation.'

The IRA was known for mounting audacious escapes from Irish prisons, north and south. One such escape occurred in 1973, when a hijacked helicopter landed in the exercise yard of Mountjoy, picked up three prisoners and flew off into the sunset.

In the same report, Mulderrig expressed concern about the FBI's description of Joe in their wanted poster as an 'explosives expert'. 'A subversive organisation,' he wrote, 'may have some interest in rescuing him in return for the benefit of his knowledge of explosives.' The police officer had no knowledge of Joe being involved in subversive activities, helping the IRA in particular, but he asked the Special Detective Unit to look further into the matter.

Mulderrig's report was strangely prophetic. In June 1985, a few days after Judge Hussey approved Joe's extradition, media in Ireland reported that the defendant had offered $50,000 to a prison guard to smuggle explosives into Mountjoy.

Joseph Kennings, a spokesperson for the government, told Rochester's *Democrat & Chronicle* that officers 'acting on a tip' discovered a key to a prison gate alongside fuse material in a toilet in the prison section that housed Maloney. 'Explosives detective equipment was brought to the prison, but a search for explosives proved negative,' he said. Kennings said the key would have given Maloney access to the prison yard. Explosives, combined with a fuse, could have blown a hole in the wall, granting him freedom. Joe was summarily moved to a maximum security cell. Bribery, explosives, a hidden key: textbook Joe Maloney.

Howard Relin, the DA awaiting Joe's return in Rochester, was unnerved. Irish officials were not taking this man seriously enough. 'We're extremely concerned about this news,' Relin told reporters in Rochester. 'We've communicated our concern [to Irish prosecutors] that given Maloney's past history he's capable of doing anything.'

Joe's prison break was prematurely scuppered, so he tried another tactic: he went on hunger strike. Hunger strikes were zeitgeist in Ireland. Four years previously, IRA volunteers in Northern Ireland had stopped eating as a protest against the British government's refusal to recognise them as political prisoners.

One prisoner, Bobby Sands, was elected as a member of parliament during the protest, and Sands and nine other prisoners died before the strike ended. There was widespread sympathy over the deaths, and the protest propelled Sinn Féin, the political wing of the Republican movement, from the margins into the mainstream. Mountjoy had precedent for this form of protest. Five hundred Irish Republican prisoners went on hunger strike in 1923 over poor prison conditions and charges without trial.

Joe, of course, refused to eat not because of political ideals but because of a stubborn refusal to accept the court's judgement over his extradition. His hunger strike began in late July 1985. Mountjoy's cafeteria had a self-service system, whereby prisoners took away their meals and returned the plates later. Officers didn't notice Joe had stopped eating until he informed them. He apparently went 16 days without food before he ended the strike to lodge another request for bail: a request that was again denied.

In a further snub, the High Court told him he still needed to pay the travel expenses of George Reiss Senior from Rochester to Dublin from his bail hearing six months beforehand before they'd consider another application. Joe was infuriated. He returned to Mountjoy and went back on hunger strike.

After a number of days on strike he appeared to be growing weaker, and Mountjoy's warden moved him to Jervis Street hospital in Dublin's city centre, where he continued to refuse food. As his appointed chaplain, Bishop Michael Cox was granted permission to visit Joe at the hospital, and he was struck by his friend's appearance: 'He looked like a skeleton.'

Joe was being moved around in a wheelchair and refused to accept treatment from a nurse who came in to see him when Bishop Cox was talking to him.

'You're in our hospital and we're responsible for treating you,' the nurse said.

'Then I'll roll over on my belly and cry like a baby,' Joe snapped.

Cox was flummoxed by Joe's response. 'That's what he said. Imagine a grown man going over, rolling over on his tummy and crying like a baby.'

When the Monroe County DA heard Joe had been moved into a hospital they panicked. This sounded like 1967 all over again. They advised the Irish authorities that it was a ruse. 'Our feeling was that he wanted to get to the hospital so he could escape again,' said Howard Relin. Officials listened and took Joe back to prison, where he continued to shun food.

Rumours spread amongst his friends in the outside world: Joe was a shadow of his former self. He was hardly able to walk. He had arthritis. He would die within a month. Meanwhile, prison officers believed he was faking it and squirreling away food to eat when no one was looking. According to one officer, 'he would be shuffling along, playing the old soldier routine, until his wife came to see him and he would perk up and run to the visiting box'. The officer laughed. 'He was good and fit.'

Joe was certainly healthy enough to continue fighting in court. In October 1985, his bail application was denied again after George Shultz, the US Secretary of State, personally signed and sent a diplomatic cable to the Irish prosecutors, which described Maloney as 'dangerous' and said the US Justice Department was convinced 'he would once again become a fugitive if he were released on bail'.

Sheila was a nervous wreck trying to raise money for her husband's defence. She held a yard sale and sold off his collection of antiques, guns and books (most of them on the subject of war and weapons). She routinely visited the Fennings' new home in Sandycove, where she paced around and ranted about her disgust over Michael's treatment. The Fennings were kind to Sheila, and she became a surrogate part of the family, helping them with DIY, sticking up wallpaper and painting walls, in-between running errands for her jailed husband.

'Sheila, you're very good. Thanks a million,' they told her.

'Look, it's giving me something to do,' she said.

Joe continued to claim deterioration of his health into the spring of 1986, according to the records of prison counsellors, which I unearthed in the Monroe County DA case files. He begged the court to give him 30 days bail to allow him to put his affairs in order. Knowing these appeals were unlikely to be heard, he decided to take matters into his own hands and break out of Mountjoy Prison.

* * *

In April 1986, prison staff at Mountjoy were keeping Joe under surveillance, having heard 'underworld rumours' that a gang from Dublin's northside was planning to help him escape. In spite of their surveillance, Joe Maloney was ready to outfox them all over again. Mountjoy was an ancient, imposing fortress built in 1850 in the classic Victorian prison design: a radial atrium like the wheel of a bicycle that opened out into four main wings. Its spokes were named A through to D. There were three landings and an underground basement, each labelled A1, B1, A2, B2 and so on. Joe shared a cell with another inmate on C1, on the ground floor. The other inmate was much younger, in his twenties, and agile.

Joe offered his cellmate a sum of money, and the younger man agreed to help break him out of prison: a similar bargaining relationship to the one that occurred between Joe and the 16-year-old patient in the Rochester hospital before Joe's 1967 escape. Mountjoy's cell doors were built with a receiver that ensured the doors locked firmly at night. During the afternoon of Sunday, 13 April 1986, Joe's cellmate cut the receiver from the lock of their door, perhaps using a piece of hacksaw blade stolen from the prison workshop.

Prisoners were locked in their cells at Mountjoy at 7:30pm. Later on, towards midnight, officers initiated a master lock, which ensured all the doors were completely secured. The officers were not to know that Joe and his cellmate had wedged their door closed at 7:30pm, so, although it had the appearance of being locked, it was open.

As midnight passed, the two men stayed awake and alert, monitoring the movement of the officers who patrolled the cellblocks every half hour. At around 4:30am, they put pillows under their bedsheets, in order to convince patrolling officers that they were sleeping, and made their bid for freedom. They climbed the steps from C1 up to C2, then C3 and above that to the grimy and unkempt attic, which they accessed through a window.

Joe and his cellmate skirted the water tanks that had supplied the prison since the 1800s and broke open a doorway that led from the attic onto the prison roof. This escape was weeks in the making. The men had crafted a 13-foot rope from bedsheets, which they'd torn into strands, plaited together and hidden in their cell. The younger man lowered Joe from the prison roof to a lower kitchen roof, and from there they ran to a perimeter wall. The younger man climbed onto the wall and threw the makeshift rope for Joe. But the 50-year-old American, possibly weakened from months of starvation, struggled to climb it. Then a night guard on patrol turned a corner in the prison grounds and was surprised to see two prisoners: one on top of the wall, the other struggling to climb up.

The game was up. Joe was apprehended and the younger man clambered down to be taken back into custody. Joe and his cellmate were taken to the basement floor and thrown into two separate cells until they could be dealt with the following morning.

The story immediately leaked to the press. 'Murder Suspect in Jailbreak Bid', read the *Evening Herald*'s front page. 'Attempted Jail Break Out Foiled', bellowed the *Irish Press*. The prison initiated an internal inquiry with input from the Department of Justice as to how the men had escaped their cell. Three officers were suspended over dereliction of duty. Privately, prison staff were impressed with Joe's ingenuity.

'That escape was very, very clever,' one Mountjoy officer recalled.

The incident confirmed everything Monroe County's DA had been trying to impart to Irish authorities. This was a dangerous, ingenious individual who should not be underestimated. 'It further demonstrates the nature of this defendant,' Howard Relin told the *Democrat & Chronicle* in Rochester. 'He obviously doesn't want to come back here and face a trial.'

* * *

Officials in Ireland were not taking any more chances. They transferred Joe under heavy guard from Mountjoy in Dublin to Portlaoise Prison, a high-security facility in the midlands that held 350 IRA prisoners. Deemed the only 'non-terrorist' prisoner, Joe was separated and kept in solitary confinement 'under guard 24 hours a day'. He had come full circle. Capard House, the mansion that took him to the foothills of Irish aristocracy, was nearby, and Portlaoise was only half an hour away by car from Raheen in Laois and Roscrea in Tipperary, where his parents had grown up before migrating to the US and where Joe had visited in his childhood.

Not long after this new chapter in his incarceration, Annette Sullivan, the woman who had purchased the house in Castletown from Michael O'Shea, as she knew him, was working at her restaurant in Portlaoise when two women walked in. One was Erika Lotze, the caretaker at Capard House, who often came here for lunch when she was in town. The other was a dark-haired woman with a crisp south county Dublin accent.

'Annette, I want to introduce you to this lady,' said Lotze. 'This is Sheila. Her husband is in the prison in Portlaoise. We're going to visit him.'

Sullivan had a brief chat with Sheila before she went back to work.

Capard House was moving through bankruptcy proceedings, and Joe was about to be extradited to America to face a murder trial over the death of June Fisk almost 20 years beforehand. In Rochester, Wendy Lehmann, Monroe County assistant DA, was relieved to hear that Joe was in a high-security prison. Everything was in motion.

But a dark undercurrent was now taking this case in a new direction. Since the moment of his arrest in Ireland, Joe's future had been wrapped up in the fate of the three other men also facing extradition to America. And those men were not going back to the US without a fight.

13.

The Dirty Pool

April 1952

It was past 1 am in the west side of Toronto, and the city was asleep. A lone car approached the crossroads at Bathurst and King Street, where a green light beckoned them onwards. The driver was halfway across the intersection when another car came out of nowhere, travelling 80 miles per hour. The driver hit the brakes and avoided the speeding vehicle by inches. Seconds later, as the driver sat stationary, clutching his steering wheel in white terror, a police car sped past in pursuit.

Inside the getaway vehicle, 19-year-old Norman Douglas MacCaud fixed his eyes upon the road ahead and accelerated some more, ignoring the screams of the 22-year-old woman in the passenger seat. No way was MacCaud getting caught. A year ago, he'd been sentenced to a year in reformatory after he used a stolen car to force a US tourist off a highway north of Kingston,

Canada, robbing them of the princely sum of $10. The *Toronto Star* said the crime 'added a modern touch to the methods of highwaymen of old'. MacCaud liked that description, but he was on parole and determined not to get caught again.

'Stop the car, let me out,' screamed Gladys Mullen, a dark-haired waitress.

She was terrified. MacCaud had offered to take her out for a drive. She'd had no idea the car was stolen or that any of this madness was going to occur. The driver ground his car into second gear and took the corner of Spadina Avenue and King Street on two wheels.

In the police car behind, officers Johnny Murray and Bob Kerr struggled to keep up. Neither of them had ever experienced a chase as fast as this in the densely populated heart of the city. Thank God it was past midnight and the streets were empty. They'd started the pursuit eight miles ago on Lake Shore Road and broken countless red lights since.

MacCaud skidded into a lane near Adelaide Street West and Spadina Avenue. It was a dead end. He slammed on the brakes and floundered out the door, scrambling over an 11-foot fence, leaving the car with its engine smoking and tyres melting and the waitress screaming inside. Murray and Kerr leapt out of the squad car, now accompanied by other officers from other cars who'd joined the chase. One traffic cop tried to follow MacCaud over the fence, but he impaled his hands on sharp open wire and fell back down. Two officers rushed through another entrance to the builders' yard, where MacCaud fled. They drew their revolvers and yelled at the boy to come out of a large scrap tin which he was hiding inside.

MacCaud's head emerged from the top, and he gave himself up.

After the waitress was taken from the car, officers found an unloaded .45 revolver in the glove compartment, which they later identified as being one of several firearms stolen from a house in Toronto. MacCaud was charged with car theft, housebreaking and possession of a dangerous weapon, and he was sentenced to two years in prison.

* * *

Thirty-two years later, Norman MacCaud was the first of three men wanted for extradition to appear at Court Number Four in Dublin District Court in Ireland, situated at Bridewell, near the Four Courts complex. It was 18 December 1984, a couple of weeks before the arrest of Michael O'Shea. MacCaud did not look like a career criminal. Short, balding and 52 years of age, he was casually dressed in a grey jacket and reclined back in his seat in the courtroom smirking while Justice Mary Kotsonouris read the charges.

MacCaud had been arrested two days prior at his detached rental home near Ashbourne in County Meath. He was an Irish and Canadian citizen, the court heard, with more aliases than a secret agent: Aubrey McClelland of Ohio, Carl Johnson of Cleveland, Donald Goud and John Sullivan. He was mostly known as 'McCaud', having dropped the first 'a' from his name in a bid for anonymity. In Ireland, where he'd lived for the past seven years, he was known as Norman Sullivan, and he had a home in Blessington, County Wicklow, and Limerick before moving to Meath. He was wanted for extradition to Buffalo in the US, Kotsonouris told the court, for the alleged murder of an underworld figure.

Onlookers found it hard to associate this man's extensive rap sheet with the mild, unassuming middle-aged person before them. But he was, the court assured them, one of America's most wanted criminals.

* * *

MacCaud was barely out of prison in the 1950s when he was behind bars again: a pattern repeated across his life. In 1956, he was chased by cops when he and an associate stole computers from a business. Detectives fired shots at his getaway car and one slug narrowly missed MacCaud. Another detective was in a lane when the car turned a corner and the driver, MacCaud's associate, gunned straight for the officer, hitting him and sending him spinning through the air to land on the hood of a parked vehicle. The detective escaped with a sprained ankle and cuts. MacCaud was arrested at gunpoint and somehow escaped serious jail time.

A year later, he appeared in a photograph on the front page of the *Kingston Whig-Standard*, wearing a head bandage and a white shirt splattered with his own blood beneath the headline 'Suspect is Caught in Montreal'. The 27-year-old had been arrested in connection with the theft of $25,000 in cash from a supermarket. Two fellow bandits held the storeowners hostage while MacCaud marched the manager to the city bank to make a withdrawal. He was caught at the wheel of the car used in the robbery and an officer whacked him with a baton when he tried to escape. MacCaud was sentenced to seven years for his role in the supermarket heist and received another five years for stealing cash and gold worth over $20,000 and airline rebate slips worth $400,000.

After serving four years of his sentence, MacCaud was back on Canada's streets, where he found a new profession: forgery, counterfeiting and fraud. He was busted for running a phony cheque ring and thrown back in prison. This compulsive miscreant may have been careless, but he was no dope, and he gained a reputation as a jailhouse lawyer. In one hearing at Ontario Appeal Court in 1965, he argued his own case for four hours with the assistance of a student lawyer and a large stack of law books, which he read from to support his arguments.

'You could have become a successful lawyer,' the judge announced before dismissing his appeal. 'Your case is a tragedy. You're so well qualified to make a good living honestly.'

MacCaud continued to study law behind bars, and his pursuit of knowledge paid off. 'He Hit the Books and Cut Jail Time', read a headline in the *Toronto Daily Star* on 16 March 1969. MacCaud argued that the courts had miscalculated his jail time due to a lack of consideration for amnesties and remissions. A judge agreed and the jailbird was freed.

But by the summer of 1970, he was back in prison on a charge of using counterfeit US dollar bills and spraying mace at three police officers in an escape attempt. He was incarcerated at Kingston Penitentiary in Canada at the same time as a five-day riot that involved over 500 inmates and left two prisoners dead. Inside, MacCaud was a model prisoner and moved to the relaxed Joyceville Farm Annex institution. Outside, he was a liability. In late 1971, when the prison gave him a six-day pass to visit his mother in Toronto, he disappeared. FBI agents arrested him weeks later in Buffalo across the Canadian border in upstate New York. He was driving a car that contained two police uniforms, badges, a car siren and an ID for the Police Lieutenants Association of Buffalo. All these items were stolen.

MacCaud demanded to be deported to Ireland. He'd obtained an Irish passport on the grounds that his grandfather was born there, but his appeals dragged on for years, leaving him stuck in Buffalo and out on bail. When he was arrested for cutting alarm-linked telephone cables in the Tonawanda area, presumably to commit burglaries, a US judge deported him to Canada, ordering that 'he never return to the United States'.

Back in Canada, he beat the charge of his unlawful abscosion from Joyceville on a technicality. This time he was not sticking around. He left for Ireland, and Ireland opened its doors despite his criminal record that stretched back 25 years. He knew that authorities in the US would soon come looking for him on more serious charges, and he needed to be far away from the heat – preferably in a country without extradition to the US.

*   *   *

MacCaud's criminality took a more sinister turn in Ireland. At 11:15pm on the night of 5 April 1978, a young woman by the name of Michelle Dempsey was walking home in Kildare town when a man stepped out of a car to ask her for directions. After she told him the way, he grabbed her by the arm and pressed a knife to her stomach. She screamed, but he put his hand over her mouth and ordered her to follow him. Dempsey broke loose and ran to a pedestrian on the other side of the street. This witness and others in the locality who'd been alerted by the screams chased the would-be abductor and were ready to catch him when he stopped and threatened them with the knife. They backed off and the man escaped.

When Norman MacCaud was apprehended by police later that night in his car he was trying to conceal a wig. He was identified in a police line-up and in court as being the assailant and sentenced to the maximum penalty of six months imprisonment in Mountjoy Prison. MacCaud listed his occupation as working in the amusements machines trade. Even that occupation wasn't legit. After serving his sentence in Mountjoy he appeared at court in Donegal on a charge of stealing £271 from slot machines in three centres around the county.

Wanted notices were now circulating in Canada that described MacCaud as one of the country's 10 most wanted men. The US also sought him for questioning about a crime that occurred 11 years previously. In the 1970s, Buffalo (an hour's drive west from Joe Maloney's stomping ground of Rochester) was like the Wild West. Gangs like the Mad Dogs, Allah Turks, Matadors, Pythons and 49ers ruled parts of the city, warring over turf.

'Everybody had a shotgun in those days, slinging them over their shoulders and letting them hang down along their side,' said Leo Donovan, a Homicide Bureau chief who worked the city. Buffalo's mafia crime family controlled the city's financial rackets – extortion, bookmaking, loan-sharking, gambling.

On 11 June 1970, a local underworld figure by the name of Gino Albini was found in a car dead: shot in the face, arm and back. A year later, a woman's skeleton was found in a sewer beneath Buffalo's streets. That woman was Elayne Stec, the 22-year-old former girlfriend of Albini. The Buffalo homicide squad put the pieces together. Albini and his associate Carmen La Bruna had murdered Stec out of fear she was going to testify against Albini after she witnessed him kill a man in a bar fight. Albini was murdered a week after Stec.

La Bruna turned state witness and pointed the finger of blame for Albini's murder at Norman MacCaud. According to the supergrass, MacCaud had robbed a suburban supermarket in Buffalo and Albini tried to muscle a cut. MacCaud agreed to meet Albini and shot him. In 1977 (by which time he'd fled to Ireland), MacCaud was indicted by a federal grand jury on a charge of murder. Further adding to his notoriety, authorities in America wanted MacCaud for his involvement in a $330 million drug-smuggling operation, importing heroin to the US from Italy and France: a case the press nicknamed 'The French Connection'.

In 1981, the news broke in Ireland. 'French Connection Fugitive Is Here', read a headline on the front page of the *Evening Herald*, which detailed the warrants for his arrest over Albini's murder. Irish, US and Canadian authorities had to wait another three years before the extradition treaty between Ireland and the US was signed, though, and when MacCaud was finally apprehended at his home in Kildare, he denied the accusations against him, as did his Irish wife. 'It's a load of rubbish,' she told the *Sunday World* newspaper.

But as the hushed Dublin District Court heard his long history of criminality – robbery with violence, auto theft, possession of stolen goods, weapons possession, bail breaching, escaping custody, housebreaking, forgery, fraud counterfeiting, conspiring to sell narcotics, indecent exposure, assault, alongside the accusations of murder and international drug smuggling – it was difficult for anyone in that courtroom to deny that this short, smirking, middle-aged man was very, very dangerous.

*   *   *

The second defendant who followed Norman MacCaud into the dock in Dublin District Court on 17 December 1984 cut a different picture. He was trim, bearded and wore a flamboyant navy pinstripe suit and a monogrammed shirt with gold cufflinks. Thirty-seven-year-old Charles Joseph Walsh ran an accountancy practice at 68 Fitzwilliam Square in Dublin city centre, and he'd enjoyed the good life until his arrest 24 hours after the signing of the extradition treaty.

Walsh lived with his wife Dana in a large rented Victorian mansion in Grangecon, County Wicklow. His house was furnished with antiques and gilt-edged mirrors and surrounded by well-kept gardens. He employed two live-in housekeepers and a butler and owned 12 prize racehorses, which he'd bought for £40,000 at markets in Kildare and Dublin. He kept his horses in stables on his property and trained them locally. Walsh moved among the elite of the racing world and was often observed sipping champagne in the exclusive Owners & Trainers bar at the Curragh Racecourse in County Kildare.

All that privilege seemed meaningless in the Dublin court, where he sat a stone's throw from MacCaud. Justice Mary Kotsonouris told the room how Walsh was wanted in the US on charges of tax fraud that cost the US Treasury $6.8 million and made him $2.5 million in profit. Walsh, in an affected British accent, denied everything.

The accountant's problems began at his former home in Georgetown, a neighbourhood of Washington DC. A graduate of the University of Maryland, he started his career as an accountant for Price, Waterhouse & Co. before taking over a construction firm and establishing his own accountancy firm in Georgetown in 1978, which he boasted had branch offices in London, England, and Nassau in the Bahamas. He and his wife Dana had a lavish lifestyle in the US. He owned a farm in Virginia, which was stocked with horses, and he once celebrated his birthday floating down the Potomac River on a boat with luxury catering. His office was well-equipped with liquor, which he dished out at business meetings, and his clients came from across the US and as far away as Switzerland and Spain. Walsh liked to brag about his wealth – a habit that proved to be his undoing.

On 28 December 1981, an article appeared in the *Washington Post* with the headline 'Buying Art as Deadline Tax Shelter Could Prove Big Risk for Wealthy'. In the article, Walsh was quoted as offering tax shelters through investments in lithographic art prints for people about to file end-of-year tax returns.

'We sell it as a quick fix,' he declared.

A spokesperson for Internal Revenue Service (IRS) was quoted expressing scepticism about the validity of Walsh's business.

'The response to that,' Walsh said in the *Post* article, 'is that I own a house in Georgetown, a Bentley and an office with a fireplace.'

When the article came to the attention of the IRS, they launched an investigation, and two undercover agents equipped with hidden microphones met him in his office. According to transcripts of their tapes, Walsh offered to erase their tax liabilities if they each invested $16,000 in lithographic plates. More agents later arrived at his workplace with a search warrant and Walsh 'offered them drinks and sipped vodka as they carted records out', according to another article in the *Washington Post*. The accountant was charged with the promotion and sale of fraudulent and abusive tax shelters.

Walsh's indictment, filed in a US District Court in 1984, laid out his alleged crimes in detail: how he'd allegedly run the fraud through advertisements in national newspapers, leased 'largely nonexistent marine shipping containers to 309 unwitting investors', and supposedly laundered funds through companies in Panama, Liechtenstein and the Bahamas. Two accountants who helped Walsh were arrested and sentenced, but Walsh wasn't present for his own indictment. He fled to Ireland, where he first settled in Delgany in Wicklow. Walsh's lawyer told the US court that he'd tried to persuade Walsh to return, but his client planned to stay in Ireland indefinitely.

'He shut everything down and took off,' shrugged the attorney.

Walsh was facing a sentence of up to 196 years in jail plus substantial fines, and he was certainly not about to fly home of his own accord. But the signing of the extradition treaty and his arrest took that decision out of his hands. After his hearing outside the District Court in Dublin, a reporter asked him, 'Why don't you go back to the US to face the music?'

'Shucks,' Walsh replied, his confidence not wavering a jot. 'I'm not a great dancer.'

* * *

Norman MacCaud and Charles Walsh were both denied bail and carted off together in a van to Mountjoy Prison, leaving one more defendant to hear charges. His name was James Hildage Gilliland, a 54-year-old retired businessman who lived in Salthill, County Galway with his wife and daughter under the name James Stewart – and he was wanted in the US on charges of racketeering, bankruptcy fraud and obstruction of justice.

Jim Gilliland, as he was known to family and friends, was born and grew up in Dumbarton, Scotland, before migrating to Canada with his wife Betty in 1954. He worked for a ship-building company until the early 1970s, when he moved to Quincy, a city in Massachusetts, where he became assistant manager of the ship-building division in General Dynamics, one of the world's largest defence contractors.

Authorities alleged Gilliland and a former executive at General Dynamics took millions of dollars in illegal payoffs in return for handing out $45 million of subcontracting work, building tankers and submarines, to a company called Frigitemp. Two former Frigitemp executives were charged with arranging and paying the kickbacks as part of an indictment in New York in 1985.

Gilliland fled to Britain and then to Ireland, where he moved his family into a two-bedroom seaside apartment overlooking the Atlantic. Despite protestations from the chief investigator in the US, Ireland's High Court granted Gilliland £50,000 bail pending the outcome of his extradition hearing and ordered him to report to the police in Salthill twice a day while on bail. Gilliland hightailed it back to his apartment, telling a reporter who thrust a microphone along the way: 'I am very happy here in Galway, the people are very nice and friendly. I intend to remain in Ireland pending the determination of these extradition proceedings which I plan to contest vigorously.'

Gilliland's lawyer tried to mastermind a rebuttal to the state's efforts to extradite his client, but it went nowhere; his extradition was approved, and he was thrown in Mountjoy Prison, alongside Norman MacCaud, Charles Walsh and Joe Maloney, to await his transfer to the United States.

Over the course of 1985, MacCaud and Walsh ran out of appeals. MacCaud was returned to Buffalo to face charges over the 1970 mob murder; Walsh was sent back to Washington to be trialled for tax fraud. Now only Gilliland and Joe Maloney remained.

In the process of their appeal, Gilliland's legal team found a chink in the armour of the US-Ireland extradition treaty. The treaty, according to the team's interpretation, allocated public funds for the payment of lawyers, judges and court workers, who processed extradition cases. Ireland's constitution required Dáil Éireann, the principal chamber of the Irish parliament, to approve any legislation that required public money.

In this light, Gilliland's lawyer argued, the treaty was unconstitutional.

On 7 October 1985, a High Court judge concurred with the interpretation of Gilliland's lawyers, declared the treaty invalid and referred the matter to Ireland's Supreme Court. Prosecutors in Ireland and the US were confident that the court would uphold the treaty, but now it was a waiting game. Gilliland and Joe were both being held in Mountjoy, and their fates were inextricably entwined. On a trip to Ireland from Canada (prior to Joe's move to Portlaoise high-security prison), the doctor Brian Hanlon paid a visit to Mountjoy.

'This is all a false accusation,' Joe told him in the visitor's box. 'This isn't true. I have my lawyer working on it. I should have never been arrested because there wasn't a proper treaty signed between Ireland and the US in relation to the legal technicalities.'

'Well, when you get out,' Hanlon told him, 'get in touch with me. You know where I am.'

* * *

On 24 July 1986, Joe Maloney was in solitary confinement in Portlaoise when he heard a knock on his cell door. He expected to find US marshals outside, ready to transport him back to America. Instead, it was prison staff telling him he was free to go. The Supreme Court had declared the extradition treaty between the US and Ireland invalid, having upheld Gilliland's challenge that the treaty involved a charge on Irish public funds that hadn't been approved by the Irish parliament. Joe Maloney had escaped custody again, only this time it wasn't through his own ingenuity. This time, institutional failure set him free.

Joe's solicitors sprung into action. They contacted the governor of Portlaoise prison, who discharged him from custody, and he was transported to the High Court in Dublin. Following what one newspaper described as a two-minute hearing, the judge released Joseph Maloney, aka Michael O'Shea, from custody.

'He scarpered,' his lawyer, Derek Greenlee, told me. 'He was out the front door of a court, into a car and gone. He wasn't hanging around. He had that already arranged.'

According to the Fenning family, the faithful Rod Fenning came to the rescue. Rod had parked his car in a road next to a side entrance to the courthouse, presumably to thwart waiting reporters and the possibility of law enforcement officials planning to re-arrest Joe.

'Rod had a fairly good inkling he was going to be released,' said his brother, Patrick Fenning. 'The judge indicated there was no way they could continue to hold this man. Rod was there waiting and had the car ready to go.'

The way Rod told the story, 'Michael' was unrecognisable to the person that went into prison, perhaps on account of his time in solitary confinement in Portlaoise and the after effects of several months on supposed hunger strike.

'He looked like the picture of that Led Zeppelin album cover,' said Patrick, in reference to *Led Zeppelin IV*. 'An old man. Gandalf. Unrecognisable, balding. I remember Rod saying, "He was gone. The Michael that went in was just not there anymore." He could barely talk. Rod almost had to carry him out to the car and throw him into it.'

Reporters sped across Dublin to Joe's home on Kent Terrace in Dalkey, where an estate agent's sign describing the property as 'Sold' was posted outside the front door. A journalist rang the doorbell and a dark-haired woman answered. When asked if Michael O'Shea was present, the woman said 'a man of that name is not here' and slammed the door. The press visited the Chandler family home in Glenageary, where Sheila's father spoke. Vincent Chandler described Joe as 'a sick man. He is not well after 18 months in prison and the ordeal of several court appearances.' Chandler didn't know where Joe was, 'and if I did I wouldn't tell you. We are not telling anybody. We don't believe he did what they say.'

He had one more thing to say before closing the door on reporters. 'I don't care what the witnesses from Rochester said. They are going to have to live with their consciences.'

Those witnesses woke up in Rochester to a flurry of headlines: 'Ireland Frees Maloney', 'Maloney's Charmed Escapes' and 'Fate Has Favoured Fugitive For 19 Years Across Two Nations'. Sheila's father was correct in one sense. Wanda Mordenga, June's neighbour and friend, who was 19 at the time of June's murder and was now in her late thirties, had lived with the events of the past weighing on her conscience for two decades.

'I was always this bubbly person,' Wanda said. 'I no longer associate with the neighbours too much. I'm a little less trusting of people than before.'

Wanda thought about June often.

'She was a wonderful person. Full of life. Kind. Loving. A good person.' Sometimes she harboured the fanciful notion of visiting Joe in jail and asking him to his face, 'Why did you do this? What was the reason? You could have gone and lived your life. She could have gone and lived her life.' Wanda knew the answer, of course. Joe's behaviour was about control: '"If I can't have her then I don't want anybody else to have her." That's all I kept on thinking about sometimes. He didn't want her but he wanted to possess her. He didn't want anybody else to have her. He didn't want her to move on.'

When Irish authorities set Joe free, Wanda's trauma resurfaced. 'I thought, 'Oh my God, you've got to be kidding me. They finally got him and then they lost him again? How idiotic is that?'

Detectives in Rochester who investigated June's homicide understood her frustration. One retired cop with the Rochester Police Department, Norman Knapp, described their department as doing 'a bang-up job' in 1967 in bringing Joe Maloney to justice. 'I hate to see it all go down the drain . . . I only hope the powers that be won't let him get away.'

Wendy Lehmann, the assistant district attorney who helped Dún Laoghaire District Court in its decision to extradite Joe Maloney, felt helpless when she heard the news. Her boss, Monroe County DA Howard Relin, tried to maintain a brave face, telling reporters that he hoped Maloney would not avoid prosecution for much longer.

'We plan to get him back . . . We expect he'll stay in Ireland. If he goes to another country we could extradite him. I think we will be able to locate him. Ireland is not a large country. He's in a *Catch-22* situation. If he leaves and we trace him, he will be extradited. If he stays and the treaty is ratified, we'll extradite him. All we can do now is wait.'

The Irish Supreme Court stated within its ruling that parliament needed to ratify the extradition treaty. While those wheels shifted in motion, there was little Irish authorities could do to keep tabs on their murder suspect. Joe was not wanted for a crime in Ireland, and local law enforcement didn't have the manpower to keep him under constant vigil.

People who had been close to Joe Maloney in the US were in no doubt as to what would happen next. 'I have a feeling he'll be gone five minutes after the night falls on the moors,' said Joseph Picciotti, the suburban Rochester cop who knew Joe in his youth. 'He's an extremely clever, clever man. For him to have been out this long, he has to be clever. He seems to be able to find the cracks.'

Prosecutors in Rochester and Ireland harboured notions that Joe Maloney would soon be arrested and extradited, but another of the fugitive's former associates knew the game was up. George Reiss, the retired police officer who identified him at the High Court bail hearing the year before, was certain that this was the end of the story.

'The only thing I can say is that if I know Joe Maloney,' Reiss told a reporter in Rochester, 'he'll disappear and they won't find him.'

14.

Twisted Odyssey

September 1991

JOEY AND HIS WIFE DONNA WERE AT HOME WATCHING TV WHEN A TEASER CAME ON FOR THE FOLLOWING WEEK'S EPISODE OF THE CRIME RE-ENACTMENT SHOW *UNSOLVED MYSTERIES*.

'Next, an international fugitive is wanted for the cold-blooded poisoning of his own wife,' announced a voiceover, describing how the alleged crime occurred at their son's fifth birthday party. 'You know, Joey told me this was his best birthday party ever,' the actor playing Joe Maloney said to June as their child played beneath a canopy of red balloons.

Joey, now 28 years old, turned to Donna.

'See that boy with the balloons?'

Donna nodded.

'That's me . . . We need to talk.'

*   *   *

Joey never dwelled on his pre-1967 life, but he also never forgot it. That era came back in flashes. 'Even now I'm remembering things I didn't recall at the time,' Joey told me at his home in Florida. 'Different things that happened.' Now and then, when he was growing up, he would read an article in the Rochester newspaper *Democrat & Chronicle* about Joe Maloney and wonder, 'Where is he at? What's he doing?'

Joe never tried to contact Joey, but once in a while the boy talked with his adoptive mother about him. 'She definitely kept her ears to the ground, but it wasn't talked about a lot. If a news story came out, she'd pull me aside and say something, but it wasn't a big deal at the time.' The dominant theory in his family across the 1970s and the first half of the 1980s was that Joe Maloney was in Ireland. This rumour likely emerged from the brief spate of press reports falsely announcing his Dublin arrest in 1973 – reports the police later retracted.

When the US-Ireland extradition treaty was signed and Joe was arrested in January 1985, Joey was 21 years old, fresh from college and living at home in Rochester and working at a car dealership. ('My profession out of high school was auto repair. Go figure, right?') His mother showed him the article about Joe's arrest.

'Oh my God,' she said. 'Did you see this?'

Rochester was a small city, and this was a big event. For weeks the story was all over the news: on TV, radio and in print. Joey's mind raced into overdrive. If they brought Joe back to the US, should he reach out and visit him? He didn't know. There was no way he was able to see him in Ireland. 'I didn't have the means to do that.'

By the time of the treaty breakdown, 18 months later, Joey lost interest. He found it a non-event, and he didn't lose sleep over it. As the years continued, after he moved to Florida and met Donna, who he married in 1990, he kept the story to himself.

'It was just something I never really talked about. I don't know. Maybe because we grew up with the stigma attached. I just never advertised it.'

After Joey told Donna about his pre-1967 life, she called the producer of *Unsolved Mysteries*, Stuart Schwartz, and asked for a videotape of the Joe Maloney episode. Schwartz promised to send a tape after the episode aired the following week, which he did. The producer told them that June's family, the Fisks, dearly wanted to contact Joey, as they had drifted out of contact over the years. But Joey didn't feel ready for this level of reconnection with his past. 'We were young, starting a family, and it just wasn't our time,' he explained.

After hanging up, Joey and Donna received a call from the FBI, who wanted to know who they were, what they knew about the case and if Joe had ever contacted them. The couple knew nothing, but they found it interesting how the feds wasted no time in getting in touch.

* * *

Irish politicians were outraged when the extradition treaty collapsed. 'Despite fanfares' it wasn't 'worth the paper it was written on,' Michael Woods, Fianna Fáil TD for Dublin North-East, raged in the Irish parliament. Woods lambasted the government's 'clumsy mishandling' of the case and labelled it a fiasco. Liam Hyland, a politician from Laois, argued that the treaty's collapse raised doubts about Ireland's 'capacity and willingness to come to grips with international crime'.

James Gilliland and Joe Maloney had 'driven a coach through the terms of the treaty because of our failure in this House,' he claimed. Gillian Hussey, the Irish judge who'd approved Joe's extradition, was also discouraged: 'I thought

I was dealing with an extradition and apparently I wasn't. It wasn't a proper extradition.'

The treaty was ratified in February 1987. Irish police were tipped off 12 weeks in advance and started looking for Maloney, but they were too late. He was gone, and his wife Sheila was gone too, and nobody, least of all the prosecutors, were surprised. 'It was really disappointing,' remarked Wendy Lehmann. 'We wanted to bring justice for the person he had murdered. That's what prosecutors do. They bring justice for the victims. That's what we were trying to do, and it seemed to be slipping away.'

John Mulderrig, Joe's arresting officer, tried not to be frustrated. The way he reasoned it, the courts made decisions he disagreed with, and that was their business. In his estimation, Joe 'got as far out of Dún Laoghaire and possibly Ireland as he could. Then he most likely repeated what he did when he came here: taking on a new identity that would be hard to trace, which took [his disappearance] a step further. It definitely does take a con mind to do what Maloney did, from the identity he took on and the troubles he must have gone to.'

Authorities considered the type of assistance Joe might have received in order to escape from Ireland. Special Agent Gene Harding had been aware of the Joe Maloney warrant since he joined the Rochester branch of the FBI in 1980. He took over the case a couple of years later and was tasked with locating the fugitive after the treaty collapse. In the FBI office in Rochester, there was a theory that Joe had had assistance from the Irish Republican Army (IRA).

'I think there was some information we had received which led us to believe that at the time. The prevailing thought on the street from a number of individuals was he was getting assistance from the IRA in Ireland to go underground.'

Joe may have encountered the IRA during his time at Capard House. The local area in County Laois was a hotbed of rebel activity. In 1975, Dutch industrialist Tiede Herrema was kidnapped by the IRA, blindfolded, moved about by car and held for over a week at a safe house in Mountmellick, a few miles from Capard. O'Shea, with his guns and knowledge of explosives and vast swathes of land, would have proven useful to the Republican movement, and they in turn could have assisted him in finding him false documentation for his out-of-state travels prior to 1985.

'IRA connections?' said Tony Gilfoyle, who worked at Capard. 'Oh, I'd say he had. I definitely say he had.'

FBI Agent Harding explored every avenue. He issued wanted posters to regional bureau offices around the US using Joe's 1967 mug shot and physical description: 'scar over his right eyebrow', 'red hair, blue eyes'. Harding sought publicity for the case on prime-time TV, where re-enactment crime shows had proven successful in leading to the capture of fugitives.

In 1989, *America's Most Wanted* profiled John Emil List, a man who murdered his wife, mother and three children in New Jersey in 1971 before vanishing. Following the show's broadcast, a viewer identified List as a man posing under another identity in Richmond, Virginia.

'*Unsolved Mysteries* and *America's Most Wanted* were very popular,' remembered Harding. 'In consultation with the local authorities in Monroe County District Attorney's Office and the US Attorney's Office, the FBI said, "Let's give this a shot. Maybe there's a chance people watching this would have some information and we could generate new leads."'

Thomas Bush, who worked in the FBI Fugitive Unit, was also a fan of these shows. 'There's a right time to get publicity. Sometimes it's not right after an incident, it just depends on the type of crime. But the public has always been another tool in the toolbox of helping us apprehend bad guys.'

Unsolved Mysteries was keen to get involved. 'A hideous crime has been committed. And that's the type of case they're looking for,' Harding told the *Democrat & Chronicle* newspaper before the episode featuring June's alleged murder. 'If we can get the latest possible information and the latest possible pictures, I think this has a good chance.'

Neal Dunkleberg, assistant DA Wendy Lehmann and Wanda Mordenga were among those interviewed, and Neal testified to Joe's coercive control and domestic abuse: 'June confided in me that Joe had roughed her up a couple of times. He didn't hit her. She wasn't bruised, but he wasn't above . . . turning bright red, and jumping around, hollering and yelling and looking very dangerous. And perhaps grabbing hold of her and shaking her. And that's pretty intimidating.'

He described Joe's visit to his basement, in which he 'showed interest in one particular chemical: a clear liquid which is odourless, tasteless and lethal when ingested in sufficient amounts'. And he explained how Joe showed up at the house a few days later and 'sweet-talked his sister' into letting him into the laboratory and giving him poison.

The episode of *Unsolved Mysteries* re-enacted June's death, detailed Joe's dubious explanations that it was attempted suicide, his escape from the Rochester hospital and subsequent discovery in Ireland. 'Incredibly, the twisted odyssey of Joseph Maloney was not over,' announced the narrator, Robert Stack, at the episode's denouement, before detailing the collapse of the US-Ireland extradition pact.

Two years later, in 1993, the story was profiled on *America's Most Wanted*. Karen, one of two daughters from Joe's first marriage to Joan Howland, had moved in her early twenties from

New England to Texas, where she was married and had children. Karen's mother had kept the story of Joe's arrest in Ireland hidden from her, and Joey was unaware of Karen's existence, so she was oblivious to events surrounding her biological father since 1967. She was watching TV at home when a bulletin appeared for *America's Most Wanted*, featuring a man who gave his wife a drink laced with methyl alcohol on their son's fifth birthday.

'Wow,' she announced to her kids, 'that must be my dad.'

* * *

A flurry of tips came in from viewers after *Unsolved Mysteries* and *America's Most Wanted*, and FBI agent Gene Harding travelled to the studios in Los Angeles to assess their credibility. One viewer claimed to have seen Joe in Puerto Rica; another thought he was in Jamaica. The investigators thought Canada was a likely bolthole. (Sheila's sister lived in Canada, as did Joe's friend Brian Hanlon, but neither the sister nor the doctor claimed to have any idea where he'd fled.) 'I heard on the grapevine South America,' suggested Hanlon. Another former colleague suggested Malta, the island where Joe had worked on *Remington Steele* in 1984 and abandoned his camera tracking vehicle. None of these tips amounted to anything.

'My recollection,' said Harding, 'is we didn't have any positive leads.'

The FBI kept tabs on Joe's associates in Ireland through their legal attaché office in the UK and the US Embassy in Dublin, who in turn liaised with the Irish police and government. 'They exchanged information, kept files and records, and acted on any leads,' explained FBI agent Tom Bush. They seemed acutely aware of Joe's inner circle in Ireland, frequently questioning people like Bishop Michael Cox.

'There was an agent from the American Embassy who used to visit me to ask for information about Michael O'Shea,' recalled Cox. 'I wouldn't have any information for him, of course. [As a priest] I can't interfere with things like that with the state.'

The FBI was aware of Rod Fenning's importance in Joe's life. In the early 1990s, Rod's brother-in-law was working in Mexico when an FBI agent contacted him and asked if he knew of Joe's whereabouts. The brother-in-law knew nothing. Another agent interrogated Olga, Rod's youngest sister, who lived in California.

'It was very tiring talking to the feds, because they kept asking questions and then they'd ask them again in case you changed what you said,' Olga told me during the making of *Runaway Joe*. The agent phoned on Olga's birthday, and she asked if he'd like to come to her party that evening. He declined over the phone but turned up on the night. A friend answered the door, asked who he was and, upon hearing he was FBI, slammed the door in his face.

Gene Harding and his colleagues in Rochester routinely checked to make sure their state warrant for Joe's arrest remained active, and New York's state department periodically asked the Monroe County District Attorney's office if they were still willing to proceed with extradition and prosecution if Joe was found. The DA also checked with witnesses to see if they were willing to testify. They were, so the warrant remained active . . . for now.

Some people in Rochester still feared Joe Maloney, including Dale, June's brother. 'My parents were concerned about his whereabouts and if he would ever come back to the United States,' said Dale's daughter, June's niece, Amy Emerick. 'I think that did bother them for a time. They were afraid for our family's safety because he's a dangerous man.'

Even prosecutor Wendy Lehmann felt haunted by Joe. In the 1990s, she returned to Ireland with her husband Gary for a vacation themed around sites relevant to St Patrick. During their travels they visited Rosenallis, home to Joe's former property, Capard House, in County Laois. 'We were in a restaurant that night and there was a party of several people and I just remembered this man's eyes. Maloney's eyes were very distinctive. I remember a man looking at me with those eyes. I got scared and we left. Piercing. I can't really describe it. And he had a grey beard. I tend to think it was my imagination, but I don't know.'

Over time fears faded. People moved on with their lives. Gene Harding retired from the FBI in 1997. Joe Maloney's case files were secreted in five or six large cardboard boxes and tucked away in a storage room at the DA's office in Rochester. Once in a while, when there was a suspected sighting, the files were resurrected, but those occasions became more and more infrequent. Dust gathered, and details of the case were forgotten.

It was a situation that suited Joe Maloney and his wife Sheila Chandler just fine.

*   *   *

On a hot summer's day in 2001, a young Englishman walked into the foyer of a post office in Ames, Iowa. Serendipity or maybe plain bad luck brought him here. The previous day he'd been caught jumping a train boxcar, was arrested and thrown into the county jail for the night.

Michael Nagy, known to his friends as Mike, was a drifter and a nomad, a man driven by wanderlust. He had grown up in Cambridge, England, and excelled in music as a child, learning piano, violin, viola and organ, and singing in choirs at Westminster Abbey and Durham University. Education (a degree from Durham and a Master's at Bradford) gave way to travel, and he abandoned his classical instruments for an acoustic guitar and a mouth organ in the manner of his idols Woody Guthrie and Bob Dylan.

Once he left, he never returned on a full-time basis to Cambridge, but instead travelled the world teaching English, busking on the street and cadging paid gigs in bars and restaurants. He taught English in Slovakia, Mexico, Hungary and Taiwan, worked labouring jobs in Guatemala and travelled light across America's great sprawl, hitchhiking and living out of a rucksack, riding boxcars and relying on the kindness of strangers for accommodation and food. It was not an easy life, but he found it liberating.

Nagy stared at a board pinned to the wall of the post office that displayed a long list of fugitives from justice. It intrigued him. The oldest poster on the board dated back to 1967: Joseph Michael Maloney. Thirty-four years on the run. How had he managed that? Had he been recaptured or died long ago? The man speculated for a moment and then moved on.

This was the spark behind Nagy's hunt for Joe Maloney. What drove him? Innate curiosity and something to aspire to: a goal, a purpose in an existence that in his thirties was becoming increasingly less tenable. Maybe he had a future as a successful novelist, maybe a documentary maker? Perhaps finding Joe Maloney was his ticket to a new start in life.

Nagy recounted his investigation in a series of emails sent to Linda Chamberlain, one of June's classmates at Albion High. Nagy asked that Chamberlain pass on his discoveries to June's other friends, and his emails are reprinted here in abridged form.

From: Mike Nagy
To: Linda Chamberlain
Subject: MIKE NAGY, MALONEY FISK STORY

Well, here is the first instalment. Over the next 12 days I hope to send you the complete story, though please bear in mind that power cuts can and do occur with frustrating irregularity where I am.

Reunions are exciting affairs giving people a chance to share memories, relive precious moments and renew old friendships. At the same time all of you will be aware of those of you who are not or cannot be present. Death is cruel enough when it strikes in middle age but when your life is taken at the age of 26 it seems totally unjustifiable. I am referring of course to June Fisk and the grisly circumstances that surround her death.

Poisoned by wood alcohol at her son's fifth birthday party in May 1967. An accident? No. Suicide? Hardly. Murder? Most probably. The poisoner? Undeniably her estranged husband Joseph Michael Maloney.

From: Mike Nagy
To: Linda Chamberlain
Subject: ENTER THE BIOGRAPHER

A year elapsed [after seeing Joe's wanted poster in Iowa] before I was in a library in 2002 wasting time on the internet. For the sheer hell of it, I keyed in Maloney's full name on the internet and up came an International Crime Alert giving me a brief outline of an intriguing case. A party in Rochester, June Maloney's agonising death, his escape from custody, his arrest in Ireland 18 years later, where he had assumed the alias Michael O'Shea, and his subsequent release and disappearance with his new wife Sheila. If he was still alive he was 67. I tried to visualise the scene of the crime.

I was due to fly back to Britain a month later and decided I'd pay a visit to Rochester to do some research with a view to writing an article on the case. (An elderly astrologer had once told me, when I was a disbelieving 25-year-old that I could write thrillers. Maybe there was a grain of truth in his words after all). Rochester's Central Library proved to be a mine of information providing me with a background, facts, and names of important people to contact. Soon I was having lunch with Maloney's old buddy Neal Dunkleberg, and later with his former apprentice David Farrell. Dunkleberg was inclined to suspect Maloney was dead; Farrell felt he was alive. From what they told me I was quite convinced neither of them or any of his family had heard from Joe since his escape in 1967. Both agreed that if he had kept in contact with anybody from Rochester it would have been with Warren Daansen.

I made trips to photograph Maloney's boyhood home on Linden Street, the crime and escape scene, and Brockport Cemetery where June Maloney was reburied on the first anniversary of her death. I made a flying visit to Albion but nobody in the library remembered her or the case. Genesee Hospital had also since closed but the archivist responsible for handling its records provided a photo of June Maloney.

Feeling confident, I contacted *Master Detective* magazine. They had done a feature on Maloney in 1973 and knew nothing about his subsequent recapture in 1985 and release the following year. My optimism in their initial enthusiasm proved to be unfounded.

I then tried to interest a TV station about making a documentary about my search for Joe Maloney but they rejected me on the grounds that it might be dangerous were I to find him. In my idle moments I wondered if he was still alive and with Sheila O'Shea who was ten years younger. Given that she wasn't wanted for anything I figured she would almost certainly keep in contact with her family and maybe even visit them. And maybe Joe did too on a false passport. Maybe they had even returned to the very different Ireland of today where people can lead anonymous lives in new suburbs on the edge of Dublin.

* * *

Over the winter of 2002, Nagy travelled to Dublin, where he spent Christmas and New Year, between his shifts as a cleaner at Dublin Airport, 'observing' the Chandler house on Arkendale Road in the hope that Sheila might show up. It resulted in nothing other than 'shivering and feeling rather silly', he wrote. Instead, his breakthrough came by accident. He was hitchhiking into Dublin when a woman stopped to offer him a ride. By coincidence, the woman was from Dalkey and had known Joe in the 1980s.

Nagy and the woman went to a café, and she gave him the names of Rod Fenning and a painter and decorator who worked with Joe until the time of his arrest. The painter told Nagy how his former boss 'could convince you that night was day', 'never had the change to buy a newspaper', was 'forever scrounging tea and biscuits off his workers' and 'invariably paid the wages weeks in arrears'. With his savings from the airport job, Nagy paid a private investigator to track down Sheila, providing him with her date of birth and maiden name. The investigator traced a woman of the same name to County Meath. 'Sensational news,' wrote Nagy. Only it wasn't. When he investigated the suspect, Nagy realised the detective had identified a younger woman of the same name. Were Joe and Sheila really in Ireland? Unlikely. It was only when Mike Nagy paid a visit to Capard House (which had by now been purchased by a legitimate antiques dealer from Dublin) that his investigation grew legs.

From: Mike Nagy
To: Linda Chamberlain
Subject: ENTER THE BIOGRAPHER (CONT'D)

Strolling up the half mile long driveway of Capard House I bumped into a gamekeeper who smiled when I explained I was trying to locate the property's former owner.

'Captain O'Shea I presume. You'd better come this way.'

I was led into a kitchen where Joe's former housekeeper, Erika Lotze, was enjoying a cigarette. Michael O'Shea, as she knew him, was a confusing topic. On the one hand she'd been well treated by her former employer and she liked him a great deal. On the other, from her dealings with the journalists that visited her following his arrest, she believed the evidence against him and was appalled by what he had done. Then she told me what I wanted and by now probably needed to know.

'After Michael's release in 1986, Rod Fenning helped smuggle him out of the country on a trawler.

Michael and Sheila made it across mainland Europe to East Berlin where they lived until 1990. Rod Fenning has since got a job at the British Embassy but he still hears from them from time to time. All their money has gone. Sheila now has a tumour on her head which they can't afford to treat and so she wears a wig to disguise it.

They're in Cyprus. Please don't tell him I told you.'

15.

Behind the Wall

WHEN I STARTED MAKING THE *RUNAWAY JOE* PODCAST SERIES WITH RTÉ'S *DOCUMENTARY ON ONE* TEAM, THE AFTERMATH OF JOE'S ESCAPE FROM IRELAND WAS UNKNOWN. I'd been drawn to the case after reading an excerpt from the autobiography of Gillian Hussey, the judge who ordered Joe's extradition from Ireland in 1985, but neither she nor the Monroe County District Attorney's Office in Rochester nor the FBI had a clue where Joe and Sheila went after the treaty collapsed. The arrival of a package from Rochester serendipitously sent to me by one of June Fisk's friends, a package that contained the writings of Michael Nagy, changed all that.

From the outset our ambition was to find justice for June. With help from Nagy's 20-year-old investigation I was able to peel back more layers of the onion.

The mystery began after Joe's release from custody on 24 July 1986. Patrick Fenning told me how his brother Rod, after collecting

'Michael' outside the High Court in Dublin, drove him to the west of Ireland. A hotel or bed and breakfast was unlikely given the media coverage about the extradition treaty's collapse. The destination, Patrick suspected, was a house in Westport, County Mayo, owned by Rod's mother and which the family once used as a holiday home.

'Nobody ever went down there anymore. It was haunted. It had life-sized statues of the Virgin Mary all over the place. It was a weird kind of place. Sneak down there and nobody would have noticed.'

Patrick believed Joe 'took a few days to rest, get some decent food and recuperate, get a haircut and a change of clothes and off he was gone.'

Others confirmed Nagy's revelation, which he heard from Erika Lotze, that Joe escaped Ireland on a trawler. 'He didn't take a boat or a plane,' said Brian Hanlon, Joe's doctor friend. 'He used a trawler.' Rod told his partner Melinda the same thing. 'Rod told me there was a few of them involved in his escape. Rod said to me, "He left by boat". He went out to sea.' From where? 'I imagine Coliemore Harbour or Bullock Harbour.'

Both were small ports in Dalkey. Hanlon agreed that his departure point was probably Dalkey or Dún Laoghaire, 'because Michael used to work on the trawlers there'. I spoke to an old fisherman working out of a shed at Bullock, and he remembered Michael O'Shea, describing him as 'mad', but he insisted he knew nothing about his escape on a boat.

In making the documentary, we followed the money trail. How could Joe have paid for safe passage to England and life on the run without any cash? Before fleeing Ireland, Joe had spent 18 months in prison, and he faced large legal fees for his court defence and appeals. In his Garda arrest report, Detective Inspector John Mulderrig wrote that 'Maloney, alias O'Shea, was in financial difficulties when arrested'. Marylands, Arkendale Road, the house he lived in until late 1984 before moving to Kent Terrace, Dalkey, was rented accommodation, where Joe was 'in arrears of rent to the tune of £7,000'. When Maloney moved to Kent Terrace, according to Mulderrig's report, he 'sublet the premises on the pretence that he owned it'. Debt was nothing new for Joe Maloney, and financial difficulties never perturbed him in Ireland or Rochester. He owed the builder Peter Collins and his partner Frans Jansen another £7,000 for their work on the house in Castletown in Laois.

'We never got that money,' said Collins.

Joe's ambition during his house renovation frenzy of 1983 and 1984 was never to pay back his debtors. Instead, he appears to have been tucking money away and fled Ireland with a sizeable amount. Brian Hanlon learned that Sheila was complicit in aiding and abetting her husband to escape to a country without extradition: 'He couldn't do it from prison, and by the time he got out of prison, he was gone from Ireland within a week. So there had to be preparatory work done on the outside, and the only one who could have done that was Sheila.'

Witnesses recalled Sheila frantically trying to sell and auction off every item they owned while her husband was behind bars. She sold the freshly renovated Kent Terrace for £62,000, a house she'd bought three years beforehand from her aunt Isabel Grimson for £15,000. The sale agreement included Joe's counter-signature, presumably written in Portlaoise Prison. In a remarkable stroke of luck, the sale went through on 23 July 1986 – the day before the extradition treaty collapsed and Joe was released from Portlaoise.

Sheila's father allegedly assisted in paying Joe's legal fees, so it's not unreasonable to believe that, including the estimated £55,000 from the sale of the house in Castletown, he escaped

Ireland with £100,000. It was a mirror image of Joe's behaviour in 1967, cashing fraudulent cheques after escaping the Rochester hospital – amassing enough collateral to allow him to flee one country and set up a new life in another.

* * *

For a few weeks after Joe disappeared from Ireland in 1986, locals witnessed Sheila driving around the Dalkey area in a Mini-type car. She was renting accommodation in the local area, making preparations while the money came through from the sale of the house on Kent Terrace and waiting for her husband to get established in whatever country he was in. Eventually, she left Ireland to join him.

Erika Lotze, as per Michael Nagy's testimony, described how they initially relocated to East Berlin, which at the time was part of the German Democratic Republic (GDR) within the Soviet Union and beyond the reach of Western law enforcement. While stories tell of defectors from the East, some people moved in the opposite direction – most of them East German citizens who returned home because of homesickness or because they couldn't find a decent life in the West.

People from western regions were rarely integrated into the GDR, but there were exceptions. Around 200 NATO soldiers who deserted from the service came to the GDR, some of them for personal reasons, such as love. For others, it was ideological. Dean Reed, an American movie star and musician with communist sympathies, permanently relocated to East Germany in 1973. Another defector was Victor Grossman, a US soldier from Buffalo who was posted to Austria, where he swam across the Danube into the Soviet-occupied zone of Austria in 1952 due to McCarthy-era fear of prosecution over his membership of left-wing groups. Grossman earned his living in East Berlin as a journalist and a translator.

A number of Joe and Sheila's associates in Ireland heard rumours that they fled to East Germany, and among them was the filmmaker and lawyer Maurice O'Callaghan. Joe had friends in Ireland who were German and, according to Bishop Michael Cox, he had conversational fluency in the language. Neville James (who befriended Joe during his Capard House days) was also surprised to learn that the owner of the Laois estate was bilingual.

'My father had this theory,' remembered Fiona, his daughter. 'He said, "I think he went to East Germany". And I was like, "Why do you think he went to East Germany?" And he said, "Because I heard him speaking German fluently on the phone. I think he has contacts over there."'

How did Joe learn the language? Erika Lotze had a side hustle teaching people the language on the estate, and she tutored both him and Sheila (who was already versed in the language, having studied it after school). 'I heard him speak German,' confirmed Tony Gilfoyle, who worked on the estate. 'He was fluent. Mrs Lotze taught him and Sheila. Mrs Lotze had a birthday party up there and we all dressed up in German suits. O'Shea brought two lads from Germany and Bishop Cox. They came to the party and spoke German all night. They could be talking about you, they could be talking about me. I don't know who they were talking about.'

Lotze's ex-husband had lived in East Germany. Did Joe's former housekeeper, who visited Joe with Sheila when he was incarcerated at Portlaoise, give them contacts in East Berlin? Whatever Lotze's involvement, Joe and Sheila would have faced a grilling upon arrival at the East Berlin checkpoint. From there they would have been taken to Röntgental, a central admission centre and interrogation camp north of Berlin. Foreigners or returning GDR citizens could be kept at the camp for 30 days or more and were questioned about their lives in the West to ensure they were not spies.

I visited the Stasi Records Archive, part of the Federal Archive of Germany, in Berlin to learn more. 'A third of all the people that tried to move to the GDR were rejected,' Oskar Böhm, a clerk at the archive, told me. 'They didn't take everyone.'

During their interrogation, two factors may have worked in Joe and Sheila's favour: they both spoke German and they potentially had a connection in East Berlin. 'By speaking German it would be easier to convince the people who interrogated you about why you were coming and why you were motivated to be integrated in the socialist society,' said Böhm. Joe – an expert in demolitions, car mechanics and weaponry – may have been of use. As Brian Hanlon once said, 'Wherever he went, he would have been able to make a living because he had a knack of doing things. He wasn't stupid. He was very strong.'

But living in the Soviet Union came at a price. GDR was tightly controlled by the Stasi, a secret police who kept their citizens under close surveillance. That monitoring, explained Böhm, was undertaken 'where you worked and where you lived. All around you people might have worked unofficially for the Stasi. They collected information, they wrote information about you. That's how the Stasi was always aware what you're up to. Your colleagues, your friends, your neighbours might have worked for the Stasi.'

Rückkehrer (returnees), the people who came back from Federal Germany, and people from Western countries and defectors were kept under the strictest surveillance.

If Joe and Sheila were in East Berlin, the Stasi knew.

The Stasi maintained a complex index card filing system, which the archives used to trace records. Using Joe and Sheila's names and dates of birth (with two sets of details for Joe, including ones for his pseudonym Michael O'Shea), Böhm searched the system and found what he initially thought was a match. But ultimately we couldn't find information of Joe or Sheila's time in the GDR during the making of the *Runaway Joe* podcast.

I faced an Everest-sized obstacle in tracking their movements. What if they were using new fake identification and fake names? During his time in Ireland, Joe had travelled to the UK, across Europe and even to Canada, despite the existence of an international warrant for the arrest of a Joseph Maloney and Michael O'Shea. Was he travelling under a third, as-yet-unknown identity in order to evade detection?

Tom Bush, who was part of the fugitive-hunting division at the FBI, believed so. 'I'd have to assume he had some false identification, that he was falsifying his visa application, his travel documents and had somehow obtained a passport,' said Bush. 'I don't know to what level of sophistication it was, but it would have been a different name.'

There was another distinct possibility: Joe had been turned away from East Berlin. Westerners were treated with extreme suspicion, and Joe, despite his charm and spiel, may not have been convincing enough to persuade the Stasi. Victor Grossman, who, I discovered, was still alive and writing in his 90s, did not recall encountering Joe. 'Although I was in Berlin at that time and there may be parallels in our stories, including even the closeness of Rochester and Buffalo, I have no recollection of the fellow you are looking for,' he said. 'There were not too many Anglophone people in East Berlin, and we generally knew each other. If he was in East Berlin, he may well have avoided such circles.'

But even if Joe and Sheila had somehow connived themselves into the GDR and laid low, their stay in the region would have been cut short. In late 1989, the Berlin Wall fell. Germany was reunified, leaving anyone hiding behind the Soviet Bloc facing the hot glare of the West.

*   *   *

Rumours in Ireland suggested Joe and Sheila moved around before settling in one location. Some friends speculated Malta. This was where Joe abandoned his camera tracking vehicle on the set of *Remington Steele* in 1984. Rod Fenning told his partner Melinda that they spent time working on a kibbutz in Israel. 'He could have been hidden away on the kibbutz,' said Melinda. 'Nobody's going to come looking for you there, you just sort of blend in.'

Neither lead proved fruitful when I looked into them, and neither location was secure from international law enforcement: both had extradition arrangements with America. This left us with the destination of which Erika Lotze told Mike Nagy – a location off the grid and without extradition to the West. A place that Nagy visited, and where he uncovered vital information about Joe and Sheila's years on the run: North Cyprus.

16.

Enter the Bounty Hunter

MIKE NAGY LEFT IRELAND IN THE SUMMER OF 2003, CERTAIN HE'D COME CLOSER THAN ANYONE ELSE TO DISCOVERING JOE MALONEY'S FINAL DESTINATION. He felt he had nothing to lose by following his hunches and flying to North Cyprus while still enthused. If all else failed, he could make a living there playing music in bars and restaurants. Before leaving, he penned two identical letters, one to Rod Fenning (who he'd met for a pint in Sandycove in south Dublin, but who was reluctant to offer information about Joe and Sheila) and the other to Sheila's family on Arkendale Road – announcing he'd be in North Cyprus in two weeks' time and would be happy to meet 'Michael' or Sheila for lunch at Niazi's restaurant close to the harbour in the city of Girne. He suggested two separate meeting dates in case the first didn't work out.

Cyprus is in the Eastern Mediterranean close to the Turkish mainland and Syria, a place with a millennia-old history of conflict. The island was ruled at various stages by the ancient Greeks and the ancient Egyptians. The Roman Empire controlled Cyprus for almost 400 years before the Byzantium Empire and then the Ottomans, under the Turks, stepped in. By the turn of the 20th century it was the turn of the British Empire. The island was divided then by people who identified as either Turkish Cypriots or Greek Cypriots. During the 1950s an armed Greek Cypriot militia group fought to rid the island of British colonial rule and unify Cyprus with Greece. Britain withdrew in 1960 following the signing of a treaty that established an independent Cyprus, jointly governed by the Turks and the Greeks. Greek Cypriot extremists, unhappy with this shared solution, overthrew the president and launched a violent uprising against their Turkish counterparts, prompting Turkey to send 40,000 troops to the north coast of the island in 1974.

A truce was eventually enacted, prompting the creation of two separate states divided by a 112-mile UN peace line. To the south: Greek Cyprus, part of the European Union from 1981. In the north, the Turkish Republic of Northern Cyprus (TRNC). For the most part, TRNC was a peaceful and welcoming place where residents left their doors unlocked and crime rates (petty ones at least) barely registered.

Nagy settled in quickly, finding down-at-heel lodgings in a cheap pension. He had a few days to kill before his first meeting at Niazi's, and he split his time between trying to get gigs in bars and restaurants and showing a photograph of Joe (given to him by Pat McMahon, the Irish film industry armourer) to long-term residents. There were no plausible leads.

From: Mike Nagy
To: Linda Chamberlain
Subject: ENTER THE BOUNTY HUNTER

It was a hotter day than usual when I walked down the quiet streets to Niazi's an hour before the appointment. I chose to sit at a cafe opposite. If Maloney were to show up at least it would give me the element of surprise. I drank a coffee and then another. A yellow Fiat full of young people and a film camera on the back seat went by. I was so absorbed watching them, I scarcely paid any attention to a woman who stopped by a parked car and turned to take a good look inside the restaurant before walking on.

The second appointment wasn't for another four days. Sunday was even hotter than Wednesday and I'd still not gotten around to buying suitable clothing. Dripping with sweat I decided to stand outside Niazi's so there could be no mistaking my arrival. Almost an hour had gone by when from around the corner came the same rather peculiar looking lady who'd passed by before. From about 15 yards away she fished a mobile phone out of her handbag.

'He's here,' she said, loud enough for me to hear before walking straight by me speaking Turkish.

Dark glasses covered her face, her head covered by a wig. A wig! It had to be.

'Sheila,' I cried out, but she carried on walking, quickening her pace.

Instead of hurrying after her I watched her until she disappeared. The encounter was almost a confirmation that she and Maloney were both alive and living in North Cyprus.

Now I had the daunting task of finding them in any one of the hundreds of villages spread out across a 150 mile diameter.

Nagy described his next few months in Cyprus as a catalogue of failures. Following his sighting of Sheila, he penned two more identical letters to Rod Fenning and Sheila's family. 'Only this time more out of frustration than malice, and probably to my detriment, I lied.'

He claimed he was not acting alone and that his 'assistants' had followed Sheila and 'got some interesting pictures'. Nagy told Linda Chamberlain in an email that he was not vindictive but that he couldn't walk away from his investigation empty-handed. In the letters, he 'strongly advised' Rod and Sheila's family to tell Sheila to attend another meeting at the same venue in two weeks' time or he would reconsider his options, 'which included going to the press or the police'. Unsurprisingly, Sheila didn't show up at the proposed time.

Nagy asked around boating businesses, auction rooms and gun clubs. He took out an advertisement in the local newspaper, *Cyprus Today*, and made inquiries in TRNC's German community in case Joe and Sheila's suspected time in East Germany had given them roots there. He even showed Joe's picture to people in the local Roman Catholic Church in case Joe's involvement with Bishop Cox in Ireland had inspired him to keep the faith.

Nagy was no fool, but he knew how he must have appeared. 'To the majority I came across as an idiot or a nutter. Even within the minority, a lot assumed I was related to June Maloney and wanting revenge.' Sometimes his persistence paid off. Denise Phillips, an expat from Britain who presented an interview programme for Bayrak Radio and Television Corporation (BRTK), the national broadcaster in TRNC, interviewed him about his hunt for the fugitive.

Nagy provided a detailed background on the case and played a song he'd written about it called 'The Ballad of Joe Maloney'.

The presenter was unsure if Nagy was having her on, but he won her over with his oddball charm. 'We didn't know whether this was true or not,' said Denise. 'It was such a good story, though, and he told it so well. I erred on the side of believing him, but I couldn't do any sort of research to find out. I met him several times afterwards because he used to play around some of the bars. He was always out and about working, busking, singing for his supper. Everybody loved him. He was just such a lovely chap.'

With his search reaching a dead end in Cyprus, Nagy flew back to America, where he returned to his usual pattern of 'working odd jobs in odd places alongside odd people'. In time he was drawn back to Rochester, where he learned that Joe's younger brother, James, had died in 1998. He visited Aquinas School, which Joe attended, and met Joe's friend Warren Daansen, who claimed to have no clue were Joe was hiding out.

'When you meet him please say "hi" to him from me,' Daansen told Nagy.

From: Mike Nagy
To: Linda Chamberlain
Subject: ENTER THE BOUNTY HUNTER (CONT'D)

Linda, here is my final e-mail. Hope you enjoy the high school reunion. Let me know if you can get any new information out to me.

Browsing on the Internet, I discovered that since Maloney had appeared on the FBI Most Wanted List twice his finder was technically entitled to two $50,000 rewards. Maybe it was time to switch from biographer to bounty hunter and hope he was not acting as a gun dealer between the local mafia and the IRA. Assuming he was still in North Cyprus that is.

A forthcoming referendum to decide the future of Cyprus was causing many fugitives to have sleepless nights. The referendum had been called for both Greek and Turkish Cypriots to vote on whether they wanted to end the partition. North Cyprus would be no more, the embargo would go, and extradition would come in. In April 2004, the Turks voted Yes [but] the Greeks voted No, leaving the north out in the cold. For the time being at least Maloney is still safe.

It was a loathsome obligation to leave America once more but I resolved to return to North Cyprus with the proviso that if I didn't find him this time then I would give up on the case. I knew I could earn a living playing in bars and restaurants around Girne. At the same time I could not afford to get too distracted in looking for a man who has already outlived his brother in spite of spending the greater part of it on the run.

In the past two months in Cyprus I am still running into plenty of new people that have been living here for years. There's a chance that one of them will recognise Maloney. Of course I might have walked past him in the street, by his front door or even spoken to him. Just about every possible scenario has gone on through my mind. Were I to find him I sense my actions would depend as much on his reactions and state of health and mind as it would on my initiatives. I would like to hear his account of what happened all those years ago. Could I come from nowhere and succeed where everybody else has failed and bring Joe Maloney back to Rochester to stand trial for the murder of his wife 37 years ago?

The messages ended there. In July 2004, Nagy gave a second and final interview to BRTK in North Cyprus, in which he seemed despondent and admitting defeat.

'I was trying the write the biography of this man who I believe might be living in North Cyprus,' he told the interviewer. 'His original name is Joseph Michael Maloney. He's eluded me. It would make a very interesting life story. With that project shelved, I've refocused my energies into music and playing in bars and restaurants around North Cyprus.'

A few months later, Nagy had an article published in *Cyprus Times*, a regional newspaper. He described this as 'his last chance to solve a fascinating real life murder mystery'. But nothing came of his appeal for readers to dish up information about Joe's location. His time in North Cyprus had reached an end – and so too had his search for Joe Maloney. Nagy returned to Ireland, where he worked odd jobs, played music for money and learned the Irish language in his spare time.

In the summer of 2006, two years after leaving TRNC, he was hired as a piano player at a hotel on the shores of the Atlantic in the wilds of Connemara, County Galway. Shortly before noon on Sunday, 10 September, Nagy spoke to the hotel's deputy manager while practising piano in the restaurant area. He was to provide the music for a wedding party that evening and was popping out, but he assured the manager he'd be back by 6pm. Only he never returned.

On the morning of 27 September 2006, 17 days after Mike Nagy went missing, a farmer from Louisburgh in County Mayo was driving his tractor along the seashore when he noticed what he thought was a sheep resting on the sand. Upon his return he had a closer inspection and was shocked to discover the body of a man. The body was removed from the strand and identified as Michael Nagy. A post-mortem carried out the following day found his most likely cause of death was asphyxia due to drowning.

At an inquest, investigators theorised he'd been trying to swim out to an island off the Connemara coast but had underestimated the power of the tide and had drowned, and his body had been swept to a beach 14 miles north of the place where he entered the sea.

Mike Nagy was 39 years and ten days old when he died.

Family and friends, many of them in North Cyprus, mourned his loss, and spoke of his energy, his enthusiasm and his worldliness. For me he was a fellow investigator, a colleague even. We never met, but were united across time in the same campaign: find Joe; get justice for June.

'Mike was such a gentle soul: an old soul,' said Denise Phillips, the presenter at BRTK radio. 'I really do believe that somewhere, on some level, he knows about this renewed investigation into Joe Maloney and he's happy the story's carrying on and that he was on the right track. It seemed to be a bit of an obsession with him. I don't know, but I think it's a little bit like that for you as well, Pavel.'

17.

Where I Live, I Don't Exist

February 2025

A VEIL OF DUST ROSE BEFORE ME AS I DROVE THE COASTAL ROAD OF NORTH CYPRUS EAST TOWARDS THE MUNICIPALITY OF ÇATALKÖY. Cars, trucks, trailers, tractors and other jalopies in differing states of disrepair filled both directions of the two-way thoroughfare, moving at a crawl even though rush hour was hours away. Buses honked their horns at people wandering beside the strip, inviting them to get onboard. The occasional hitchhiker stuck his thumb up like it was 1976.

Lining the sides of the highway was a parade of electronic stores, supermarkets and garden centres. I'd seen a mosque after leaving Girne, a city otherwise known as Kyrenia, described as the cultural and economical capital of the Turkish Republic of Northern Cyprus (TRNC), but beyond that the only places of worship were to commerce and construction.

The Mediterranean Sea loitered out of sight to the left, but the Kyrenia Mountains were not for hiding, rising into the sky with crooked fingers and shooing away the outside world. Beyond this jagged peninsula to the south was the central Mesaoria Plain, and further still the Greek-controlled southern Cyprus and European Union. The geography complemented the region's political isolation. I felt hidden and secluded here in TRNC, and this ramshackle highway added to the remoteness. There was no ring road to circumvent Girne, so travelling from the western coastal road had meant driving through the city's congested streets, providing a further layer of protection for what lay hidden in the east.

As I continued I saw a land in flux. Shrubs and trees were outnumbered by rocks and construction materials, traffic cones and dirt roads leading to nowhere. There were apartment blocks under construction and ongoing building work everywhere: modern designs contrasting with older, simpler architecture. This world felt unfinished.

I passed a sign for the Courtyard, a long-standing Indian restaurant and lodging, where a kindly couple took in Mike Nagy when he first arrived in TRNC in 2003. A lot had changed in the 20-plus years since he was here. This was my second trip to the region in the space of a year, trying to find information that supported Nagy's discoveries. So far my investigation had proved fruitful. I'd learned the names they used here. Sheila Chandler-O'Shea, Joe Maloney's wife, lived here under the name Maria. And Joe? He was known by locals as Mick O'Shea, the same pseudonym he'd used in Ireland. He was either thumbing his nose at authorities or had an inability to cut loose his most successful character.

I was driving to Çatalköy following a tip-off at the home of a German couple, Rica and Andreas, who I met during the making of the *Runaway Joe* podcast. They lived in a house on the outskirts of Girne, surrounded by an orchard of apple, orange, lemon and black and green olive trees. Rica made me tea with ginger and lemon, which I sipped while she smoked a cigarette and Andreas called an old friend, a Turkish-Cypriot called Kutlay Keço.

'Keço is a good friend of ours,' said Rica. 'Actually, he helped us build this house.'

The couple met Keço at the Grapevine, an old colonial bar and restaurant in Girne, which he managed, and where he was fondly known as 'Jimmy' by regulars. 'The Brits all met there,' Rica continued. 'We were 30 Germans on the island at that time and hundreds of British. We didn't have lots of restaurants. So this Grapevine was a meeting point.'

Keço answered the phone and, after some small talk, Andreas explained there was someone from Ireland with him who wanted to ask a question. He put the phone on speaker and held it up to me.

'Keço,' I said, 'do you remember a man who used to live on the island called Mick O'Shea and his wife Maria?'

'Why, yes,' he replied without hesitation. 'Yes, of course.'

* * *

During the broadcast of *Runaway Joe* in 2024, listeners who knew Joe and Sheila contacted us with more information, and we heard multiple testimonies that supported Nagy's belief that they'd fled to North Cyprus. Nagy got his information from Erika Lotze, his former housekeeper at Capard House. Lotze, we discovered, received a postcard from TRNC in the mid-1990s in which the anonymous sender expressed interest in Michael O'Shea. Lotze immediately recognised the handwriting as belonging to O'Shea, and she understood the subtext of his message: it was an acknowledgement that he was alive and well.

Peter Collins, the builder in Rosenallis, saw the postcard. 'Erika showed it to me and said, "What do you think of that?"' It was genuine, he said. Peter's daughter Esther saw it too. Sometimes when Esther visited Lotze at Capard they talked about it. 'It kind of came up every now and then,' she said – 'and is he going to send another postcard?'

A second confirmation of their relocation to Cyprus came from Bishop Michael Cox. Cox had lived a colourful life since Joe fled Ireland. In 1992, he performed an exorcism on the RTÉ studios in Dublin after watching two TV sketch shows that 'jeered at Mother Teresa' and made 'a skit of His Holiness Pope John Paul II'. Cox told the press that he 'did the exorcism to free them from satanic influence'. Not long after the exorcism, Cox 'inexplicably' fell over and smashed his leg. 'The Devil hates people like me who help God,' he said.

A few years later, he set up a telephone confession service in which callers were charged £1 a minute in exchange for a shout-out at his Latin Mass. In 1999, the former Dún Laoghaire harbour policeman hit headlines again when he was reported as ordaining the singer Sinéad O'Connor as a Roman Catholic priest in a hotel bedroom in Lourdes. Another Tridentine priest in Ireland criticised the ordination, but the singer (newly named Mother Bernadette Mary O'Connor) and her bishop stood their ground.

'I'll stand by the decision until I die,' said Cox.

Cox purchased a fishing trawler, which he consecrated and planned to use as a floating chapel for a missionary tour around Ireland, 'to challenge the abortion ship which offers abortions'. He also stood for election in the Laois-Offaly constituency. (The boat burned down and sank after an apparent electrical fault, and Cox was not elected to political office.)

When I met Cox at his home in Offaly, he had an important point to make about all his press coverage. 'I would be very thankful if you'd straighten something out for me regarding a location. I did not ordain Sinéad O'Connor in a bedroom, as stated in the media. It was in her living quarters like this one we are in here.'

Cox was in no doubt about Joe Maloney's new home. 'Michael and his wife, they took off, and I can tell you straight up they went to Cyprus. I don't think there's any extradition treaty there. He would have to go to a place where there's no extradition treaty. I often wondered what happened to them, because I had no account of the matters, but they did go to Cyprus. I have a reliable source, which I cannot reveal, that they went to Cyprus.'

In a subsequent conversation, Cox revealed his source: Desmond 'Dessie' Monks, since deceased, who lived close to Mountjoy Prison. The exact nature of Dessie's relationship with Joe, aka Michael O'Shea, is unknown.

During my first visit to North Cyprus in 2024 with Tim Desmond, co-producer on *Runaway Joe*, I brought a collection of photographs to show to residents. Rica and Andreas had been living in the region since 1984 when they came for a holiday and never left. We showed Rica a number of photographs of Joe, spread across a single page.

She stared, fascinated.

'I don't say anything. Andy, look. There's one picture. Yes and that man I might have seen, just seen. Never spoke to him.'

Andreas looked at the page and nodded. 'Yeah. Same.'

He pointed out a picture of Joe from the early 1980s in Ireland under the guise of Michael O'Shea. His face and hair were wild and rangy; his eyes narrow and inscrutable.

'Andy shows the same,' said Rica. 'Both of us. I gave the pictures to Andreas without saying which one. And he showed the same picture. Like me.'

'Where did they see him?'

'Maybe in harbour in Kyrenia, Girne, having a brandy sour,' said Rica. 'It was meeting point for all of us. That might be. Or some restaurant. We didn't have so many restaurants at that time. There were some special points. The Grapevine, for example. An old Cypriot had that restaurant. Maybe we have seen him there.'

Rica and Andreas sent the photograph of Joe to their German friend group. A woman, Yasmin Fein, who worked for the German Embassy in Nicosia, recognised him. I phoned her.

Where did she see him?

'In the harbour in Girne,' replied Fein. 'He was sitting in the harbour many times when we were there as well and especially the eyes I can remember very good. In the 1990s the harbour was always very empty and not a lot of people were sitting there and in this time you were always able to remember all people you have seen there. I remember that we talked about him even, that he looks like a man who is going to the sea.'

'His face stood out to you?'

'Yes and I remember the eyes especially.'

'Do you remember him being with other people?'

'No, I think he was sitting alone and this was the reason why I recognise him,' said Fein.

'You're positive?'

'Yes, I'm positive.'

Before we left North Cyprus on that first trip in 2024, I had one more question for Rica and Andreas. Was it common, during the mid-1990s, to send postcards from the region? Rica nodded. It was how they communicated with the outside world from the isolated territory of TRNC. 'At that time you could rely on postcards. When you put a postcard in the box, it really arrived. Nowadays I never would send a postcard . . . because of the Internet too, of course. When a postcard was sent from here, it must have had a picture on the front.'

'What kind of places would you see on the front of postcards from North Cyprus?'

'Normally they showed the harbour. The harbour in Girne.'

*   *   *

Since TRNC was not recognised as a legal state by any country in the international community other than Turkey, it lacked extradition treaties with other parts of the world. Fugitives could rest easy here. They lived in the sun in a place that was low cost, low rent and low fuss. At the time of Nagy's arrival in 2003, a number of British criminals were hiding out in the north of the island – among them Peter Roberts, aka Maggot Pete, a British man who fled justice after receiving a six-year jail term for selling contaminated chicken to supermarkets, schools and hospitals. Asil Nadir, a Turkish-Cypriot entrepreneur accused of stealing £150 million from his Polly Peck business empire, was one of the island's most wanted.

In January 2003, the BBC broadcast an investigative documentary about suspected criminals living on the island called *Kenyon Confronts: Fugitives' Paradise*. In the show, journalist Paul Kenyon confronted Gary Robb (a former nightclub owner from Teeside who was wanted for skipping bail while on charges for running a large narcotic ring) and Brian Wright (another alleged drug dealer known as the Milkman 'because he always delivers'). Kenyon and his undercover team covertly met and recorded Stanley Rankin, a former lorry driver from Liverpool who jumped bail in 1995 after being found in possession of £2.5 million in forged bank notes. In August, a few months after the documentary aired, the same month as Nagy's arrival, Rankin was shot dead at his home in Girne.

Rica and Andreas described the region in those days as 'Mickey Mouse Land'.

'You were allowed to do whatever you wanted,' said Rica. 'It was easier to hide here than on the south. There were several people on the run. Nobody knew that they were on the run.' How did they make a living? 'Everybody could work here,' she continued. 'You could have an agency for selling houses which you don't have. Selling land you don't own. Selling insurances that didn't exist. You could make money or find people who wanted to launder money. It was an ideal island for criminals. *Für flüchtlinge.*'

Fugitives? 'Yes, yes,' said Rica. '*Flüchtlinge.* Fugitives.'

TRNC had changed a good deal since those days. 'They are stricter now,' said Andreas. There was still no extradition in the 2020s, but authorities had made residency procedures more complicated. I met Elizabeth Forsyth, an elderly expat, in Karaman, a mountainside village up a narrow winding road that overlooked the city of Girne.

'I'm notorious,' she announced. 'But I didn't escape here.'

Why was she notorious?

'Well, I didn't expect to be.'

Forsyth had been Asil Nadir's personal banker and was convicted of handling stolen cash for her boss. She served 20 months in prison before her conviction was overturned on appeal. 'It would be more difficult for someone to hide themselves here now because of all the regulations,' she explained. 'Things have become not over-restricted but normal. If people live here for more than three months they've got to apply for residency. That stops a lot of people from just coming here.'

But back in the 1990s? She smiled. 'It was like the Wild West.'

Nowadays it has become more difficult for fugitives to hide out here, because TRNC authorities deported criminals to the Turkish mainland, where Interpol could get their hands on them. Yet the region was still an off-grid haven for runaways wanting a fresh start. 'We don't exist' was a common refrain in a place still unrecognised by international law.

TRNC society was earmarked by duality. Places were known by both their Turkish and Greek names: Girne was known in Greece as Kyrenia; Lefkoşa was the Turkish name for Nicosia, the capital city of Cyprus; and the city of Gazimağusa was known by Greek Cypriots as Famagusta. Even the foundation of TRNC, following Turkey's attempted coup d'état of 1974, was considered an 'invasion' by some and an 'intervention' by others.

Some expats came here to retire because they fell in love with the island, its rugged beauty, its kind-hearted locals and slow pace of life. Others were escaping something or someone – history, trauma, grief – and they created new identities and forged new lives. North Cyprus had a fitting nickname amongst these locals: the Land of Reinvention.

*   *   *

The coastal road east of Girne was opening up, leaving the heavy traffic and construction sites behind in favour of rural panoramas. I rounded a corner and the road led downwards. A small town appeared in a cove to my left and I took a slip road signposted Marine Turtle Conservation Project. This was Algadi, the home of Kutlay Keço, founder of the conservation project and the man who claimed to have known Joe and Sheila.

I drove down into the village. Like other places along the coast, there were half-completed buildings here – residential homes and holiday retreats – and not a soul in sight aside from a few sheep that loitered in pastures next to the road. It felt quiet, remote. I parked the car outside our designated meeting place, St Kathleen's restaurant, and walked to the covered patio, which was furnished with wooden chairs and tables and potted plants.

I was the only customer. Sezgin, the elderly Turkish-Cypriot owner, appeared and I explained I was here to meet Keço. She said she would phone him, 'but first a plate of fish and mezze'.

Keço established the Society for the Protection of Turtles (SPOT) in the late 1980s with two local British expatriates to study and conserve the creatures, which were native to the local area. SPOT became one of the most active turtle protection organisations in the Mediterranean, facilitating research and student expeditions to the area, and Keço was honoured by the International Sea Turtle Society for his efforts. Keço arrived as I was finishing off Sezgin's feast. He loaded his pipe with tobacco, lit it up and talked.

'I used to see Baxter Soups. They used to sell turtle soup in the early 1960s in England. The Israelis used to harvest them and freeze the meat and sell it to England. And the turtle population went down. But now the population is as high as it used to be in the 1960s. So they are not endangered anymore. We increased the number by 75 per cent.'

How long does a turtle live? 'Only Allah knows. Maybe 100 years.'

Keço had been around a long time too. Born in Pelathousa, Cyprus, he was in high school in the second half of the 1950s, during the Cyprus Emergency, when a right-wing Greek Cypriot organisation was formed to violently oppose British rule and Turkish presence on the island. At 16 years of age, Keço joined an underground Turkish-Cypriot organisation, Türk Mukavemet Teşkilatı (TMT), with the ambition to overthrow the Greeks and force partition of the island.

'I became an outlaw for three years on the mountains fighting,' he told me, proudly.

When the Emergency ended and Britain handed shared control of Cyprus to the Greeks and the Turks, Keço travelled to England to study textile engineering at the University of Leeds. Following Turkey's intervention of 1974, he returned to North Cyprus and established a home here in Algadi in the municipality of Çatalköy.

Why did Keço choose to live here at a distance from the city?

'Because my father was a customs officer while the British were in Cyprus. He always lived at seaside. I wanted to live beside the seaside and far away from everybody.'

In 1983 an American visited him in Algadi with an offer. The Grapevine, an old bar in Girne, was for sale, and he thought Keço was the right person to take it over. So he did. Under Keço's ownership it transformed into a thriving meeting point for expats. He employed 10 or 11 people there during the 1980s and 1990s.

'My customers were mostly ancient Brits. We used to call them ancient, although now I am more ancient than they are. I was a young man then. They were all mostly ex-colonialists: from Africa, Australia, you name it.'

And Mick O'Shea?

'Yeah, yeah, yeah. He was very tall and his wife Maria looked very small. But actually she wasn't very small. Standing next to him, she looked short, of course. He was a regular there.'

Joe was six feet two inches in height, so this made sense. But in terms of personality there was nothing about Joe that stood out to Keço. He was unexceptional.

What was his profession?

'I didn't get friendly with him. There were some that I got friendly with, like a Scottish man who was in charge of the railways in India when it was a colony. He became a colonel in the Indian regiment, fighting the Germans, during the war. There were some characters.' Keço understood these former soldiers. 'Being an outlaw myself and fighting, I got closer to them because we had something in common.'

I showed him the photograph of Joe Maloney from his Michael O'Shea days in Ireland.

'There is him.'

You recognise him?

'Yeah, yeah, of course. This one, yes,' he said, pointing at the photo with the stem of his pipe. 'That's him.'

Before I met Keço, another source had given me snippets about Joe and Sheila's life on the run. They bred rabbits, which they sold or swapped with neighbours for food. Sheila apparently became adept at killing them. Keço confirmed that wild rabbits were a traditional dish in Cyprus. When he was a child, growing up, every family had a few of them.

How long ago did he remember Joe and Sheila from the Grapevine?

'Thirty years.'

This placed them in TRNC in the mid-1990s.

Did he think they were British or Irish or American?

'British, but you can be Irish or Scottish. He could be Welsh. I mean, it doesn't matter.'

After a few decades in the saddle at the Grapevine, Keço sold it on to new owners. He was now retired, albeit an honorary member of SPOT.

'I have sheep. I had a lot of goats, but I sold them. I have two donkeys, turkeys, ducks.'

Where did Mick O'Shea and his wife Maria live?

'They maybe lived in Çatalköy,' he said, gesturing inland. 'There were no houses when I came here. Nothing. There was hardly any development.'

The other source told me that Joe and Sheila had no electricity. They were living remotely on an island that was already off grid and they grew their own vegetables. 'Sheila was always a good cook,' confirmed a member of Sheila's family. 'Certainly [Joe] wasn't.'

Was it possible to be self-sufficient within the municipality of Çatalköy? Keço took another puff from his pipe and nodded. 'I lived here 11 years with no electricity, no plumbing, nothing. A simple life. I grew vegetables, I had animals, eggs, you name it.'

* * *

I left Keço to tend his sheep and drove inland, back onto the coastal highway and into the village of Çatalköy. I sat in a bar that overlooked a valley leading to a beach and wondered where Joe and Sheila once lived and if it was now hidden beneath a canopy of construction and development. From all accounts, the landscape had changed a lot since Michael Nagy was here 20 years ago. Denise Phillips, the radio presenter who interviewed Nagy, arrived here in 1980, when those colonial British who Keço spoke of were still around.

'Those people that might have met Joe, they're no longer here and probably no longer alive,' she said. 'He might have moved in those cocktail party circles. Maybe he bought a small house or a piece of land and lived very quietly. But from what I've read and heard in your podcasts, Joe Maloney would not have wanted to be completely off grid. He knew he was lucky. He thought he wasn't going to be found. I think he was more likely to have been somewhere like [the] Grapevine, holding court every Saturday, talking to everyone and telling his story. That's my feeling – he would have been a bit of a *bon viveur*.'

Joe and Sheila did frequent the Grapevine, but the impression I was getting was of a muted, stilted character. A man reduced to a whisper. Was this a repercussion of his 18 months in prison? It was his extravagant lifestyle that got him caught. Maybe he learned from his mistakes. Or maybe Sheila was now calling the shots and he was following her lead. If he was not content at being incognito, she certainly was.

'Sheila would have loved to have kept a low profile,' said someone who knew them in Ireland. 'Sheila was like a mouse. Very protective of him.'

A source in Ireland told me they had two English friends, a couple who lived close to them and knew them as Mick and Maria. I was unable to discover the identity of those friends but I pieced together some of Sheila's life from the mid-1990s onwards – because that was when she started to come back to Ireland.

*   *   *

In the summer of 1996, Sheila appeared on the doorstep of her family home on Arkendale Road. Catherine, her mother, was shocked by her daughter's appearance. Sheila was practically in rags. Catherine 'thought it was a terrible come-down for her daughter,' said a family friend. Sheila explained she'd returned out of necessity, because she'd been sick for a long time and couldn't hold it off any longer. She was taken to a family doctor, who diagnosed her as having advanced metastatic breast cancer. The cancer was no longer localised and had spread to other parts of her body. The doctor had never seen such advanced yet untreated cancer before.

'Why did you not get your cancer looked at?' asked a friend. 'The doctor said it's so bad.'

Sheila replied: 'Where I live, I don't exist.'

Sheila was very sick on that visit home in 1996, but she had treatment in hospital and fought it. She was, according to a family member, a positive person. 'She waited a long time,' they told me. 'Maybe there were reasons.' But there was a psychological impact to coming back home after a decade away with no contact with home. Her elder sister Joan died a couple of years after Joe's release from prison. Sheila's father Vincent passed away in the early 1990s and Sheila had known none of this until her return home.

'She missed out,' remarked a relative. 'She didn't know her dad had died, she didn't know her older sister had died. She had to cope with that as best she could.'

One day during that visit one of Sheila's family members received a phone call. It was Joe (or, as they knew him, Michael). He was calling at a designated time to speak to Sheila, but she'd been held up in hospital. The call was not long. The family member described her diagnosis – stage four cancer – and explained she was in hospital undergoing treatment.

There was a pause on the other end of the line. Then Joe said: 'I didn't know how sick she was.'

That was the extent of their conversation, recalled the family member.

Sheila responded well to the treatment and announced she was ready to leave Ireland again. Life expectancy for some women with stage four breast cancer is only one to two years, and her family were unsure if they would see her again. But Sheila came back over subsequent years for further treatments: 'three to four times' according to Vanessa Fenning, sister of Joe's most loyal companion in Ireland, Rod. 'Sheila would come back periodically always well-tanned and she'd be in Ireland for a while and then she'd disappear. I'm sure if we really wanted to we could have figured out where they'd got to, but we didn't.'

Olga Fenning, another of Rod's sisters, added: 'She went to so many countries to get home so [authorities] would lose track of her. But I have no idea where they were.' Sheila 'zigzagged' her way across Europe to Ireland in an effort to cover her tracks, according to people who knew her during this time. This was a necessity when travelling from North Cyprus. Due to its unrecognised status, the region was only accessible via air through Istanbul.

During her visits home, Sheila stayed at the house on Arkendale Road, where her mother now resided in a 'granny flat' at the back of the property. Between treatments she occasionally met a friend for coffee at the Royal Marine Hotel in Dún Laoghaire, a few hundred feet from the site where Joe opened his first car repair business in the early 1970s. They talked for hours but never discussed the elephant in the room.

'The reason I kept meeting her was I felt I was the only person she ever saw beyond her family, who she was driving crazy,' said the friend. 'We could talk about our mothers, our grandparents, our schooling. Books, which was our main interest in life and all the rest.'

Family members were careful not to grill her about what was going on with her and Michael: 'You didn't ask questions.' Sheila, according to a relative, 'used to come back and forth and back and forth and disappear and come back and go away again'.

By the time Michael Nagy discovered that Joe and Sheila were living in North Cyprus, they had spent all their earnings from their Ireland property sales and were broke. Every time Sheila came home, she hit her mother up for cash and carefully choreographed her departure. She'd ask a relative to drop her somewhere discreet, like a local train station, and make her own way out of the country.

'She was very careful,' said the relative. 'Both, I suppose, to protect us and to protect him and herself. You find the woman, you find the man.'

The millennium came and went and Sheila continued to respond positively to treatment. She appeared to be living healthily in TRNC.

'They lived a very simple life,' the relative continued. 'From the sound of it, they ate healthily. I'd say that's one of the reasons she lasted as long as she did with the extensive cancer she had. She was physically strong.'

But the breast cancer progressed into a brain tumour, and by April 2008, the month when her mother Catherine died at 97, Sheila was living on a permanent basis in Ireland. Once a week she visited a charitable hospice in Blackrock, a coastal suburb of south county Dublin, where she swam. She counted only one friend in Ireland but kept in touch with her former English neighbour (presumably in Cyprus), who emailed her on a regular basis. Every week she visited the local St Vincent's hospital for treatment. 'When the team comes to see me,' she told her friend, 'they can't believe I've had cancer for so long.'

In 2010, her Irish friend phoned Sheila's family to ask how she was. 'She's in a nursing home,' they said. Peter Collins in Rosenallis was among those who expressed a desire to visit Sheila, but she didn't want to see anyone apart from close family and a single close friend. 'We had to respect that,' said Collins.

'She never had other visitors except her family,' recalled the friend, who asked to remain anonymous. Sheila was still not opening up about her years on the run, but 'whenever she mentioned Michael I could tell she was mad about him'.

On 23 June 2010, Sheila Mary Chandler died in Dalkey Lodge Nursing Home, half a mile from Kent Terrace, the last place she and Joe called home in Ireland. Sheila's family quietly cremated her remains. It was a muted end to a life that went off the rails the moment she met her next-door neighbour, Michael O'Shea: a fantasy character created by the fugitive Joe Maloney. 'I don't know if she'd ever had a proper boyfriend before Michael,' said her friend. 'I don't think she'd ever had a nice relationship with somebody.'

Peter Collins described Sheila's life as tragic. 'When she realised what was happening I think it completely destroyed her personality,' he said. 'She wasn't robust in that way. Sheila committed to Michael and gave him her all. He took it up and it didn't come back to her. That was the harm he did in life.'

* * *

Sheila's death left a glaring question unanswered. Where was Joe? Rod Fenning was one of the few people from Ireland, perhaps the only person, who kept in touch with Joe Maloney after he fled Ireland. Rod occasionally visited Erika Lotze at Capard House in the 1990s and 2000s, by which time the estate was under new ownership, and the pair chatted about their fugitive friends. But Rod wasn't blabbing about their whereabouts outside of these conversations.

'Roderic would not talk to anybody in the family about him,' said his sister Olga Fenning. 'It was all very hush-hush. He was very protective.'

Melinda, Rod's girlfriend, was privy to rumours. In the mid-1990s, the teething era of the Internet, Rod asked her to check the FBI Most Wanted List to see if Joe was on it. Melinda checked but couldn't see his name. Rod was irascible and occasionally volatile: a trait that became acute at the age of 34, not long after Joe fled Ireland, when he was diagnosed with diabetes. In Rod's mind, dark forces had conspired to victimise his friend. 'He was really infatuated with Michael,' one of Rod's sisters told me. Rod was convinced Joe Maloney was innocent, that he had been framed and hadn't killed June. Sometime in the early 2000s, he told Melinda that the man he knew as Michael was beyond prosecution.

'Rod told me even if they had arrested him, they couldn't do anything because he was not of sound of mind,' said Melinda.

'Rod told me Michael O'Shea had Alzheimer's.' Before her death, Sheila slipped the same information to her friend. This master of disguise who outfoxed the FBI for decades, who skirted extradition and vanished, had dementia.

* * *

A full moon hung loosely above the dilapidated two-storey structure in Alsancak, a few miles west of Girne on the north coast of Cyprus. I stood in the dark looking at the abandoned building while traffic belched around a roundabout and the Mediterranean breeze whipped the cuff of my neck. In my hand: a photograph of the building as it was 21 years ago, in 2004. The Ravine had been the only Irish pub in the region, and it catered to a litany of expats, most law-abiding but some of them Britain and Ireland's most wanted men.

The Ravine was owned by Michael O'Sullivan, a man from Bantry in County Cork. In 2004, O'Sullivan posed for a photograph and gave an interview about the island's fugitive class to the *Telegraph* newspaper. He told the reporter: 'All these characters have had a drink in my bar but I never ask questions. I could write a book every week on the stories I am told, but I've learnt to believe nothing that I hear and only half of what I see.'

O'Sullivan's clientele included Mick O'Shea.

A local described him as 'one of the guys at the bar': big, unkempt, with long, straggly grey hair: 'unattractive'. That was all. There was no charisma, no big dreams, no ambitions, no can-do attitude. He was just a barfly and a forgettable one at that.

I looked at the remnants of the Ravine, which, like many buildings along the TRNC coastline, seemed trapped between renovation and demolition. The bar didn't last long and neither did its owner, who allegedly screwed people over for money and was run out of North Cyprus and told not to come back. O'Sullivan fled to Scotland, where he died a few years later.

Nothing is as it was, I thought. People who encountered Michael O'Shea in Ireland recalled him vividly as a rambunctious lunatic – here in North Cyprus he lingered on the margins of memory like a wisp.

'I know Mick O'Shea,' a barmaid at a local British pub in Alsancak told me. 'As soon as you said it I knew that name. Part of me thinks I can see him as well.' But she couldn't be sure.

As I imagined an aging Joe Maloney walking into the Ravine 20 years before me, four dogs pelted from behind the ruined structure. I ran down the road as they gave chase – barking, snarling, growling – until they gave up. I stood there panting, looking back to where one of the hounds was perched on the wall outside the former bar, howling triumphantly.

* * *

Before Sheila moved back to Ireland on a permanent basis, a few years before her death in 2010, she phoned a close relative from overseas.

'He's gone,' she said. The relative was positive Sheila was telling the truth. 'I don't think if he wasn't dead Sheila would have left and come back to Dublin. My only belief is that he is dead, without a doubt. I have no doubt in my mind.'

Sheila told her friend that Michael had Alzheimer's and was dead. Olga Fenning, Rod's sister, heard the same: 'He's definitely dead. Roderic told me that – and that's why Sheila came home.' Vanessa Fenning added: 'Because he died there was no reason to stay.'

The news reached Peter Collins in Rosenallis: 'I believe he died in Cyprus. I just heard he died so you know I just accepted it.'

Sheila told her friend she had a property that she had to abandon after Michael's death 'because it was in someone else's name'. If these accounts are to be believed, Joe Maloney, aka Michael O'Shea, died in the mid-2000s. Rumours of his demise added another layer of mystery. If Joe died, then there was nothing left to hide other than a body. There would be no more arrests, no more extraditions, no more hiding. Why didn't Sheila spill the beans to her family about their years on the run?

'Oh, but she was quite a private person in her own way,' said a relative. 'Very private. She never gave anything away. She'd had years of hiding things, when you think of it. We learned that she closed up if you asked questions. Her attitude was you're better off not knowing. She was a past master at evading questions. Even in the latter years she didn't really open up. We were aware that what you were told might not have been. It could have been fictionalised to some extent. I thought she'd make a mistake at some stage. But she was ultra careful. I'm sure she'd had years of practising. And she had a past master teaching her.'

The family member paused.

'Or maybe it was the other way around, I'm not sure. I don't know, to this day, whether she believed or didn't believe he killed June Fisk. I couldn't say categorically whether she believed he did at the end or whether she didn't. She always claimed he didn't. And he said he didn't. Whether that changed over years, I don't know. But she stood by him the whole time.'

Before Sheila died, when she knew the end was coming, she destroyed all her photographs and documents. Everything. She was determined to take her secrets to the grave as a final two fingers to the persecutors who tormented her and her beloved 'Michael'.

* * *

In May 2009, 11 months before Sheila's death, Erika Lotze was sitting at a dressing table in a nursing home, making preparations for a party taking place at Capard House the following day. Age and illness had forced her to move from her beloved Capard into this facility, much to her displeasure. But Frau Lotze remained fiercely independent. She didn't need anybody else, and it never occurred to her to leave Capard, no matter who owned it, until health issues overtook.

The antiques dealer who'd taken possession of Capard had renovated the property and its land with care, and this was a consolation. Lotze was content that her beloved home was in safe hands. She laid her jewellery on the table neatly as night fell over County Laois.

The following morning an employee of the nursing home entered Lotze's room to find her slumped on the floor beside the table. After 48 years in Ireland, her story had reached an end and with it her secrets about Joe's years on the run. Lotze had been a closer ally to Joe in Ireland than many people, even his intimate business partners, realised, but she was also a woman with a moral compass who was shocked when the truth emerged about his true identity and his alleged role in the murder of June.

Lotze wished to be buried in Capard, where Charles de Jenner, her former employer and the man who brought her to Ireland in 1961, was interned. Instead, she was given a plot at Rosenallis cemetery. The headstone included a photograph of Lotze in her finest jewellery, set against the backdrop of a blue sky. Imprinted directly beneath her name was the location that defined the greater portion of her life: Capard House, Rosenallis.

* * *

By the time the RTÉ *Documentary on One* team and I began work on the story of Joe Maloney, many of the key players in this story were gone. James Maloney, Joe's brother, died in New Haven, Connecticut in 1998 at the age of 61. There was no indication that Joe had stayed in contact with his brother, who led a quiet life apparently free of any criminal conduct. I learned that Warren Daansen, who spoke to Joe over the telephone in the years following his escape from Ireland in 1986, passed away in 2015.

Four years later, Rod Fenning died of cancer, shortly after his retirement from the British Embassy in Dublin. Neal Dunkleberg, Joe's childhood friend, passed away in the months following the release of the *Runaway Joe* podcast. Now there were only architectural remnants of Joe's time in Ireland: the iron cross and memorial stone he erected at Capard in memory of the IRA man killed there; the arch he built in the lane behind Kent Terrace; the hole in the wall behind Castletown House, which once held the sheela na gig that Joe sold at an auction.

The resting places of these people were easily found, but Joe's remains were elusive. After the podcast finished, I gathered up my leads and returned to North Cyprus one last time in February 2025 to see if I could discover a resting place. Sheila told a friend he died in a hospital, which narrowed my search to Girne State Hospital or the State Hospital in Lefkosa, the largest in TRNC, but these facilities were reluctant to disclose identities of people in their care 20 years ago.

Muslim countries like TRNC do not permit cremation, which meant Joe had to be buried in a grave. Westerners of Christian or other denominations were kept separate from Muslim dead, which narrowed my search to specific areas of graveyards. Locals knew him as Mick O'Shea, so this seemed the most obvious name to look under. The first and most obvious location was the British cemetery in Girne, tucked behind an old Greek cemetery near the harbour. I scoured each headstone with help from Andy May, chairman of the British Cemetery Committee, but they all drew a blank.

'No record of a Mick O'Shea there,' concluded May.

The British cemetery was declared full in 2010, at which point Green Hill cemetery opened nearby to cater for deceased expats. But there was no trace of Joe there either. Westerners who died in the eastern region of the north part of the island tended to be buried in Famagusta cemetery, 50 miles from Girne, but the local council had no record of him here. And there were only a handful of expat plots at Bellapais, a private cemetery in idyllic surroundings in the Kyrenia Mountains outside Girne.

I spoke to the custodian of Wayne's Keep, a resting place for British military dead located in the UN buffer zone between northern and southern Cyprus. Perhaps Joe's wartime fabrications found him a space here? 'The latest date I have for the whole cemetery is 1961,' responded the captain in charge.

Perhaps Joe Maloney was not buried under his birth name or Michael O'Shea. I'd established that he and Sheila had a house, off grid and without electricity, which Sheila was forced to abandon after Joe's death because 'it was in someone else's name'. Surely this referred to another pseudonym, perhaps one he used for officialdom during his time on the run. If he was buried under another name, a name I didn't know, then his remains could be untraceable.

In Lapta cemetery, a few miles away from Alsancak, where Mick O'Shea had been known to drink at the Ravine bar, I encountered a series of unmarked graves. Anonymous graves were not uncommon and indicated a pauper's burial, Andy May explained. Some people travelled to North Cyprus to escape or forget their past. By the time they died, oftentimes alone and penniless, their past had forgotten them too. There was no procedure here for people who died alone, under pseudonyms, with no money. Only charitable contributions from expat cemetery groups granted these faceless individuals a resting place.

I drove 70-odd miles along the Karpas peninsula, a rugged finger that tapered up the north-eastern end of Cyprus along the coast. Resort-style hotels and unfinished developments gave way to miles and miles of unspoiled, dramatic countryside beside the two-lane highway. Eventually I reached Dipkarpaz, the last town on the map close to the tip of the peninsula and pointing toward Turkey's Iskenderun Bay.

North Cyprus was already off grid, but this place felt like another level. I walked through town as the sun set, men playing backgammon in brightly lit coffee houses after a day of toiling in the field, the call to prayer broadcast from a mosque and accompanied by a chorus of cicadas. Further outside town was another graveyard: stony and silent, decorated with wildflowers and orchids and rich with the scent of jasmine and honeysuckle. I found a handful of Christian graves a distance from the Muslim section, and among them were eight unmarked, inscription-free headstones. The dead lay beneath them, anonymous and invisible, indecipherable in their cradles at the end of the world.

18

Footprints in the Snow

JOE MALONEY WAS DEAD, WE CONCLUDED IN THE *RUNAWAY JOE* PODCAST. But questions lingered. If he had Alzheimer's, who diagnosed him? If he died in hospital, who cared for him? Someone put the lid on his coffin – surely they'd recognise him? Was he even dead? In a further pollution of the record, Sheila Chandler's family listed Sheila on her death certificate as 'separated' rather than widowed. Was Sheila muddying the waters from beyond the grave? (Most people took Sheila at face value when she told them 'Michael' had died. She'd been too besotted by him, they said, to return home for good if he was still alive.)

In 2003, Michael Nagy apparently encountered Sheila in North Cyprus and was pestering Rod and Sheila's family with letters. At the same time, Scotland Yard and other law enforcement agencies were zoning in on wanted criminals in North Cyprus with help from the Turkish government, who wanted to shed the region's reputation as a fugitives' paradise.

Runaways were making moves to leave the island for places like North Africa and South America. With that in mind, there was another plausible eventuality. What if Joe and Sheila, scared by Nagy and the authorities, had fled TRNC, and Joe perished in another country?

A few years before Rod Fenning's death, Rod was with his brother Patrick in Fitzgerald's pub (the same place where Rod entertained Mike Nagy) in Sandycove, Dublin. They'd had a few pints when the subject of Michael O'Shea was raised.

'That was some weird story. Do you think he did it?' Patrick asked, referring to June's murder.

Rod shrugged his shoulders and muttered, 'I don't really know'.

'What happened to him?'

'Ah, he's gone,' said Rod. 'Dead. No idea where.'

Patrick pushed him. 'Go on, where did he go?'

Rod shrugged again and said, 'Andorra', referring to the tiny nation between France and Spain in the Pyrenees Mountains, a nation without extradition laws with the United States. Patrick felt his brother was telling him the truth, because 'Rod had a few pints'.

Rod mentioned nothing about Andorra to his girlfriend, Melinda. Was he misleading his brother? It was possible, Patrick told me. You never really knew with Rod. I sent an inquiry to the civil registry office in Andorra to see if they had a record of Michael O'Shea dying there. There was nobody with that name in their records. Then I was given information about a possible final destination in the serpentine saga of Joe Maloney. In 2008, Sean Wisely (the Laois haulier who'd worked with Michael O'Shea at Capard House and played the accordion at O'Shea's parties) happened to meet Erika Lotze on the street in Mountmellick, the town a few miles from Capard House.

'Your old friend died,' she told him.

Wisely recalled: 'I didn't know who she was talking about, and I said, "Who? Who was my friend that died?"'

'Michael O'Shea,' she said. 'He died out in Moscow.'

Lotze didn't tell Wisely where she got this information.

'I didn't hear any more about it then after that,' said Wisely.

* * *

Most of her life, Wanda Mordenga wondered what had become of June's children. The last time she saw them was when social services had taken them away. If she happened to be in Rochester and saw a red-headed boy, she wondered if it was Joey. She always thought she would see him again one day, but it never happened. Eventually she became a mother and had two children of her own, and they gave her three grandchildren. Still, she wondered. Were Joey and Patti-Ann OK? Was anybody mean to them?

She need not have worried. Joey was raised in what he described as a great family. For 12 years he worked in dealerships for General Motors, a continuation of his childhood fascination with cars, and then he changed careers and became a custom furniture builder. 'I'm very mechanical and I like to fix things,' he said. 'If something's broken, I like to fix it. I guess if it's a trait that I inherited from Joe it's not a bad one.'

Joey looked like Joe but did not inherit his height and had none of the psychological peculiarities that defined his biological father. Instead, like June, he was kind-hearted and generous and loving of his family. 'Patti and I both live good lives. Patti has two of her own that she loves dearly. I've got two of my own that are great boys.'

Joey was proof that trauma need not be passed down through generations. The podcast series *Runaway Joe* reunited Joe with his cousin Amy, who he last saw as a small child in 1973, and it also introduced him to Karen, a sister he never knew existed.

'Life worked out fine for us,' said Karen. 'It's most likely Joe isn't with us anymore. I don't know what else to say. It's just a closure to the story.'

The series also reunited Wanda and Joey.

'To know that you and Patti-Ann are safe, that you were happy growing up, that gives me a lot of peace,' Wanda told Joey in their first conversation together in 57 years. 'I know your mom is looking down and smiling and throwing kisses for you.'

After Karen and Joey met, Karen took a DNA test on Ancestry. com and a hit came back for another sibling. Mike Horn grew up in an adoptive family and knew little about his real identity other than he was born on 28 May 1965, at Genesee hospital in Rochester: the same hospital where June worked. (Coincidentally, he was also born the same day as Joey, only three years later.)

When Horn was a child, his parents told him his real father was a doctor and his mother was a nurse. Like many adopted adolescents, curiosity got the better of him, and he petitioned the state of New York. The state protected the anonymity of his biological parents but offered a scintilla of information: his mother worked at Strong Memorial Hospital in Rochester and gave him up for adoption because she had no plans to marry his father, who was already married.

'Your mother felt it would be selfish to keep her baby and have you grow up without a father,' read the document. 'Your father agreed with your mother's decision. She never named your father.'

Horn left it there, assuming this was the end of his search. But in 2009 he was getting married and as a Roman Catholic needed to contact his former parishes to obtain his sacramental certificates: baptism, confirmation and first communion.

He phoned the Catholic Church in Rochester and 45 minutes later a clerk called back. They had discovered his identity. His birth name was Michael Joseph, and they told him his biological mother's maiden name.

'I was like, "Holy shit. Okay, now I've got my name."'

Horn wrote a blurb on the genealogical website Ancestry.com with the details he knew thus far and was contacted by a relative of Joe Maloney who knew the whole story. The relative wrote: 'Joe was a con artist. He claimed he was a doctor. He claimed he was a hundred other things as well. He was also your biological father.'

When Horn asked more questions, the Maloney relative advised him to watch the episode of *Unsolved Mysteries* featuring Joe's case. Horn knew it was true when he saw the mugshot. Horn looked just like Joe. Then he received a message on Ancestry.com from another sibling match whose story was uncannily similar.

This man was born a few weeks before Horn, in May 1965, and he too was named Michael Joseph. His mother was a nurse at Genesee hospital and he'd been adopted through the Catholic Family Center in Rochester. At first the sibling wondered if they might be twins, but their birthdates suggested not. They had different mothers.

Joe had pretended to be a doctor when he met Carol Reckahn in the late 1950s, hanging out in the student nurses' dormitory. Evidently he was still using this disguise to attract women five years later while married to June.

'There was some weird thing with Joe and these two hospitals, Genesee and Strong Memorial,' said Horn. 'They seemed to be a hunting ground for him.'

In the same month that Mike Horn and his brother were born, June was pregnant with Patti-Ann: three women pregnant by Joe at the same time. How much of this June was aware of we will never know, but since Mike was born at June's workplace of

Genesee hospital (and since his brother's mother worked as a nurse there), it's likely she knew all of it.

Joey and Patti-Ann, Karen and Deborah. Mike Horn and his brother. Joe had six children to four different women before fleeing Rochester. Six we knew of. Then Horn began to receive more connections through Ancestry.com: a man from Scotland 'whose mother was made pregnant by an Irish-American'; another potential match from a person in New South Wales in Australia. In late 2025, he received a positive DNA match for another sibling in Rochester: a woman born in 1958, a year after Joe's daughter Karen was born, a couple of years before Joe met June.

'I think that there might have been another two more,' said Horn. 'There's this massive iceberg under the water.'

Tony Gilfoyle at Capard House once asked Sheila why she and 'Michael' had no children and Sheila had answered: 'He isn't having kids. I got him neutered.' Despite Joe's reputation as a philanderer in County Laois, Tony and others 'never heard of anybody in the area having a child with him'. But I hadn't forgotten the story of Rosie Morgan, the woman who worked with Joe at the furniture shop in Dolphin's Barn, about encountering him in Dún Laoghaire in the mid-1970s with a woman and a child in a pram.

Horn was in no doubt about his biological father.

'Did Joe have kids in Ireland? I'm sure there's a bunch of them. Why would he stop? There's got to be some, right? There are probably kids everywhere.'

* * *

Most crimes happen in the moment. They are crimes of passion: violent acts encouraged by emotional distress or self-defence.

Or they are crimes of desperation: robberies, drug-related acts or public order offences. Those felonies tend to be impulsive. Then there are premeditated crimes – fraud, assault, murder – which are carefully planned. Joe Maloney's alleged actions fit into the latter category. This was a man who took the time to come up with a plan, not only for the crime that occurred but for the story of his persona. His cover-up was not just the crime; it was his entire life.

Laura Meade, the Rochester *Democrat & Chronicle* reporter who followed the case and travelled to Ireland in 1985 after Joe's arrest, had many years to think about Joe's behaviour.

'There is a whole host of criminals who think that they are cleverer, better, more cunning,' she said. 'They have a mindset that they are smarter than everybody; they can outsmart the police. Some serial killers – Jeffrey Dahmer, Ted Bundy – have the same mindset. "I can get away with this. I am stronger. I can target whoever I want. I can live a dual-personality lifestyle and convince people that's who I am." Simultaneously they have a corrupt side that nobody sees. I'm not saying Joseph Michael Maloney was in the same calibre as those serial killers, but it's the same mentality. "I can do whatever I want. Nobody will touch me."'

In investigating this story, I was surprised by the number of people who were quick to defend Joe – from the hospital staff in Rochester who believed his claims that June had attempted suicide, to people in Ireland who couldn't countenance the idea that Michael O'Shea was not who he said he was (despite his admittance of his true identity following his identification by the Rochester detective in Dublin's High Court). Some people who knew him created a blanket of conspiracy around him, spurned by his intelligence and survivalist instincts ('maybe he was an international spy', more than one person told me).

Others accepted that he may have killed June, but they made excuses that it was just 'another domestic homicide' and did not deserve international scrutiny.

It was the oldest story in the book: a story of coercive control and domestic violence. Joe had been arrested and charged with third-degree assault of June a few months before her death and had assaulted her on numerous occasions before that, according to the testimony of her friend Catherine Blair. He was engaged in a campaign of intimidation against June, which included threats and having her followed by private detectives. When June finally broke free and met another man, Joe allegedly made the decision to kill her.

'If I can't have you, nobody else will': a cowardly perspective from a man who was sleeping with multiple women outside his marriage to June. Laura Meade described his crime as a cold-blooded calculation: carefully plotted, choreographed and executed. Yet it was still one of the oldest stories ever: male violence against women.

Then there were the allies who allegedly assisted Joe in his criminal behaviour – including people who may have financed Joe and Sheila during their years on the run. Gene Harding, the FBI investigator who worked the case, described this as discouraging for June's family. 'I'm shocked at the fact that people would help someone who killed another person,' said Harding. 'Does it happen? Yes, but it's unfortunate. I don't know how he manoeuvred those people into believing him, but that just goes to show you the type of man he was.'

Many people I spoke to could not countenance the idea that Joe, or Michael as they knew him, was capable of murder. They liked him – he was good to them – and to accept he was not who he said he was required admitting to themselves he had fooled them. Joe had a con mind from an early age: an ability to deceive and to deceive completely. Colleagues, friends and associates of white-collar criminals like Elizabeth Holmes and Bernie Madoff were just as dumbfounded and in denial when their crimes came to light.

'Joseph Michael Maloney needed to do something,' said Laura Meade. 'He had a problem in his mind that he had to take care of by killing his wife, and he compartmentalised it and then said, "I'm better than this and I am getting away with it."'

She paused.

'And if somebody did it once, you have to wonder if they've done it again.'

* * *

Who was Joe Maloney? What was he? Joseph Picciotti, who shared an organic chemistry class at the University of Rochester with Joe and later became a local police chief in a city borough, described an air of mystery around the man.

'People who had contact with Joe Maloney have perpetuated the myths, the half-truths. They've filled in the spaces. It's hard to know what's true about him . . . Someone should write a book about him, but only Joe Maloney could write it. He's the only one who knows the truth,' Picciotti told Rochester's *Democrat & Chronicle* in 1985.

In March 1967, the same month that Joe allegedly stabbed himself and attacked June and her new partner, Lee DiClemente, a physician called Francis W. Kelly met Joe on three occasions. In a letter posted to Joe's attorney on 3 July 1967, two days before June's death, Kelly diagnosed Joe as manifesting emotionally unstable personality disorder, a condition otherwise known as borderline personality disorder (BPD). Symptoms can include a fluctuating sense of identity, unstable mood and relationships, and impulsiveness. It was only during Joe's two weeks in Rochester State Hospital after his indictment in 1967 that a clearer diagnosis emerged, a diagnosis that went far beyond the manageable traits of BPD.

On 29 September 1967, four days after Joe escaped from the hospital, Benjamin Pollock, a psychiatrist at the facility, submitted the following evaluation:

Joseph M. Maloney ... was interviewed on numerous occasions by duly qualified examiners. He was guarded, tense, and gave many conflicting stories which were not always credible. He gives a superficial appearance of being sincere, honest, and helpful, but it is obvious that he is only presenting information which he believes will be helpful to his care. He objects to disclosure of other material or even to the admission of details of his past life which were obtained from sources elsewhere. He talked freely, coherently, and relevantly, and he displayed no signs of mental disorder. He spoke in a cultured manner and with good choice of words which were much above his formal education. At times, he appeared somewhat irritable and suspicious of the motives of others, but for the most part he has been quite cooperative. His background is that of a sociopath, with lack of insight and judgment.

His psychological examination revealed that in spite of the fact that he was observed under tension, he was functioning in the superior range of intellectual ability, with a wide range of information, a high degree of apprehension and sensitivity to the world about him. His replies were deliberate, precise and somewhat pedantic, indicating the value he placed on purely intellectual pursuits.

There were no signs in his psychological or psychiatric examinations of any type of mental disorder, except for that of a psychopath.

J. Reid Meloy, author of *The Psychopathic Mind* (1988), is one of the world's leading authorities on psychopathy. A forensic psychologist, he worked as a consultant on criminal and civil cases across the US and Europe, provided advice for the FBI's Behavioural Analysis Unit in Quantico over two decades, and was a technical consultant for the TV show *CSI: Crime Scene Investigation*. After reviewing Joe Maloney's behavioural traits and Benjamin Pollock's 1967 diagnosis, he concurred that Joe ticked all the boxes. The warning signs began early in Joe's life and continued throughout his adulthood in the form of compulsive lying.

'Psychopaths will lie regardless of person, place, time or circumstance,' Meloy explained. 'Everybody has lied, we've all lied at different points in our lives, but we typically lie for situational reasons. Oftentimes we lie to manage anxiety, to not anger somebody, to maintain a relationship that might be threatened if the other person knew the truth. But psychopaths lie – and this is very important, the line is very endogenous – to dominate their objects. Objects being people, relationships, entities: the University of Rochester Medical School, the psychiatric hospital where Joe's dad worked as a custodian. The social paradigm of the psychopath is dominance-submission. He's always working to move himself into a position of dominance over his objects. That is the place from which he has encounters with other people literally throughout his lifetime.'

Another way to think about psychopathic behaviour, Meloy continued, is in terms of a predator-prey dynamic. 'This is in contrast to how most of us build our social paradigm, which is through affectional relatedness: reciprocal, affectional contact with other people throughout our day.'

Joe displayed all the signs of what psychologists Delroy Paulhus and Kevin Williams described as a 'dark triad' personality –

narcissism, Machiavellianism and psychopathy – and he showed evidence of a fourth trait in what has been described as a dark tetrad: sadism. He also met most of the criteria on psychologist Robert Hare's psychopathy checklist: sexual promiscuity, charm, the ability to manipulate, a lack of empathy, a mask worn to reveal his true self from others, repeated attacks on the vulnerable and the ability to evade capture.

Joe was repeatedly able to outthink and outfox authorities. When it comes to intelligence, psychopaths are like the rest of us, and this is where Joe was probably exceptional, according to J. Reid Meloy.

'The distribution of IQ in the psychopathic population is normal. Most psychopaths are of average intelligence. You have psychopaths that are less than average intelligence and a lot of those guys end up in prison because they're not very smart. But it sounds like Joe was in the superior or very superior IQ range, which makes a psychopath like that quite dangerous.' In tandem with danger comes violent impulses, because 'psychopathic individuals have a lower threshold for being violent'.

I asked Meloy why some people in Joe's life, like Sheila and Rod Fenning, were utterly faithful to him and why others refused to countenance his guilt. The psychiatrist assigned this to what he described as 'predatory acuity' in extremely intelligent psychopaths.

'They can read what you're about and what you want in your encounter or relationship with them, whether it's casual or long term. They're very chameleon-like, so they can mimic behaviours that are appealing to you. Their goal, of course, is to dominate the object. Oftentimes the means to that goal is to provide you with what you want in the relationship with him. He will appeal to that and provide you with that as a way to ingratiate himself to you. It sounds like Joe was very good at that.'

After three years investigating this story and following Joe's labyrinthine passage through life, I felt I was no closer to understanding the man. There was a canyon-sized gulf between us, and although I could see his faint figure in the distance, he remained a cipher and an enigma. I felt as though I was chasing a shadow. Meloy assured me that these feelings are common when trying to understand a psychopath.

'There's less there than meets the eye. Psychopaths don't have the internal psychological structure that normal individuals have: an internalised value system otherwise known as conscience. Internalised values are not there. But what comes with that absence of conscience is a remarkable freedom. Psychopathic individuals do things beyond the pale of anyone else and that's how some of them, if they're bright, can get away with extraordinary behaviours. It doesn't cross people's minds that somebody would even attempt to do that. They are like footprints in the snow that melt away.'

Yet there was one aspect of Joe's story that remained a mystery even to J. Reid Meloy. What might happen to a psychopath's brain if, as Sheila told her family was the case with Joe, they were to contract dementia? How would this degenerative disease impact an already compromised mind?

'There's no formal study I know of anywhere,' said Meloy. 'I looked to see if dementia in psychopathic individuals has been studied, and I don't know if anybody's done that yet.'

In Ireland, Joe Maloney lived as Michael O'Shea with his head above the parapet. He befriended policemen, travelled freely outside of the jurisdiction and lived in Laois, close to where his parents surely had living relatives who recognised him. It must have made him feel untouchable and invincible – for nothing fans the ego more than the success of getting away with a lie. Yet his year and a half in Irish prison may have knocked the wind out of him. In the end, Joe Maloney never faced justice, but neither was he redeemed or ever truly free.

Reports of him in North Cyprus painted a picture of a solitary individual – unattractive and isolated – no longer the flamboyant raconteur go-getter. A strange, abstract character, sitting alone in a café in the Girne harbour, waiting for a boat that never came to take him out to sea, his mind washing blank, slipping through the cracks and fading from the light.

Epilogue
June

5 June 2007

A PROCESSION OF CARS FILED INTO LAKEVIEW CEMETERY IN
MONROE COUNTY, NEW YORK, AND TRAVELLED THE TREE-LINED
DRIVE, PAST THE CHAPEL, POND AND FOUNTAIN, AND ALONG A
WINDING PATH UNTIL THEY CAME TO A HALT. Two dozen people,
all in their mid-60s, emerged from the vehicles and walked
through the maze of headstones. This was the Class of 1959,
and they were here to pay respects to June Rosalee Fisk on the
40th anniversary of her death.

June was initially buried in Mount Hope cemetery in Rochester,
17 miles away, but a year later her family decided to bring her
closer to her father Ward Fisk's home in Albion and to Brockport
where her brother Dale lived with his wife Gladys. So June was
reinterred in Lakeview, where she rested alone until 1986, when
her father Ward was laid next to her. The former tenant farmer
lived a long life – he died at 90 – but the sadness of June's loss
never left him. Next to Ward and June were the graves of Dale

and Gladys; nearby was her mother Marie, who had separated from Ward and remarried.

The gathering of former classmates circled June's grave and bowed their heads.

The Class of 1959 had by their own admission not been particularly special at Albion High. Like any school, they'd fallen into cliques. Some had been sporty and outgoing, others studious and reserved; some were popular, others less so. But over the intervening decades, as they married and had children and then grandchildren, the class became closely knitted. They drove each other to hospital appointments, volunteered for hospice care if a classmate needed help with an elderly relative, offered advice and provided emotional support for one another. They reunited a few times a year, going for lunch at local diners. They kept in contact over the phone and formed close bonds. The reason for their uniqueness and closeness, they acknowledged to each other and to local newspapers, was June.

'We've lost 18 members of our class and we grieve over every one of them,' said Sharon Howard, the class's de facto spokesperson. 'But this one you don't get over.'

Visiting June's grave on this day was something they felt they needed to do. Most of them had not been particularly close to June at school. She was a quiet girl who kept to herself, but they each felt a loss of innocence when she was killed.

'We felt we were invincible, that nothing could touch us,' said Howard. June's murder 'changed all of that. It was the first time we thought anything could happen to us.'

What happened to June made them recognise the preciousness of life and the importance of friendship and community.

Standing around June's resting place, the members of the Class of 1959 placed their hands upon June's headstone. Some of them whispered little prayers and placed flowers and notes on her grave. They bid June goodbye and weaved their way back through the headstones to their cars, to their lives and loves and families beyond the walls of Lakeview, the blue sky above them alive with the first promise of summer.

*   *   *

October 2025

Dear Aunt June,

I was never able to say hello or goodbye. You were taken from our family before I was able to meet you. I would visit the cemetery and see your name, but I never knew you. I missed having you as my aunt.

I am grateful now and thank you for my cousins Joe and Patti.

You are forever in my heart for your bravery and courage to become the wonderful woman you became. You endured more than any person should in their life.

Love,
Your niece, Amy

Dear June,

Though I was too young to remember you, I've always known who you were. You, your story, and your life have never been forgotten.

I was lucky to grow up in a big family – with Joey by my side the whole way. That meant more than I can put into words. We had each other, and we had a lot of love around us. That foundation helped shape the happy life I have now.

I've had a really happy life. I've been married for over 30 years to a wonderful man, and we have two children who are absolutely thriving. They bring so much joy and pride into my life. I'm so grateful for everything life has given me, and I feel incredibly lucky.

What truly makes me happy today is being with my family. The time we share – both the family I grew up with and the one I've built – means everything to me. I know in my heart that you would have loved being part of it all – and we would have been lucky to have you with us. I think of you often.

Love always,
Patti-Ann

Dear Mom,

Even though we were only together for a short time, I've carried you with me my whole life.

I want you to know that I'm doing well. I grew up in a big, loving adoptive family – one that took both Patti and me in and gave us stability, joy, and a forever family. I promise you, I had a happy and full childhood. I've built a good life for myself. I have been married for 35 years and have two wonderful sons and three amazing grandchildren. I'm healthy and I'm surrounded by people who love me. If I have one regret, it's that I didn't get the chance to know or stay in touch with your parents – my grandparents. I often wonder what they were like and what they might have shared with me about you.

I hope you're at peace, and I hope somehow you can see the life Patti and I were able to build. We were okay – more than okay.

With love,
Joey

Acknowledgements

OUT OF THE GATE, MY HAT IS DOFFED TO THE RTÉ *DOCUMENTARY ON ONE* TEAM, WITHOUT WHOM . . . WELL, YOU KNOW THE DRILL. My co-producer Tim Desmond was indelible during production of the *Runaway Joe* podcast: guiding my microphone hand, inspiring new investigative leads, editing episodes from my messily written drafts, compelling the story in new directions.

Series producer Liam O'Brien was our unflappable captain (even when the ship veered close to krakens) and Nicoline Greer a tireless barrelman who scouted new shores and interviewees in Ireland, Cyprus and beyond. Credit to Peadar Kearney, sound engineer and to composer-musicians Martin Klusák and Tomáš Borl, who made the podcast sing. (Go stream their heart-rending *Runaway Joe* soundtrack on podcast platforms.)

Edie, my beautiful daughter, for providing another musical score: Eddie Van Halen guitar licks from her bedroom while I was writing this book. (Her friends call her Edie Van Halen).

Petronella, my mother, for inspiring me to take on this story in ways she might not have expected (and for taking care of Edie on the days I skipped the country for this book).

Brian Langan, my incredible agent and editor. Deirdre Nolan, my publisher at Eriu. Lisa Gilmour, Assistant Editor, copyeditor Neil Burkey, proofreader Liam Maguire and the team at Bonnier Books – thanks all for guiding me toward and over the finish line.

Joey and Donna, for your friendship, hospitality, rollercoaster rides at Busch Gardens and Pop-Tarts. Joey's sons Logan and Austin (you've got one hell of a dad), the extended family (especially Aunt Laurie) and a special thanks to Cheyenne for inspiring a crucial part of this book. Robert Connors, a Maloney relative who connected me with Karen and Chris. Thank you Karen for being part of this journey, which I know hasn't been easy for you.

Amy, I hope I have provided some justice for your Aunt June.

June's friends and schoolmates who spoke with me – Sharon Howard, the late Carol Reckahn, Kay Zatine, Linda Chamberlain, Kay Walter, Marsha Curry, Sandy O'Mara, Joan LaBue and Carol Severns. Cecile, who welcomed Tim and I into your home and gave us precious time with the charming Neal Dunkleberg. Rest in peace, Neal.

Gary Craig, retired Rochester *Democrat & Chronicle* reporter/ sleuth, who covered the podcast series and helped me out with investigative bits and bobs for this book.

Rochester DA's office, in particular Sandra Doorley, for allowing us access to the Joe Maloney files. Wendy and Gary Lehmann for your knowledge and support.

In County Laois, Kitty, Tony, Aila Nikka-Conroy, the Collins family. In Dublin, the Fennings and other families (some named within these pages, some not) for their memories and generosity. Nick Ryan and Ian Sorensen: cheers chaps.

In North Cyprus, Liz Moore and Chris provided smoked salmon, Bloody Marys and great company. Denise Phillips and Can Gazi invited us through the doors of Bayrak Radio and TV, scoured their archives for Mike Nagy memorabilia, and hosted Elaine and I with our dubious music selections on their *Main Event* radio show (without losing their licence!) Thank you Julian and Pauline Mawdesley for accommodating us at your home in Karmi, and the owners of the Crow's Nest bar for not kicking us out after closing time. Rica and Andreas and everyone else in TRNC who provided guidance, direction, friendship, tea and mezze.

Peter and Anne Nagy, thank you for trusting me with Mike's research. I'm glad we got to share time together in Cambridge.

John Burns, my former editor at the *Sunday Times*, who assigned me the task of editing *Culture* magazine on the weekend judge Gillian Hussey's memoir, *Lessons From the Bench: Reflections from a Life Spent in Ireland's Criminal Courts*, was reviewed. This was the catalyst. I read a paragraph mentioning her interactions with the strange case of Joseph Maloney, purchased the book and the rest is borderline obsession.

Finally, thank you to my friends, family and extended family, who have to put up with me. You make it all worthwhile.